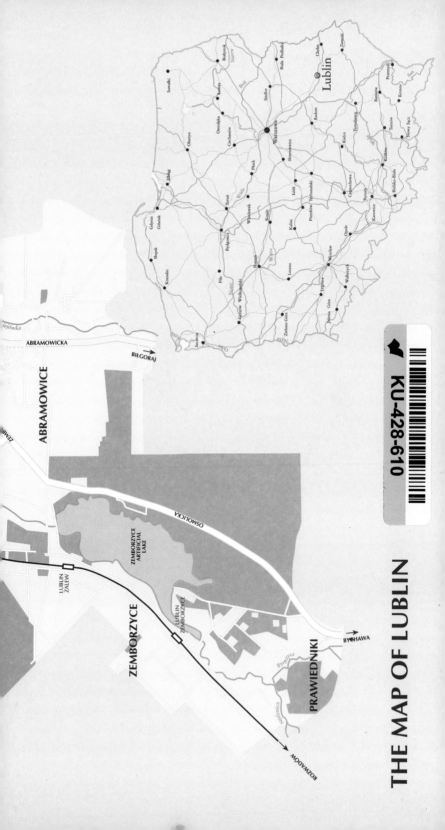

KU-428-610

THE MAP OF LUBLIN

LUBLIN
AND ITS VICINITY
THE GUIDE

The main text:
Marta Denys, Marek Wyszkowski
Preface:
Jan Lewandowski
The outline of the history of Lublin:
Konrad Zieliński
Translated:
Wiesław Horabik, Anna Winiarczyk

Photos:
Irena Rolska-Boruch (IRB), Tomasz Buczek (TB), Adam Chlebiński (AC), Stefan Ciechan (SC), Karol Dromlewski (KD), Czesław Herda (CZH), Monika Konkolewska (MK), Piotr Maciuk (PM), Jan Magierski (JM), Stanisław Turski (ST), Jan Żaczek (JŻ) Other photographs by Piotr Maciuk

Consultation: Grażyna Jakimińska

Idea and Graphic Design:
*idea*MEDIA

The First Issue

ISBN 83-88104-09-8

Contents

From the Publisher

This is the first – since the printed word was invented – classical Lublin and it's Vicinity guide. Over 200 pages of the text, 2 individual language editions (polish and english), 20 routes marked on the plan, including 5 special, almost 500 photos and directory about adresses of cultural institutions, offices, hotels, restaurations, banks... Finally the knowledge and good writing shills of authors, not only experts in the region's past but also guides.

This vivid account about monuments, people, special and peculiar places is professional and interesting, full of anegdotes and curious details. But it would have never been created but for many thousands km walked on foot, hundreds groups of different age, state and nationality, countles number of questions, recollections, comments.

But can a good guide be written by knowing the city from the windows of library, without the contact with tourist?

Before you go off "on route" I recommend to read the introduction by Jan Lewandowski and the short story of Lublin by Konrad Zieliński. These are the best texts of our city, that I have ever read. Concise, reliable and excellently written.

Waldemar Żelazny

The Location Privilege from 1317 (rep. – PM)

LUBLIN – THE TOWN OF VARIED CULTURAL AND RELIGIOUS TRADITION

Towns – like people – have their ups and downs, their good and bad periods as well as their light and dark sides. Each town or city has its own characteristic feature, which makes it special among other places, which have similar function. There are numerous things that distinguish Lublin from other well – known places e.g.: location, unusual topographic profile, and varied monumental architecture being the reminder of a troubled history. Many of these factors changed over time, which strongly shaped the role of the town, its image, ethnical and religious composition.

During a thousand-year-old history the face of the town and its territorial shape largely changed. There were times when Lublin would disappear from the map of Poland. Having remained located among the same hills; surrounded with marshes at the estuary of the Bystrzyca, the Czerniejówka and the Czechówka it used to be the eastern Polish frontier. As the winds of history blew it used to move into the very heart of Poland. During the Partitions, it was a peripheral town near the north-eastern border of the Habsburg Monarchy. Later, it was the capital town of the Duchy of Warsaw and the Kingdom of Poland, separated from the former Commonwealth with Galician border to the south and with the river Bug to the east. During the times of the second Commonwealth the region having its centre located in Lublin was the only one that did not share any border with its neighbours. Following the World War II the Polish-Soviet border (known as "the border of friendship") – separated the region from its eastern part located on the eastern side of the Bug. Today Lublin shows the desire to be the gate to the east both for Poland and for the European Union.

The winds of history left their mark on today's Lublin. The historical events seem to have changed its architecture, landscape, legends and anecdotes, which comprise the city's cultural heritage. Jokingly, the Lublin is often called "the town of a goat". This must be a reference to its remarkable coat of arms: the goat standing on its rear legs, leaning against the grapevine tree.

During the Piast Dynasty, Lublin played the role of administrative and military defensive fort. One hill was the location of defensive settlement and trade; the other was the centre of Christianity. At that time Lublin was to safeguard the eastern frontier regions from foreign invasion: the Russian tribes, the Lithuanians, and other Slavic peoples. Lublin was also the hinterland for Poland's expansion towards the Polish-Russian frontier and further into the Russian lands. At the turn of 12th and 13th century, the town was the seat of the archdiocese and the governor's office.

Further history of Lublin reflects the good and bad periods of the whole country. After the union, which took place during the reign of King Władysław Łokietek, Lublin was given the city rights in 1317. The policies of King Kazimierz Wielki diminished the danger of Russian invasion. The incorporation of the Duchy of Wołyń and Halicz by the last King of the Piast Dynasty helped to tighten trade and cultural bonds with the Russian lands being a part of the Eastern Slavic Empire and having different cultural heritage of which the most important element was the Eastern Orthodoxy.

The Eastern Orthodoxy was the dominant religion of the power, which competed with Poland for the Russian lands. Its name was the Great Duchy of Lithuania and it was growing in strength in the 14th century. On one hand, the Lithuanians posed a potential danger for Lublin and the surrounding areas; on the other hand, they were the most attractive political and trading partners for Poland. It was not by accident that amongst the great landowners who once offered the Polish crown to King Jagiełło and who were one of those who signed the Act of Union in Krewa, was the former administrator of Lublin. Earlier, the inhabitants of Lublin were given the official privilege (the privilege from King Jagiełło) of crossing the Polish- -Lithuanian border without paying any custom duty.

After the Union of Krewa Lublin became the most prominent town within the Crown; the town in which the Great Duchy of Lithuania acknowledged the formerly approved resolutions and where the great Polish landowners accepted the historic act of union. Ever since, the history of Lublin came to be influenced by the fact of its geographical location between the two important Jagiellonian capitals: Kraków and Vilnius. Initially, the typical borderline settlement under constant danger of foreign invasion, Lublin turned into one of the finest urban centres of the large Polish-Lithuanian Commonwealth located within the very heart of its geographical, trade and political life.

The most famous and the most historically meaningful reminder of Jagiellonian reign is the Holy Trinity Chapel. Its western Gothic architecture has been enriched by the elements of the eastern culture: a set of Byzantine-Russian frescoes including the portraits of their founders – the great Polish-Lithuanian King Władysław Jagiełło. This is the example of the merging of two artistic styles: western European architecture and eastern religious painting. King Jagiełło was a son of a Duchess representing the Russian Orthodox Church and a pagan father. Most of his subjects were Eastern Orthodox. As a Polish King, Jagiełło was a Catholic but the frescoes are the proof that deep inside he remained the great admirer of the Eastern Orthodox religious art. Jagełło was not the only person to have the privilege of spending hours praying within the walls of the Castle Chapel. One of the greatest

Jerzy Braun, Abraham Hogenberg, The Oldest View of Lublin. 1618 (rep. – PM)

Polish historians – Jan Długosz – who apparently did not show much liking for the King – was educating his grandchildren, the sons of Kazimierz Jagiellończyk who later became the sovereigns of Poland, Lithuania, the Czech Kingdom and Hungary. The Chapel, which had been restored for the last century, was the place where many of the monarchs' servants left the traces of their presence. The splendour of the Polish-Lithuanian Empire had direct impact on Lublin which in 1569 witnessed the final union between Poland and Lithuania that marked the new political shape of the country known as the Commonwealth of Two Nations. The situation remained stable until the Partitions. It is not by accident that in the Castle Museum the most visibly exposed (and the largest) painting is the one by Jan Matejko entitled *The Union of Lublin*. It is worth mentioning that one of the most prestigious high schools and the most luxurious hotel in Lublin have both been named in commemoration of this great historical event – the Union of Lublin.

The "golden age" of King Zygmunt's reign were the times of the great splendour and opulence for Poland. Lublin fulfilled many important functions. It was one of the greatest international trading centres. The famous fairs made the people richer and the prosperous business opportunities attracted traders from the west and the east who brought in their customs, religions and family heritage adding to the city's variety and spice. The urban complex was soon inhabited by many Russians and Jews. The Jews created their own urban area – the Podzamcze District – which existed until the tragic events of World War II. The famous fairs attracted merchants from Russia, the Armenians and the Greek. Among those who came from the west were the French, the Germans, the Dutch and the English. As Poland was tolerant to different religious and ethnic minorities, it became a home to numerous victims of 15th and 16th century religious oppressions and wars: the Spanish Jews, refugees from as far away as Germany, the Netherlands, France and Scotland. There were many others coming from different parts of religiously fanatic European areas and not a few of them chose to settle down in Lublin, which was the important centre of the Reformation in Poland.

The remainders of the city's architectural Renaissance splendour can be seen looking at the Old City monuments and the interiors of a few churches. The Renaissance decoration show the richness of the people (especially the nobility, which patronised the churches) and their attitude towards life and death. The portraits of the dead, which can be seen in the form of the Renaissance tomb sculptures are totally different from the Medieval and the Baroque ones showing the terrifying perspective of living and the dangers of dying. The sculptures seem to be emanating the inmost calm and dignity; they seem to be sure that the afterlife stands open to the man and is as friendly as the earthly journey, which allows one to make noble sacrifices and experience the joy of living. In order to find it out, do not fail to visit the Dominican Church and Monastery.

The great peculiarity of the Lublin architecture – the Town Hall, which is now situated outside the walls of the Old City (the New Town Hall) – dates back to the Renaissance period. The middle part of the Market Square is occupied by a large, great building called the Crown Tribunal. This institution used to play a very important role in Lublin's history and topography.

In 1578, the highest court of appeal was created for the Polish part of the Commonwealth. It was known as the Crown Tribunal. Its sessions were held in Piotrków Trybunalski (for the Great Poland) and in Lublin (for the Little Poland). The 16th century judicial province of the Little Poland ranged as far as 100 kilometres beyond Kiev towards south-east...

The historical echoes of the Crown Tribunal, which was a legal institution until the final years of Old Poland, are far more than the famous legend of the devil's court preserved in the name of a popular cafe "Czarcia Łapa" (the Devil's Paw), and the actual impression of the devil's paw against the table (belonging to the Collection of the Museum of Lublin). Most importantly, the remainders of the Crown Tribunal having its seat in this town are evident in architectural and urban shape of the contemporary outskirts, especially the areas lying outside the urban walls. Within a few decades the City of the Crown Tribunal was enlarged by the sprawling chain of magnate mansions. The dignitaries coming to the Tribunal were in need of proper accommodation, which resulted in the sudden mushrooming of the residencies belonging to the finest Polish families: the Czartoryskis, the Radziwiłłs, the Sobieskis, the Potockis, the Tarłos, the Lubomirskis, the Sapiehas and the Sanguszkos... In the later centuries – after the Partitions – they were no longer needed. Many were either sold or leased. Some changed the initial purpose. Looking at the tenement houses at Królewska Street (former Korce) you can hardly find any remainders of the former magnate splendour. Only a few buildings have managed to regain their initial beauty and glamour now serving as the seat of educational institutions. It may look like the continuation of the aristocratic tradition but only in the metaphorical sense. The palace which once belonged to the Czartoryski Family is now a seat of Lubelskie Towarzystwo Naukowe (the Lublin Scientific Society) and Instytut Europy Środkowo-Wschodniej (the Institute of Central and Eastern Europe). The Radziwiłł Palace has been turned into the Department of Political Sciences of the University of Maria-Curie Skłodowska. The Sobieski Palace is now a seat of the Technical University in Lublin. The residence of the Potocki Family was not as lucky – it first served as an Austrian prison. More recently i.e. during the years of the Communist regime it was the seat of the state police known as ZOMO. Its new owner – the Catholic University – may bring the better decade for the building, which is located almost in the heart of Lublin.

"The Fire of Lublin in 1719" (rep. – P. Maciuk)

Another important element of the urban topography are the monasteries built outside the Old City walls. Apart from the oldest ones, most date back to the epoch of the Counterreformation. The building of monasteries started at the turn of the 16th century and was initiated by the Jesuits who settled near the town walls. In less than a century, they built a huge and extensive monastery, which consisted of the Baroque temple (now the Cathedral), the Jesuit college complex for noble gentlemen, which had functioned until its liquidation in 1773. There were many other monasteries, for both boys and girls, which despite being less opulent and resourceful have quite fine architecture which stood the test of time and serve many important purposes e.g.: hospitals, cultural and educational institutions, even a brewery.

The mid 17th century marked the beginning of a severe decline, which lasted until the half of the next century. During that time the magnate residences along with monastery complexes largely dominated the urban and the suburban topography. The next epoch of King Stanisław Poniatowski meant the better times for Lublin. The first thing to be done was reorganisation of the urban economy. The results can be seen today. The Royal initials decorate the two major city gates: Brama Krakowska and Grodzka. The Crown Tribunal situated in the middle of the old Market Square was given the new Classical character. The sign of religious tolerance prevailing during the age of Enlightenment was a newly built Evangelic Church which, for the contemporary inhabitants of Lublin, brings to mind the popular tiny wall, where one can buy the most lovely flowers. In the past, the wall surrounded the cemetery of the Protestant church.

The favourable period lasted for a short time. Following the 3rd Partition, the judicial institution of the Crown Tribunal was closed down. After three hundred and twenty years Lublin stopped being the centre of the Little Poland, which suddenly disappeared from the map. Under the Austrian rule the city was reduced to the seat of a political prison. The number of houses and people diminished, the palaces and monasteries emptied. Most of them were transformed into prisons,

Philipp Dombeck, General Zajączek's Entry in to Lublin. 1826 (rep. – PM)

military hospitals or soldier houses. To make matters worse, a fire which broke out in 1803 lasted for two weeks and destroyed the buildings in Korce, the large part of the Old City and Krakowskie Przedmieście.

Even the short period of unfavourable Austrian rule left its marks on the city's culture and monuments. The Austrians established the new cemetery – the oldest Christian necropolis at Lipowa Street. At that time, the residence of the Roman Catholic bishop was transferred from Chełm to Lublin. In 1807, Wincenty Pol was born in Lublin. He was the son of an Austrian clerk who took part in the November Insurrection in Lithuania. Pol was one of the most passionate admirers of the Polish countryside, nature and history. He became the first geography professor at the Jagiellonian University. Acquiring the Polish identity by Wincenty Pol was part of a widespread historical process, which affected the Austrian clerk families and their children. When the army of Prince Józef Poniatowski entered Lublin in 1809 they were warmly welcome by daughters of the Austrian clerks and officials who were born to Austrian families.

In 1809, Lublin was Polish again. It first belonged to the Warsaw Principality. Following 1815, it was one of the Polish cities within the Kingdom of Poland. The 19th century attributed Lublin the new function – political, economic, administrative and cultural centre of the land lying in between the rivers Vistula and the Bug. To the south it was guarded by the cordon of the Austrian police, its northern border was more open and reached as far as the southern regions of Mazowsze and Podlasie. The historic bonds with the Little Poland were getting weaker and its capital (Kraków) had been incorporated into different territorial and political section. The new political division granted Lublin the position of the biggest city on the eastern side of the Vistula. Lublin was to regain this favourable position after World War II, in 1944.

The stormy era of the Napoleon wars was followed by a short period of political stabilisation within the autonomous Kingdom of Poland (1815-1830). Lublin started to assume a new character. It was slowly becoming a governmental city and to

Andrzej Grabowski, The Holy Trinity Chapel, 1854

some extend it still has it. The Old City was no longer the city centre. Instead, the most important area was now Krakowskie Przedmieście along with a number of adjacent back streets. Within a hundred years, the existing complex of buildings had been adjusting to new functions. It was supplemented with new buildings to satisfy the needs of the contemporary authorities as well as the average people. The partially ruined Castle was restored in accordance with the contemporary Neo--Gothic architectural standards. It was turned into prison again and was to remain

Bronisław Kopczyński
The Chapel Interior Restoration, 1918

Adam Lerue, Lublin – the Castle Chapel, 1857

13

Adam Lerue
St. Michael's Church, 1857

Adam Lerue
The Lublin Cathedral and the Trinity Tower, 1857

Adam Lerue
The Lublin Magistrate, 1857

Adam Lerue
The Kraków Gate, 1857

one until the mid 20th century. The gate to the Old Town was replaced by a new Brama Trynitarska (the Trinity Gate) which still dominates the view of the Old City.

Plac Litewski (the Litewski Square) was the place where military parades were held. It was also the area where the local and district authorities resided for a number of years. Stanisław Staszic was the one who initiated the building of the cast – iron Union of Lublin Monument. A lot could be written about the place and a huge number of historical events that happened here, about various building owners and the buildings themselves. We will only mention a few historic plots. The central city square, once

The Water-Tower, a postcard from 1916

*The Russian Orthodox Church
at the Litewski Square, 1917*

*Symche B. Trachter
The Interior of the Maharszal Synagogue, 1921*

called Hitler Platz or Joseph Stalin Square, has no reminders of foreign eastern political dominion. Plac Litewski was occupied by the Orthodox church (a sort of basilica), following World War II the Monument of the Russian Soldier was erected there. During the Great War the Radziwiłł Palace served as the seat of the Austro-Hungarian, Tsarist and Royal Polish Military Governor. Here is where on November 5th 1916 the central countries proclaimed the creation of the new Polish Republic. Two years later the Palace witnessed forming of the first independent Polish government. From here the Prime Minster (Ignacy Daszyński) together with the Minister of Defence (Edward Rydz-Śmigły) set out to Warsaw in order to hand over the power to the hands of Józef Piłsudski. It was on November 11th, 1918.

The only reminder of the orthodox basilica are a few oak trees that once surrounded the sacral building. The basilica was demolished and the construction material was used to built the Polish Soldier's House. The southern part of the Litewski Square is closed by the large post office building.

During the final years of the Great War the Austrian officer, war veteran and later General Stanisław Sosabowski had been working here. He was the founder of the military parachute team, which was to support the Warsaw Uprising. Unfortunately, the team was defeated during the military operation near Arnheim.

Next to the post office building stands the monument of Józef Czechowicz. The greatest poet of Lublin, the son of a female guardian, born in the neighbouring Kapucyńska Street. In 1939, he fled the bombarded Warsaw to find some peace and security in a provincial Lublin. On the 9th of September, one of the bombs exploded into a hairdresser's shop inside which Czechowicz was sitting...

A few days later the German and the Soviet officers were seen hugging one another at the Litewski Square.

The eastern part of the square (its eastern corner, in particular) is occupied by the hotel and restaurant "Europa". For many decades it had been the most luxurious hotel in the city. The legend says that the owner built it with the money ha had embezzled from the participants of the January Insurrection. His family are said to have been cursed with misfortune for this shameful deed.

Among the places which has shaped the present appearance of the city there is also the famous nineteenth century Ogród Saski based on a model of the Warsaw park. Ogród Saski testified for the high position and the richness of the inhabitants of Lublin the final decades of the first half of the 19th century.

The most rapid development of Lublin is said to date back to the pre-war decades. It started to be regarded as the industrial centre: it served all local farmers, landowners and peasants. The goods were exported to the Russian and even the Far Eastern markets. The local industry, which was a far cry from the contemporary industries in Łódź, Warsaw and the 19th century Białystok, still had its outstanding figures. One such figure was Wilhelm Hess, the Czech immigrant, who learned the tricks of the trade in the field of fine mechanics during his stay in the USA. His remarkable technical skills helped him to start the production of scales. His factory became popular all over the region. Despite his success, he did not want to become an American citizen.

After coming back to Europe, Hess decided to seek his fortune elsewhere and set forth towards Kiev. The way to Kiev led through Lublin. At first, he earned his money mending scales. By the end of 1879, a new scale factory was opened at Lubartowska Street. In the later period, he opened a couple of branch houses in Berdyczów, Białystok, Smoleńsk and Jekaterynosław. In 1913, the company was given a new name: the Scale Factory Stock Company – "W. Hess" in Lublin. The son of a poor miller reached the apex of his career. The company was destroyed by the war, the loss of the eastern markets, competition and the general economic crisis.

Hess was a protestant. He is buried in the evangelic section of the cemetery at Lipowa Street, just like most of the contemporary industrial tycoons. The cemetery encompasses the last two centuries of the city's history. It is divided into Evangelical, Catholic, Orthodox and Military sections. The latter was founded by the Austrian authorities. It is occupied by the military quarters of the Tsar's Army soldiers, the soldiers of Marshall Piłsudski's Legions and the Polish soldiers who died in the war of 1920. Many tombs were built to honour the victims of World War II. One of them belongs to the great Lublin poet – Józef Czechowicz. There is a quarter for the Red Army soldiers from 1944 and the symbolic Katyń Tombstone raised in 1989. The soldiers' tombs from the years 1944-1948 date back to the Communistic regime: military pilot tombs, the working class activists' graves from the years 1944-1989.

The extensive Catholic cemetery is not only a place of rest for the ordinary inhabitants of Lublin. The tomb of a priest Piotr Ściegienny, raised at the turn of the 19th century, was where the first working class demonstrations began to take place. During the 1905 revolution the cemetery walls were the places of secret meetings of the Polish workers and the Jewish labourers from "Bund".

The rich 20th century history of Lublin has left the most symbolic monument: the Majdanek Death Camp – a place in which many representatives of different races, religions and cultural backgrounds were exterminated. The city was deprived of its historically – important Jewish Podzamcze District. Those who had lived there for many decades vanished into the thin air. The few things that have remained include two cemeteries (the second oldest in Poland, the first is in Kraków), the hospital building and the Rabbinical Seminar at Lubartowska Street. The bitter memories are still alive…

Łukasz Rodakiewicz
building engineer
designer of the Old Theatre

Wincenty Pol
Poet, Jagiellonian University professor
Born in Lublin in 1807

Henryk Wieniawski
composer, great violinist
Born in Lublin in 1835

Wilhelm Hess
owner of Scale Factory
"W. Hess"

Wacław Moritz
industrialist
owner of Steel Foundry
and Agricultural Machine Factory

Karol Vetter
Brewery owner

Mieczysław Biernacki
Doctor, journalist, editor

Jerzy Rudlicki
Engineer, chief constructor
of E. Plage & T. Laśkiwicz
Industrial Plant

Mieczysław Wolski
Industrialist
Owner of Agricultural
Machine Factory

Teofil Laśkiewicz
Co-owner of E.Plage & T. Laśkiwicz
Industrial Plant

Eugeniusz Kwiatkowski
Co-author of the design
project for building new
Industrial Centre

Józef Czechowicz
Poet, born in 1903, killed
in the bombardment of Lublin
in 1939

Stefan Wyszyński
Rector of Lublin Diocese
1946 to 1949

Karol Wojtyła
Catholic university professor
1956 to 1978

The post war decades marked the significant transformations. Lublin grew in size, the number of population increased. The city was preparing to hold new functions. It was turned into the educational centre. No other Polish city had more than one university. Lublin had two: the Catholic University opened in 1918 and the newly – founded University of Maria Skłodowska-Curie. In the beginning, the younger of the two universities offered the higher education in the following branches: medicine, veterinary medicine, exact sciences, natural and agricultural sciences.

The new university was opened during the lasting Nazi occupation. The first meeting of its authorities took place in the building of Stanisław Staszic high school. The noble professors sat on barrels. The historians have been long jokingly arguing whether the barrels were full of cement or… beer.

Today, the academic centre has a few thousand students who create the city's friendly atmosphere. The campuses vibrating with the energy of the young are scattered all over the area. They are associated with several universities: KUL (the Catholic University), UMCS (the University of Maria Curie-Skłodowska), the Agricultural Academy, the medical Academy and the Technical University. In recent years, many new schools have been opened. They include new private schools as well as sister universities, which so far have not gained large popularity.

Universities are often famous for their remarkable professors. They have made a name for themselves among the local students. Some have become regarded as strange and eccentric. They are known for the jokes that generations of students tell about them. Some professors, however, were held in high repute. Prof. Krwawicz (cryosurgeon) and Prof. Andrzej Waksmundzki (light pipes) are among the greatest. Student theatres are well known at home as well as abroad. The first one was "Gong 2" whose founder was Andrzej Rozhin. Scena Plastyczna KUL with its director Leszek Mądzik has visited many countries so far. Another well-known artistic formation is the Theatrical Workshop Centre "Gardzienice" founded by Włodzimierz Staniewski.

Lublin is widely known owing to the two outstanding figures standing high in the church hierarchy. These are: Stefan Wyszyński – the honourable primate, the first bishop of Lublin after the war; and Cardinal Karol Wojtyła, the former bishop of Kraków, who was the professor of ethics at the Catholic University. The two monuments erected in commemoration of the great Poles can be seen at the University courtyard.

During the last decade, Lublin has become more and more colourful and elegant. It slowly starts to live up to its glorious past. It stands wide open to the West and East, either trying to attract foreign capital to let the local trade and industry flourish, or encouraging young people to come and study here. Recently, young people from beyond the eastern border have come to study here. The old truck factory has been sold to the South Korean concern – "Daewoo". The biggest shopping centre is owned by E. Leclerc.

The Institute for Central and Eastern Europe is open to facilitate the co-operation with the scientists from that part of the continent. It has taken up the task of presenting the cultural wealth of the countries located in this part of Europe. The city of the historic Union between the East and the West is the best place to make people realise the fact that there are common cultural roots in Europe.

Today's visitors are bound to receive the traditional eastern warmly welcome and the city itself may surprise many with its quietness as well as the unforgettable views from the charming hills, valleys and lovely ravines.

Jan Lewandowski

THE OUTLINE OF THE HISTORY OF LUBLIN

*T*he area of the contemporary Lublin, which spreads along the northern tip of the Lublin Upland, has been inhabited by man since the Neolithic Era. The beginnings of the settlement on the Bystrzyca River, however, hide in the darkness of time, as does the name of the city. Although Father Kadłubek described Lublin as a very ancient city founded by the Slavonic Prince Lubl, a relative of the Roman Emperor, it is only one of the many "fables" of Master Wincenty. It is probable, however, that someone's name was the origin of the city's name. Linguists derive its name from the name of Lubel or Lublia. The oldest written source bearing the name "Lublin" comes from 1198.

*A*lthough the people would settle here since the 6th century, the municipal beginnings of Lublin should be associated with the 11th century, and a settlement called "Czwartek". It was a small trading post located on the peripheries of the Polish State. After 1138 Lublin became a part of the Sandomierz Province. During the reign of Kazimierz II Sprawiedliwy it was united with the Kraków Province thus forming one Principality. At the end of the 12th and the beginning of the 13th centuries, the settlement gained importance due to its location in the border area and to the eastern policy of the Piast Princes. It initiated the interference of various cultural traditions and intensified the trade contacts, which later shaped the history and development of the city. It was most probably in that time when the settlement increased and now included the fortified town and a settlement on the Old City Hill. According to Długosz, Lublin was in 1241 "the populous town". It was a time of great changes in the Central European trade. Lublin became then a transit post on the trading trail leading from the Greek colonies on the Black Sea to Western Europe and to the Baltic Sea. Since the middle of the 14th century, however, the city was – first of all – the borderline centre of the state power and church administration. Because of these factors, Władysław Łokietek agreed in 1317 to the location of the city on the Magdeburg rights. Maciej from Opatowiec became the hereditary governor. After the location, the town was spatially reorganised. The reorganisation included the Old City Hill as well. The spatial pattern of old Lublin is extremely interesting. It does not copy the traditional, typical pattern of a chessboard. It was probably the result of including the old settlement into the city. In Kazimierz Wielki's times, the city area of about 7 ha was marked by two gates: the Kraków Gate and the Grodzka Gate. The great moments for Lublin were yet about to come. In the 14th century it had about 1000 inhabitants.

*T*he breaking point in the city's history was the Polish and Lithuanian Union of 1385. Lublin was now located at the meeting point of three geographical zones. It was also situated at the trail that connected two Jagiellonian capitals – Kraków and Vilnius. It acquired new political importance and it quickly developed economically. Since 1448 four big fairs have been organised in Lublin. The city also became the main administration centre of the Lublin Province. The Province was created in 1474, and Lublin became its capital. The central and local parliaments held their sessions here, and among them the famous Union Sejm from the years 1568-1569 so nicely depicted on the painting by Jan Matejko. Lublin was one of the few towns that sent its representatives to the Crown Parliament. In the 15th and the 16th centuries, the existence in Lublin was marked by fairs, which were attended by the merchants from all over Europe, and from the countries of the Ottoman Empire. One of the historians wrote: "During the Lublin Fairs the East met the West and thus made Lublin an important point and the trading centre". The demographic structure of the city was altered by the profits taken from trade and handicraft and by the need to serve a large number of the people who came to the town. In 1524, there were about 4,5 thousand inhabitants in Lublin, and in 1573 – over 9 thousand. The first written accounts of the Lublin Jewish Community come from the 2nd half of the 15th century. In the next century, due to the tradition of tolerance, the Jews lived in great numbers north and north-east of the Castle. In the 16th century, the importance and wealth of the Lublin Jewish community was almost equal to those in Kraków and Lwów. Besides the Talmudic Academy and one of the first Hebrew printing shops in Poland, since 1580 Lublin had been the official seat of the Jewish "Parliament of the Four Sides of the World".

$\mathcal{I}$n the 16th century, the city became one of the major trade and cultural centres. These were not, however, the burghers that shaped its reality now. Even more so, because since the end of that century – due to the changes in the European trade exchange – the Lublin Fairs began to loose their significance. Lublin was now a place where the noblemen held their meetings and in the suburbs of the city the aristocratic palaces and manor houses of a smaller gentry began to spring up. It provided the city with a special architectural character. At the beginning of the 17th century Lublin expanded. The towers of churches and chapels founded by the magnates overshadowed its other buildings but this process was not accompanied by the promotion of the burghers. As was the case with other Polish towns, the 17th century wars ended the "Golden Age" of Lublin. In 1655, it had to "play a host" to the Cossack and Tartar troops. Then it was invaded by the Swedish, the Lithuanian and finally the Hungarian troops under Rakoczy. Before the city began to revive, its suburbs were plundered by the Tartars in 1672 who burnt the Jewish Quarters as well. All these events brought Lublin almost to a total destruction, and the pauperised and decimated burghers were unable to rebuild their trading activities. The Jewish merchants proved to be better prepared to overcome these difficulties. The Christian merchants and craftsmen, however, found the strong supporters in the clergy, especially in Jesuits. The old tolerance of the Jagiellonian Era was passing away. The economic life, however, returned to its normal course: till the end of the 17th and the beginning of the 18th centuries, all renovations and repairs of the defensive equipment had been completed, and the city had newly organised local authorities. During the Northern War, Lublin was a place of parliamentary sessions, which meant the revival of its old political functions. The city was ruined and its inhabitants pauperised again due to fires, plagues, and marches of troops and imposed contributions. In the 18th century, the damages were repaired – the new churches and monasteries were erected but the burghers and local authorities were unable to make serious, more general investments. The status of Lublin was diminishing, and the economic life began to revive only in the 80s when the standard of towns and the status of burghers was increased all over Poland. Basing on the principles of the Sejm Wielki, the administration reform began. In 1792, the Russian troops entered Lublin, and the enemies of the May 3 Constitution "that offended the national liberties" formed a confederation in Lublin. It cancelled all the previous decisions. The inhabitants of Lublin participated in the Kościuszko Insurrection but in June 1794 the town was again occupied by the Russian troops, which were then followed by the Austrians. The epoch of the Partitions commenced. Lublin became a part of the Austrian Empire and was included into the Province of Galicja Zachodnia (the West Galicia). The Austrians began their rules with the imposition of contributions and requisitions. It deepened the poverty of the inhabitants. May 1809 was marked by the victorious offensive of the troops of the Warsaw Principality. Lublin became the capital of the liberated territories in Galicia, and in 1810 was nominated the seat of a Department. The town was destroyed and neglected, and this fact was not changed by the promotion of.

*L*ublin to one of the Provinces of the Kingdom of Poland created during the Viennese Congress. The later years, however, brought visible improvement. The town was reorganised, the new communication routes were established, some churches and aristocratic homes were rebuilt, and public facilities were placed in them, and the first patches of green were established. The centre of Lublin moved in that time towards Krakowskie Przemieście Avenue. Many of these initiatives were copied from Warsaw – the Lithuanian Square, for instance, was a copy of the Saxon Square in Warsaw. The number of inhabitants gradually increased, and new craft workshops, trading stalls, shops and first factories were erected. Lublin was becoming again an important cultural and educational centre. The education in various kinds of schools developed. The first newspapers appeared, and there was a theatre in the city. The fashionable Masonic Lodges also contributed to the development of Lublin at that time. The outbreak of the November Insurrection was greeted in Lublin with an enthusiastic patriotic manifestation. The troops of the National Guards were formed. The Citizens' Council collected money for the Insurrection, and "Kurier Lubelski" promoted the Insurrection ideas. Unfortunately, two months later the Russians entered the city, and the inhabitants had to suffer all the persecution that was the fate of the defeated country. After the Insurrection the pace of life in the city was slow. The industry and the trade were in ruins, and all cultural activities that overstepped the frame of the censorship were forbidden. The visible change occurred in the 60s. Due to the news coming from Warsaw, the inhabitants of Lublin – and especially the youth – engaged in the patriotic street demonstrations and patriotic Masses, and many members of these events became conspirators. The soldiers from Lublin participated actively in the battles of the January Uprising, and the city – though occupied by the Russians – became an important centre of power of the National Government. Even during the Insurrection, many inhabitants were persecuted and many of them were killed or exiled.

*T*he rapid increase of the number of inhabitants – from about 22 thousand in 1870 to about 77 thousand at the outbreak of World War I – was the result of the economic changes undergoing in the Kingdom of Poland as a whole. In 1913, the Catholics, mostly the Poles, accounted for about 40% of the Lublin population. About 50% of the population were the Jews, over 8% the faithful of the Russian Orthodox Church, and the remaining 2% were the polonised Czech and German Protestant families. At the end of the 19th century the Christians began to leave the Old City area, and they moved to the so-called New City with the prominent Krakowskie Przedmieście Avenue. The nearby Piaski turned into an industrial and trade district. It was a result of the opening in 1877 of the railway line connecting Lublin with Warsaw and of the establishment of many new industrial plants. The deserted Old City was taken over by the Jews who earlier occupied the area of the Podzamcze, Lubartowska Street and the Wieniawa suburbs. The latter was one of the suburbs – not the most important and not the largest one – but that was the place where 100 years earlier Jakub Icchak Horowic, the famous "visionary from Lublin" resided with his entourage. The 19th century was the epoch of the social changes. The class of wealthy bourgeoisie was formed, and the growing number of workers found jobs in factories and private enterprises. Trade and handicraft remained the domain of the Jewish population. The urban shape of the city was being created although Lublin – in spite of industry – had been for a long time deprived of technical infrastructure such as sewage or water supply systems and electricity. The gap between the prosperous centre of the town and the poor suburbs was widening. Industry concentrated on the manufacture of machinery and agricultural equipment. There were a lot of processing plants and Lublin was a host of many National Industrial and Agricultural Exhibitions. In 1874, the Lublin Doctors' Association was founded, and a few hospitals were functioning in the city. In spite of the anti-Polish policies of the authorities the spiritual and cultural life developed. There were a few newspapers in the city, and a new, impressive theatre was built. In the revolutionary years of 1905-1907, many political parties became active. The revolution collapsed but it resulted with the establishment of the Polish private high schools. In 1908, the Public Library was opened, the economic institutions were developing, and so were professional and cultural societies. In summer of 1915, the Russians left Lublin. The evacuation of the offices and – first of all – the industrial facilities had a deep impact on the industrial potential of the city. The devastating policy of the Austrian and Hungarian authorities even deepened the difficulties. A certain compensation for this was perhaps the liberal attitude of the new authorities towards culture, education and patriotic activities – schools and courts were taken over by the Poles. The elections to the local government were organised. In the years 1916--1917 the suburban communities and the suburbs themselves were included into the administrative borders of the city. It meant the expansion of the city area and rise in the number of inhabitants and Lublin became a capital of the Austrian and Hungarian occupation in the Kingdom of Poland. It became second – after Warsaw – centre of the political life. In November 1918 the Provisional People's Government of the Republic of Poland under Ignacy Daszyński proclaimed its Manifesto here.

*I*n the independent Poland Lublin became the capital of the Province. This period is the time of unbalanced, and chaotic economic development. Among the major industrial plants were: the aircraft manufacturing company Plage & Laśkiewicz, and a new truck factory. New streets were being shaped, and new residential districts built. The city was provided with the water supply system, hence overcoming the centuries long "civilisation gap". The contrast between the centre of the town and the workers' districts was widening. The situation became worse in the time of the economic depression in the years 1929-1935. The pre-war time was very important in the cultural life of the city. Franciszka Arnsztajnowa and Józef Czechowicz lived and worked here. Lublin became one of the major university centres. In 1918, the Catholic University was founded, since 1926 the Jesuit College "Bobolanum" was active, and in 1930 the "Academy of the Lublin Wise Men" was opened. It was a modern Talmudic university.

*T*he years of World War II had a tragic impact on the life of the city. The Germans entered Lublin on 18 September 1939. The symbols of the long lasting occupation are the prison in the Royal Castle and the Seat of the Gestapo in the House "Under the Clock". Detentions, roundups, resettlements and executions began in November 1939. In 1941, the Russian POWs began to build a large concentration camp. It is estimated that 360 thousand people died in Majdanek. 40% of those were Jews. The Jewish inhabitants of Lublin were closed by the Germans in the Ghetto that covered most of the Jewish Quarters. In April 1942, the Jews were deported to the extermination camps in Treblinka, Sobibór, Bełżec and Majdanek, and the Lublin "Jewish town" was totally destroyed.

*T*he Resistance Movement was active since the beginning of the war. The city was its important centre. In July 1944, the units of the Home and People's Armies took part in fights against the German Garrison. The Russian troops entered the city. In August the Provisional Government (PKWN) and the National Council as well as the General Staff of the Polish Army moved to Lublin. Besides the representatives of the political parties, also men of culture and science lived here. For a few months, Lublin was indeed the capital of the so-called Lublin Poland. Then it became a major administration, cultural and education centre of the Region. The area and the number of inhabitants significantly expanded, its industrial potential was strengthened, and the co-operative housing projects were flourishing. A new university – Maria Curie-Skłodowska University in Lublin – was founded. After its reorganisation – the Medical Academy, the Agricultural Academy and the Technical University were established. Museums, permanent theatrical stages, Philharmonic Opera and Operetta, artistic and folklore groups, scientific societies, numerous publishing houses and newspapers – they all reflect the cultural achievements of the city. Lublin also participated in the historical events of the recent history of Poland. In October 1956 about 100 thousand inhabitants at a rally protested against Stalinism and in favour of the forces regarded as pro-reformist in the government. In July 1980 there were protests and strikes in Lublin and Świdnik that were forerunners of the August events at the Polish Coast.

*L*ublin – the capital of the new Province – is the largest city in the eastern and south-eastern Poland, the tenth most inhabited city in the country and its population is now close to 400 thousand. It is, however, with no doubts, the "historical" town. Its links with the past are clear – there is no district not connected with some historical event or with a historical figure. These links are vivid in the pattern of housing in the city – the Gothic Castle Chapel with the Byzantine frescos, the Old City built in the Renaissance style, the Baroque churches and monasteries, the Classical building of the former Crown Tribunal in the Old City Market Square, the eclectic houses of Krakowskie Przedmieście Avenue, "the secession" houses from the turn of the centuries, the architecture of the pre-war times at Chopin Street, and soc-realism of many districtsand public houses – this is only the most obvious review of the styles and epochs. There are places in Lublin where one gets the impression that time has stopped, and the local character of them has been preserved. The Old City – though not as crowded and noisy as before – has still its unique charm. Kalinowszczyzna Street recalls the atmosphere of the suburbs that it once was. On the market days, Ruska Street with the Russian Orthodox Church at its outlet and its adjoining streets recalls the times when there was the Jewish District at the foot of the Royal Castle. Someone has written about the Lublin Bronowice that they combine the specific atmosphere of Bałuty in Łodź and Brzeska Street at the Praga District of Warsaw. The houses near the railway station have not changed much and they still possess the features of the old industrial district "na Piaskach". Today's Lublin maintains the special balance with its old districts. Numerous parks and squares add to its charm, and so do the recreational areas situated in the direct vicinity of the compact housing areas of the City.

Konrad Zieliński

THE CITY'S EMBLEM

At first, the special sign of Lublin was a goat standing on its four clumsy legs, his bearded head turned to the left. The goat is a proof of the town's legendary links with the ancient Rome. The animal symbolises one of the Roman goddesses – the beautiful Venus. The first coat-of-arms had been widely regarded the town's official coat-of-arms until the fifteenth century. Another artefact associated with Lublin was found among the archival documents in Toruń. The document, dating back to 1401, has a stamp that reads: *Sigilium Civitatis Lublinenis*.

The 16th century brought significant changes to the historic coat-of-arms. The City Council stamps dating back to that period show a new goat standing on its back legs, leaning against a grapevine. The stamps dating back to 1535 and 1605 bear the following inscription: *Sigilium Consilium Civitatis Regiae Lublinensis*. The copy of the original jury stamp from 1575 has managed to preserve half of the contemporary coat-of-arms. There is a mayor's stamp (1536) that depicts the symbolic jumping goat, without a grapevine. The acronym "SPL" stands for: *Senatus Populusque Lublinenis*.

The 17th century mayor's stamp shows a goat standing by a grapevine, surrounded with Baroque ornaments. Another stamp dating back to the same period, presents a semi-goat with two grapes. In the further centuries the symbolic goat changed several times. There is also another coat-of-arms presenting the goat on the ornament background, jumping to the left, there is another without a grapevine. One of the stamps shows a ram's head on a shield background with palm twigs twisted around.

In the 19th century, there was one national coat-of-arms. The traditional sign of Lublin could only be seen in heraldic albums and historic registers. The symbolic goat was displayed in public places like publishing houses. You could see it on leaflets, lottery tickets etc. It also appears on many official documents and honorary budges from the Great War period. Following the Nazi occupation the stamp with the legendary symbolic goat was put on the identity cards and bus tickets. Even the Germans used it.

In 1936 the Ministry of Religious Denominations and Public Education approved the present coat-of-arms as the official and legal symbol of Lublin. Today the symbolic goat stands on its back legs, its head is turned to the left. The white animal stands on the green grass and leans against the green grapevine. The background is red. The time has brought major changes to the way it looks today.

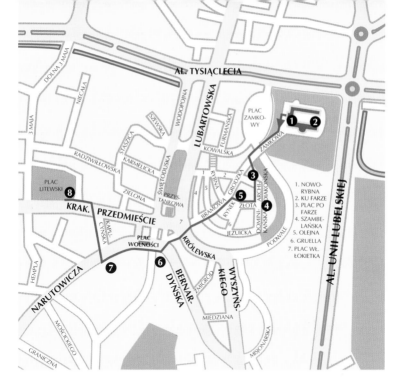

FOLLOWING
THE JAGIELLONIAN ROUTE
OF THE HISTORIC UNION

the Castle Square – Grodzka Street – the Po Farze Square – the Old Town Square – Złota Street – the Old Town Square – Bramowa Street – the Władysław Łokietek Square – Kozia Street – Bernardyńska Street – Gabriel Narutowicz Street – Kapucyńska Street – Krakowskie Przedmieście – the Litewski Square

Major objects:

❶ *The Castle Museum*
❷ *The Trinity Chapel*
❸ *The Po Farze Square*
❹ *The Dominican Basilica*

❺ *The Lubomelski House*
❻ *The Bernardine Church*
❼ *The Church of the Victorious Mary*
❽ *The Union of Lublin Monument*

"The Union of Lublin" by Jan Matejko
(Lublin Museum Collection, phot. – PM)

THE CASTLE

First stop is the Castle (see p. 56-58), the former quarters of the Jagiellonian Dynasty. Among its most outstanding guests were king Władysław Jagiełło and his wife Jadwiga. The most notable Old Polish historian – Jan Długosz – raised royal sons within the castle walls.

From January to February, and later in June 1569, Zygmunt August and his parliament held political debates which were crowned by the historic union between Poland and the kingdom of Lithuania. Among the museum collection pieces you can find a famous work by Jan Matejko entitled *The Union of Lublin* – commemorating the seminal historic event. In 1869 the painting was exhibited in Lvov, Vienna and Paris. After 1875 it was purchased by the state. The painting implies various interpretations.

Marcello Bacciarelli
"The King Zygmunt August"
(The Warsaw Royal Castle Collection,
phot. – MB)

THE TRINITY CHAPEL

The Trinity Chapel (see: pp. 59-61) is a perfect proof of the great care that the king attached to the spiritual and material condition of the place. The strong evidence for the good sense of artistic taste are the unique Russian-Byzantine frescoes dating back to the early 15th century, made at the special order of the king. The depiction of a humble and generous founder can bee seen in the middle of the fresco painting, under the flight of stairs. The depiction of the king sitting on the back of the horse (non-religious theme) is a unique example of medieval religious art.

THE KU FARZE SQUARE

Situated on a hill (the former Old Town Hill), the place was once occupied by a 14th century parish church (see: pp. 51-52) which combined two predominant architectural styles: Romanesque and Gothic. The sizeable tower, raised in the following century, is easily noticeable from a considerable distance.

Here is where the historic king's parliament of 1569 prayed for the guidance of God in making important political decisions.

THE LUBOMELSKI HOUSE

Like many other houses of the Old Town, the Lubomelski House (see: pp. 72-74) is equipped with three horizontal sections which served as the wine bar, after the reconstruction made in the 16th century at the order of the contemporary owner – Jan Lubomelski. The interiors were decorated with original frescos. The leading theme was the love of life. The wall paintings, which decorate the uppermost section of the cellar, survived the great fire of 1575. Among other leading themes, you can easily recognise the Royal Castle, the Dominican Church, the parish church of St. Michael the Archangel and Grodzka Street.

THE DOMINICAN BASILICA

The painting entitled *The Great Fire of Lublin in 1719*, exhibited inside the Tyszkiewicz family Chapel (see: pp. 47-49), shows the 18th century Lublin.

The Church played important role in the past. One of the chapels (the Firlej Chapel) brings to mind the Chapel of king Zygmunt in the Cracow Wawel. According to the chronicles, after the historic act of union was signed, the king

and his advisers expressed their deep gratitude by singing religious hymn – *Te Deum*.

The historic Cross that witnessed the great event is stored in the Dominican Monastery collection of museum pieces.

THE BERNARDINE CHURCH

According to the tradition, the extensive monastery complex (see: pp. 97-99), served as a luxurious lodging house for the noblemen who seated in the royal parliament. In this church (the second biggest temple in the city) took place the spectacular thanksgiving celebration in acknowledgement of divine favour. The celebration was organised at the order of the king and the members of nobility.

THE BRIGIDKAS CHURCH

After the happy victory in the Battle of Grunwald in 1410, king Jagiełło founded the Chapel of St. Mary. From the very beginning, it was supposed to be taken care of by the convent of Brygidki. In response to the generosity of the former Polish king, half a millennium later (in 1910), the Lublinians founded the huge commemorating tablet bearing the inscription of king Władysław. The tablet and the monument can be seen in the Church of Victorious Mary (see: pp. 90-93).

THE UNION OF LUBLIN MONUMENT

The 19th century monument commemorates the historic Act of Union between Poland and Lithuania. It stands in the place of the former 16th century monument erected at the order of the last Jagiellonian king – Zygmunt August. The monument symbolises the perfect harmony between people coming from different cultures and religious backgrounds.

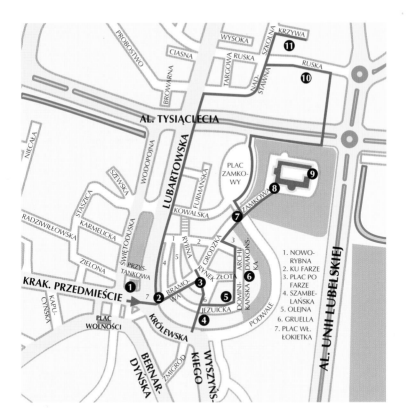

THE OLD TOWN ROUTE I

The Władysław Łokietek Square – the Kraków Gate – the Market Square
– the Rybna Gate – Teodor F. Gretz-Gruell Street – the Trynity Tower
– the Cathedral Square – Jezuicka Street – Dominikańska Street
– Archidiakońska Street – the Po Farze Square – Grodzka Street
– the Grodzka Gate – the Castle Hill – Ruska Street – the Czwartek Hill
– Szkolna Street – Lubartowska Street – the Władysław Łokietek Square

Major objects:

1 *The New Town Hall*
2 *The Kraków Gate*
3 *The Crown Tribunal*
4 *The Lublin Cathedral*
5 *The Old Theatre*
6 *The Basilica of the Dominicans*

7 *The Grodzka Gate*
8 *The Royal Castle*
9 *The Holy Trinity Chapel*
10 *The Orthodox Church*
11 *St. Nicolas' Church*

The Władysław Łokietek Square and Buildings at Królewska Street

THE WŁADYSŁAW ŁOKIETEK SQUARE

The square, built in commemoration of the Grand Duke of Krakow and Sandomierz, located outside the Old Town, marks the historic entrance to the town. In the 16th century the road was called Krakowska Street. Three centuries later it changed its name into Krakowskie Przedmieście. The history of the place dates back to the early of the 17th century. In 1601, King Zygmunt III ordered the liquidation of the embankments and the moats which surrounded the Kraków Gate. A market square was built since the Old Market Square had been overcrowded. Huge bags of grain and corn gave name to the present Królewska Street, once called Korce (korce was the Polish word for "bags" in which the large quantities of grain were stored). The shape of the present Łokietek Square, however, dates back to the 19th century. As mentioned earlier, it was the time of radical organisational changes initiated in 1780 by the city's Mayor, Kajetan Hryniewiecki – the head of the so-called Good Order Council. A new street was opened (the present Lubartowska), and Korce was extended south (the road to Zamość). In the years 1839-1890 the full name of the place was Plac Królewski (the Royal Square). The new name appeared in the official documents in 1925. It was meant to commemorate King Władysław who, in 1317, gave Lublin the city rights.

The building complex surrounding the square are worth having closer look at. To the north, you can see the New Town Hall.

The Władysław Łokietek Square

The New Town Hall

THE NEW TOWN HALL

In between the walls of the Old City and the complex of the medieval hospital and the Church of the Holy Ghost, the monks from the order of the carmelites built a new monastery and the Church. The order of carmelites was formed in 1155, at the foot of the mount Caramel. The first Carmelites appeared in Europe in the 13th century. They came to Poland at the beginning of the 17th century. They settled down in Lublin in 1610 and were brought here by the Jesuits who needed help fighting the non-Christian religions. The monastery was built between 1618-1619. The new temple was erected by the famous constructors: Jakub Balin (who rebuilt the Church in Kazimierz Dolny) and by Jakub Tremanzel of Lombardy. It was an example of contemporary Renaissance style. The Church had three isles and a narrow presbytery facing north. On the sides there were: the choir, the safe and the canteen. The isles contained chapels separated with arcade bays. The slim, richly ornamented front finished with the triangle top was opening towards the Łokietek Square and the Korce marketplace.

The great fire which broke out in the buildings at Korce on the 20th of April 1803, consumed the whole monastery. The monks had to move into Świętoduska Street. The burned church ruins were sold by auction in 1807 by the Austrian authorities. In 1826, the ruins were purchased by the municipal authorities and in the same year the repair work had started.

Within two years the old monastery was transformed into the present New Town Hall. The author of the architectural project – Aleksander Groffe – was the main Polish architect. The works were supervised by an experienced local builder – Jakub Hempel. The building was given the classical character.

During World War II, the building was destroyed two times: in September 1939 and in July 1944. In the years 1947-1952, its hall was rebuilt again. This time the author of the project was Ignacy Kędzierski who managed to maintain its 19th century classical style.

THE KRAKOW GATE

East to the Łokietek Square stands a historic Kraków Gate, named so after the Medieval trade route. Its axis turns into Kozia Street. The gate was built along with defensive walls during the reign of King Kazimierz Wielki. It was proceeded by a Tartar – Russian invasion (1341), during which the major parts of the town were destroyed. The gate was built in stages. Its lower part consisting of a square – based prism dates back to the Middle Ages. The face of a huge Gothic block was ornamented with the chess pattern of bricks and dimension stones. Its corners were strengthened with ashlars. The whole object was given a fine palisade finish. The gate was protected by a deep moat and a drawbridge. In the 15th century, a superstructure was added. The elevation was embellished with rhomboid shaped brick ornament. The cupola was finished with a huge golden sphere. In the 16th century, the Gate was added a new element – a fore-gate with palisade and tiny cupolas. The corpus was equipped with the openings, which served as shooting-ranges. Defensive character of the building was purely symbolic. The fore-gate, however, served as an extra protection of the main gate. In the later years another element was added to the existing form. The new part took a shape of an octahedron with the Baroque cupola on top. Above the cupola there is a three-letter monogram: "SAR" – "Stanislaus Augustus Rex" and the date "1782" that marked the end the building works done by Dominik Merlini, the court architect of King Stanisław Poniatowski.

The Kraków Gate was destroyed, burnt and rebuilt. In 1830 the Gate was

in such a bad technical condition that the authorities seriously considered its demolition. Since 1844 it was the lookout station of a fire-brigade. To better serve the new function, a gallery was attached to the upper part of the prism. From here a fireman had an excellent view of the city and was the first to notice the fire shortly after it broke out. The restoration works conducted in the years 1959-1964 gave the Gate its present character. Today, the Gate houses the Historical Museum (see: p. 152). From the balcony of the Gate you can hear the famous Hejnał Lubelski. Its history dates back to 1653.

Passing through the Kraków Gate and Bramowa Street you enter the Old Town and the Market Square.

The Kraków Gate view from the Łokietek Square

The Old Market Square – one of the most beautiful places in Lublin

THE OLD MARKET SQUARE

Undoubtedly one of the most popular places in Lublin. Historically – the second centre of our town. It was created in the outskirts of the Old Town after Lublin had been given its city rights by the King Łokietek. It measures 62×72 square meters. Since the Market Square had been founded on the arch formed by the former banks, its western frontage took the concave shape. The opposite eastern concave, which once clang to the banks, is convex. Like most Medieval Market Squares, the Square in Lublin Rynek had two side streets coming out at a straight angle. Later on, they were partially built up. The central part of the Market Square is occupied by a huge building of the Crown Tribunal.

THE CROWN TRIBUNAL

It once served as the Town Hall. At first, wooden, then brick, Gothic with the copula, the building had been rebuilt several times. In the mid 16th century it was given the new Renaissance character. It was enlarged by a flight of outer stairs, which led to the first floor. It looked like the contemporary halls in Tarnów or Sandomierz and was surrounded by numerous market stalls. After the fire in 1575, the hall it was quickly rebuilt. Shortly after, it became the seat of the Crown Tribunal for Little Poland – the highest judicial institution for the nobility. It had been open for six months. The head of the Tribunal was a Marshall appointed by the King. Another important figure was the main vicar. The latter was the leading figure when the accused was a member of the clergy. One of the most famous people who held judicial power at that time was a writer and a poet – Bishop Ignacy Krasicki. During their term of office, the local authorities moved to the smaller tribunal at 7 Archidiakońska Street (see: p. 50).

The next Baroque rebuilding took place in the 1680s, under the reign of Jan III Sobieski. One more floor was added and the tower was rebuilt. The contemporary view of the Tribunal can be seen in the pictures dating back to the 17th century.

The Crown Tribunal

The fire of Lublin in 1719 can be seen in the Szaniawski Chapel of the Dominican Church. The most significant changes were made between 1781-1787. In those years, the Tribunal was given its present classical character. The architectural works were supervised by the royal architect – Dominik Merlini. The whole building was enlarged and the second floor was given the last finishing touches. Its total surface doubled. When it served as the Old Town Hall, in its cellars the local merchants sold beer. The Tribunal cellars served as a torture room and a prison. In the 18th century, the ground floor was used as: a treasury (the secret royal documents were kept there), corps de garde, and chemist's shop, shopping centre and city scales. The first floor (formerly the rooms of the Town Council) after the year 1579 served as: a big hall, conference hall with the Tribunal Cross founded by Jan Zamoyski (now to be seen in the Cathedral), gathering room for members of the Tribunal, the Chapel and the portrait of St. Mary (to be seen in the Dominican Church). Once the third flood had been finished, it became the seat of the Land Tribunal. Today, the Tribunal houses the Wedding Palace and its cellars were transformed into Historical Museum of the Old Town Hall and the Crown Tribunal (see: p. 154).

THE HOUSES AT THE MARKET SQUARE

In the Middle Ages the buildings were juxtaposed in the form of the triangle running towards the Market Square. Their double – pitched roofs penetrated into the allotments. The roofs were shingled or tiled. Narrow, Gothic buildings took on their Renaissance character in the 16th century. They were rebuilt after the fire of 1575 and ornamented with mastery attics. The Old Town was given a new, representative look.

Along the western frontage, opposite the entrance to the Tribunal, there are several charming buildings. Their history is interesting enough to be mentioned in a few words.

The first house *No 2*, in known as *the House of the Klonowic Family*. At the end of the 16th century it was owned by a famous Renaissance poet and writer – Sebastian Fabian Klonowic dubbed Acernus. He suffered many humiliations, most of them were caused by his disloyal wife Agnieszka and her quarrelsome mother. Deserted and lonely, he died in the Holy Ghost Hospital at Krakowskie Przedmieście. The house was handed over to the Krokier Family – the friends of Jan Kochanowski. Here is where his famous play *Odprawa Posłów Greckich* was first performed. The house must have witnessed the death of the most famous Renaissance poet who died of a sudden heart attack on August 22, 1584. In 1785, the Klonowic House along with the neighbouring one and the house at Olejna Street was purchased by Dawid Heyzler – a banker and a merchant. In recognition for his services, Heyzler was given a noble title and a coat-of-arms known as Szyna. The new owner rebuilt his property in the classical style. A new five – isle monumental facade was added. The building was enlarged by a broad hall and an arcade courtyard. In later years, the house was added the sgraffital decoration. Here, the painter Jan Wodyński, immortalised famous figures associated with the history of Lublin: Sebastian Klonowic, Jan Kochanowski, Wincenty Pol and Biernat of Lublin.

The Klonowic House, No 2

The Western Fronton of the Market Square

The neighbouring house **No 3**, maintained its original, Gothic shape and the size of 8 m. Another typical Gothic element is a modest, late Gothic portal dating back to the early 16th century. It leads towards the shop located in the gateway, with the door-head in the shape of "the donkey's back". Since the mid 16th century, the house belonged to the family of craftsmen who produced bells – the Stanfusors. The head of the family – Alexy – made a tower bell for the Kraków Gate in 1585.

Until recently, the house **No 4** was known for the superb scene of the legendary Devil's Trial (see: p. 187). The author of the painting was Stanisław Brodziak. Little remained of his work today.

Until the mid 16th century the house **No 5** had been owned by a local official Maciej Zess. Its next owners were the family clan Konopnice who rebuilt the house several times. Until mid 19th century there was a beautiful attic, later destroyed. The adjacent Rybna Gate was also destroyed. The attic was replaced with a functional storey.

The Facade Painting on House No 4
at the Market Square

THE RYBNA GATE

The Rybna Gate was never to serve as defensive structure. Its major purpose was closing the Rybna Street, which led to the Market Square where the fish market flourished. It is thought to have been built in the mid 15th century. The gate joins the two neighbouring houses: Rynek 5 and Grodzka 2. Its housing part, located right above the Gate, added to the complex of the existing buildings. The merchants looked for accommodation, which would be within a close distance from the Square. In the Renaissance Epoch, the house got an attic which survived until 1862. After that, the attic was in a poor condition and had to be removed. The Gate an additional element, it varied in terms of architectural styles. The left side was adjusted to the facade of the house No 5, whereas the right one had to fit the house at 2 Grodzka Street.

THE HOUSES AT MARKET SQUARE

Getting back to Bramowa Street, we see house *No 20* right in the corner of the neighbouring frontage. The house is called *the Confectionery House*. The frieze of the building is decorated with several portraits. The building houses the popular cafe known as "Czarcia Łapa". In the wartime, the house was burnt. It was rebuilt during the post war period.

The front of the house at *19 Rynek* is decorated with sgraffitto made in 1954 by the Michalski Brothers, in remembrance of Jan Kochanowski. The medallion pictures show scenes from the early life of the great poet and his favourite places (Lublin, Warsaw, Czarnolas).

The house at *18 Rynek* comprises two Medieval buildings with the characteristically wide Renaissance front. In the early 17th century, it belonged to Alexander and Andrzej Konopnica, the sons of Sebastian – the owner of a gorgeous house at 12 Rynek. In 1965, during the restoration conducted by Edward Kotyłła, the working team uncovered the remains of the late Gothic walls (dating back to the early 16th century) with the Renaissance window stonework and the well-preserved fragments of mannerist (i.e. later Renaissance) portal from the early 12th century.

The House of Jan Kochanowski, 19 Rynek   *The House of the Musicians, 16 Rynek*

During 12th century the house belonged to the Konopnica Family. The portal must have been made by master architects from Pińczów, who copied the works of a superb Italian sculptor Santi Gucci.

The other part of the facade is decorated with the Renaissance wall paintings. Its authors were the married couple – the Cybis – who did the painting in 1954.

The house *No 17* was built on a lot. In the Middle Ages the lot had two narrow houses standing on it. The houses had different owners. The later owners were the families of the Stanowie and the Cholewowie. In the early 17th century, the house was given a new name – the House of Felkowski – just like its owner Wawrzyniec Felkiel – a doctor. Other owners were the Żędzianowie, the Konopnice and the 18th century family of Muratowicze. Ignacy Baranowski – a doctor, social worker and philanthropist, a Warsaw University professor, a friend of Dr Tytus Chałubiński – was born here. Two years later (until 1850) the house was owned by a well-known surgeon Dr Tadeusz Wieniawski. Here, in this house, a musical genius, world-wide famous violinist – Henryk Wieniawski was born. Ever since the house is called after his name. The younger brother of the great musician – Józef Wieniawski, the pianist – was born at Rynek. The author of the 19th century city guide, Kornel Zieliński, wrote as follows: "The house belonged to the Wieniawski family, who restored it and decorated the balcony with a symbolic figure". In 1973 (the 75th anniversary of the Musical Society of Lublin) a plaque was placed here in remembrance of Henryk Wieniawski – the Society's patron.

The Frontage of the Wieniawski House at Rynek (southern part)

Stone portal, 18 Rynek

The House of the Wieniawski Family (in the foreground), 17 Rynek

The neighbouring houses *Nos. 15* and *16* have both maintained their Gothic proportions. In 1524, the building No 16 was owned by Stanisław Mężyk. As the house had a fine decoration, it started to be called the House of the Musicians. Its nice frieze has been decorated with the portraits of the popular folk musicians. The house is a tribute to Jan of Lublin – the composer of *Tabulatura Organowa* – the greatest European collection of the Renaissance sacral songs, Polish and European folk tunes written in the 16th century. The building's façade has been ornamented with the medallion portrait of Henryk Wieniawski.

The house *No 14*, right in the corner, is called *the Fire Brigade House*. The firemen have always largely contributed to the city's safety. The tightly squeezed buildings suffering water shortages would often catch fire. The house, built in 1411, was owned by the local Mayor – Jan Kreydlar. In the early 16th century, it was a property of another leading figure – Mayor Andrzej Sadurka. During the restoration in 1938, the team of the workers discovered two later Gothic heads, rich in stone ornamental open-work dating back to the turn of the 15th and the 16th century. Having passed the house, turn right into a narrow Teodor Franciszek Gretz-Gruell Street. Born in Lidzbark, he came to Lublin in 1785 and was the pharmacist of the Trinitarians. Three years later he was the proper owner of the pharmacy. He was a medical adviser to His Majesty and a chief local health inspector. In 1791, he became the jury member and in the later years he joined the Local Council. He was the first president of Lublin, elected unanimously. The first elections were possible owing to the statutory bill passed by the Great Sejm known as "The Royal Cities". Gruell was a local president for two years, until the Partition in 1793. He contributed to establishing a new order and arranged the numbers of the tenement houses at Rynek. Amongst other important changes were: road repairing, improvements of the sewage disposal system and the better overall municipal economy.

The Jesuit Church and Monastery Complex and Buildings at Królewska Street

Passing through the Trinity Gate (see: pp. 68-69), built in 1819 in the place of the Old Monastery Gate, we are entering the Cathedral Square.

THE LUBLIN CATHEDRAL

Once a huge church complex owned by the Jesuits who came to Lublin in the late 16th century with the mission to fight non-Christian religious movements. The Jesuits were brought by Andrzej Tęczyński who offered them his own property. The church, the monastery and the college building were founded by the Archbishop of Gniezno – Bernard Maciejowski and the wife of the high Przemyśl official – Katarzyna Wapowska. The Church of St. John the Baptist and John the Evangelist was built in stages from 1586 to 1625 by the monastery architects – Jan Marion Brenardoni and Józef Briccio. The complex was built as one of the pioneer Baroque buildings in Poland at that time. Still, the predominant architectural style was the later Renaissance. The Renaissance ornamental detail has been preserved in the peculiar facade, the cornice having characteristic consoles and the scagliola with floral pattern. The Cathedral building has one nave and the line of chapels on both sides. Rebuilt after the great fire in 1752, it was given a new Baroque finish. The interior was decorated with the illusionist polychrome contrasting with the strong architectural design. The author of the wall paintings – court painter of King August III – Józef Majer was a representative of the contemporary Silasian and Moravian architectural style.

After the Jesuits left Lublin, the Church and the Monastery was handed over to the Trinities, who had no money to restore it.

The Lublin Cathedral

The buildings deteriorated. In 1797 the former Jesuit complex was handed over by the Austrian authorities who used it as a granary. After the Parish of Lublin was created in 1805, the Cathedral began to serve its original function of a sacral building. The remains of a partly destroyed Monastery College were liquidated, which allowed the temple façade to be fully uncovered. In 1821, Antonio Corazzi designed a new classical – looking front with the sexa-style porch and balcony. In 1878, the entire interior was renovated. After World War II, the building was restored according to the project by Czesław Gawdzik. All the classical details were taken away and replaced with the typical architectural Renaissance – like division.

The Copula with the Lantern inside the Chapel
of the Holy Sacrament

The Copula Paintings: the Illusionist Frescoes
in the Presbytery

The Epitaphs of Sebastian Klonovic and Wincenty Pol

The Tribunal Cross in the Chapel of the Holy Sacrament

The Crying Mary

In the side altar, situated near the passage to the left nave, there is a famous portrait of the Crying Mary, which is a copy of the miraculous portrait of Mary of Jasna Góra. It was painted by professor Bolesław Rutkowski. The portrait is famous for the miraculous event, which happened in the Holy Sacrament Chapel in 1949. The Tribunal Cross is exposed in the Chapel of the Holy Sacrament. The cross is said to have been offered by Jan Zamoyski. In 1727, it was transferred from the Tribunal to the Collegiate of St. Michael the Archangel.

The Whispering Hall exposes one of the most valuable collections of clothes and sacral objects. Until the outbreak of World War II, it had been the second Polish collection of this kind. The first and the most gorgeous one was the collection of the sacral objects at Jasna Góra. The collection contains the late Gothic clothes, ornate dating back to the 17th and 19th centuries, dishes and candlesticks. In a visitors' book exposed in the show – case there are the signatures of Maria Skłodowska and the former Polish President Ignacy Mościcki. The baptism register contains the date of Henryk Wieniawski's baptism: July 6, 1844.

The Whispering Hall of the Lublin Bishop

The Frescoes: the Allegoric Scenes Showing the Victory of the Christian Faith over the Heresy

The Liturgical Clothes from the 17th and 18th c.

The Monstrances and the Reliquaries from the 17th and 18th c.

The Visitors' Book

45

The Relief on the Facade of the Old Theatre (phot. – Archives)

Going through the Trinitary Gate, we reach Jezuicka Street. We are slowly approaching Dominikańska Street, passing by the old monastery buildings, which house the National Archives.

THE OLD THEATRE

Once called the Winter Theatre, later known as the Makowski Theatre, it was built in the Classical Style in 1822, according to the project by the first owner and a local engineer – Łukasz Rodakiewicz. It was the first theatre building in Lublin and today it is still one of the oldest in Poland. Its designer was a military officer and engineer who is said to have designed many other houses for military commanders, bridges etc. After his marriage with 15-year-old Marianna Drewnowska, Rodakiewicz became the owner of the house at 11 Rynek and the local land property in Jaszczów. His theatre had 334 seats: the ground floor, eight boxes on the first floor and the gallery. The place was tight, uncomfortable and badly appointed. The repertoire was of a low quality. The only performers were the wandering troupes who did not have much to offer to their audiences. The building works were finished in 1823. The owner purchased the French decorations from the former Warsaw theatre in the Sas Palace at a bargain price. Unfortunately, Rodakiewicz died suddenly in 1832. Following her father's death and until 1887, the daughter Julia Makowska was the hereditary owner of the property. The opening of a new Town Theatre at Namiestnikowska Street (today Narutowicza) reduced the number of the audience at the Old Theatre. In the early 20th century a new cinema called "Theatre Optique Parisien" was located there. Later on, it changed its name into "Rialto" and then into "Staromiejskie".

Strolling along the extension of Jezuicka street, we are entering the gate with a tiny chapel of St. Anton in the hidden in the niche. Passing the gate we see the monastery buildings of the Dominicans. One of the buildings houses the theatre named after H.Ch. Andersen. In the inter – war years it was the seat of Towarzystwo Gimnastyczne "Sokół" (Society of Gymnasts). Earlier, it was the tribunal archive.

To the right, along the steep Old Town slope of the hill above Podwale street, there was a defensive wall.

The Ornamental Cupolas and the Attic of a Former Tribunal Archives.
The Building of the Former Archives, the Theatre of H. Ch. Andersen

Having passed the monastery gate, we are turning left into Dominikańska Street which is leads to the Church of St. Stanislavus.

THE BASILICA OF THE DOMINICANS

The Dominicans formed in 1216. They were brought to Poland about 1260 by Jacek Odrowąż. Some of them settled down in Lublin. Until their residence had been rebuilt and enlarged the temporary place of their stay was the Church of St. Nicolas in Czwartek. Later on, the Old Town had new monastery buildings and a wooden oratory of St. Cross with the relics of the Holy Tree which were the third largest in the world. The relics, stolen at least once, were finally regained. The relics remained here until recently. A few years ago they were stolen for the final time and nothing has been known about them ever since that time.

According to the monastery chronicle, the piece of land on which the church complex was erected, was a gift from Kazimierz Wielki. The square was located at the entrance to the Old Town surrounded with defensive walls. The Gothic church of solid burnt brick, first appeared in 1342 shortly after the Tartar invasion during which the Old Town was consumed by the flames. The temple was built in stages. Firstly, it had a long, closed, rectangular presbytery. The isle and the two naves were added later. In the 15th century the ceilings were covered with the cross vaults. The church had three Gothic gables and a steep, tall tiled roof. The southern part of the monastery, including the gorgeous canteen, is the oldest architectural element dating back to the 15th century. the chapels situated near the naves date back to the 17th century. The Church was seriously destroyed by the fire in 1575. The vaults and the gables fell down and nearly entire equipment was damaged. The following reconstruction left the building suffering from the familiar Baroque additions.

The characteristic gables, divided horizontally by the Renaissance cornices had not been finished until the early 17th century. Inside the Szaniawski Chapel of St. Mary Magdalene there is a painting entitled *The Fire of Lublin in 1719*. The unknown artist immortalised the city as it is seen from the northern perspective. He added several

The Dominican Basilica of St. Stanislavus

details highly valued by the iconographers. At the end of the southern isle there is the Firlej Family Chapel, founded by Bishop Henryk Firlej. It had been decorated with the richly ornamented vault, which brings to mind the chapel of King Zygmunt in Wawel. On the wall of the copula, with the huge lantern hanging down from the ceiling, there is a fresco with the Firlej coat-o-arms known as Lewart. One of the walls has a five – storey tomb of Piotr and Mikołaj Firlej who have been immortalised in a characteristic Renaissance pose. The chapel was designed by Jan Wolff.

The Cross of the Union of Lublin
(from the Collection of the Dominicans)

The Baroque Interior of the Aisle at the Basilica (phot. – SC)

Behind the classical – looking altar there is the Tyszkiewicz Family Chapel with its elaborate stucco-work of John Baptista Falcinni.

The oval Baroque vault is covered by the wall painting, which presents the scene of the Final Judgement, by Tomasz Muszyński. The paintings on the side walls show the history of the Holy Tree.

The Katarzyna Ossolińska Chapel (see the left side aisle) has the portrait of St. Mary transferred from the Tribunal. Note the unusual combination of two pulpits and the rococo sculptures in the altar manufactured in the workshop in Puławy.

Having left the church, we are turning right towards Archidiakońska Street. Its name dates back to the 12th century when the first archdeacon was appointed in order to organise the things around here. The archdeacon was a necessary figure since the Bishop lived in Kraków.

The Tribunal St. Mary

Chrystus Pankreator, the Relief on the Façade of the Missionary House

The Little Hall at 7 Archidiakońska Street

THE LITTLE TOWN HALL

At 7 Archidiakońska Street, there stands the Little Town Hall – the seat of the local authorities during the times of the Crown Tribunal. In one of the corners of the Po Farze Square, on the right side, stands the building of the House of Social Welfare with a Latin inscription that reads: *Bene Merentibus Pax meaning* ("Peace to those who well deserve it"). In the Middle Ages the place was occupied by the church school and the wooden house of the archdeacon. Towards the end of the 17th century a huge, extensive mansion was built for him. Since 1809 the building, sold by auctions several times, was handed over to different owners. In 1912, the premises including the previously mentioned archdeacon residence were purchased by Wiktoria Michelis who turned it into the lodging house for female teachers. The construction works took a long time but owing to the financial help from the church authorities they were finally finished. The Church Authorities wanted the owner to allow the place to be used by young priests who studied at the Catholic University. The later Polish primate – Cardinal Stefan Wyszyński – lived here during his studies at KUL. From 1940 to 1944 the building was occupied by the Nazis. The teachers returned here after the war; today the place is run by the nuns.

THE MISSIONARY HOUSE

Situated near the Old Town walls, the 15th century missionary house was known as the old vicar house. It was a Gothic building having a typical 14th century tower with the characteristic cross and anvil brick setting. When the walls were no longer needed, the tower became a functional building. The whole complex was named after the contemporary missionaries who had the duty of celebrating the mass once a day. Instead, they were provided with the necessary means of living. The owners of the nearby Spiczyn – Nikodem and Anna Spiczyńscy – brought the missionaries to Lublin. In 1536, the Krakow Bishop ordered the missionary college to be built near the existing Church of St. Michael. After forming a new collegiate resulting from the college missionaries becoming the collegiate vicars in 1575, the missionary house ceased to exist. The building became the seat of the vicars from the collegiate in Lublin. In 17th century, the new buildings were added and two centuries later, in the second half of the 19th century, the whole complex was restored.

THE PO FARZE SQUARE

The Po Farze Square was once occupied by the parish church, which was one of the oldest in town. Up to now, the remains of its foundations have been preserved. The history of the parish church dates back to the time immemorial. There is a legend which says that the church was built during the reign of King Światopełk. The country of the Great Moravia was bordered by the rivers of the Vistula and the Bug. It is said that the first temple was to be built here on today's Po Farze Square. The cult of St. Michael (the holy patron of the pre-Roman church) was brought to Poland by the south Slovenes. The temple, rebuilt in the 13th century, needed further restoration after the fire of 1282. These facts are mentioned by the historian Jan Długosz in the famous legend about the dream of the ancient Polish King Leszek Czarny (see: p. 188). After the restoration (first half of the 14th century) the church of St. Michael was given its Gothic character. The presbytery (of the semicircular shape) was now equilaterally closed; the frame was supported with the counter-forts. The new chapels were added. After the Tartar invasion of 1341, the building was destroyed and needed repair. In the 15th century, the restaurateurs added a new high tower, which could be seen from far away. In the following century the church was turned into a collegiate. The local cemetery was surrounded by the complex of houses for high clergymen, collegiate members, church servicemen. The buildings housed a school and a hospital as well. After next fire, which broke out in 1575 the short and wide isle, a new high tower, a presbytery, 7 chapels and the treasury were added. The collegiate had a band of musicians. Many guilts and religious associations were formed here.

After the place become the seat of the Bishop, the church was turned into a Cathedral. Since the final decades of the 18th century, the building deteriorated. Despite the attempted rebuilding, there was a danger of collapsing. In 1846, the local authorities

The View of the Po Farze Square from Podwale Street

ordered the building to be liquidated. The Tribunal Cross was transferred to the Cathedral, the old epitaph of Sebastian Klonowic was carried to the Church of the Franciscans. The painting *The Leszek Czarny's Dream* was now transferred to the Dominican Basilica. The bricks were used to built the gardener's house in the local park. There is a gorgeous wide view of the eastern Lublin from the edge of the Po Farze Square. You can admire the view of the valley in which the three of the rivers: the Bystrzyca, the Czechówka and the Czerniejówka join to form a main stream. To the left, there is a hill of Czwartek with the St. Nicolas' Church (see: pp. 65-66). Here is where the team of archaeologists discovered the ruins of the ancient town dating back to the turn of the 6th century. Turning slightly left you can see the Royal Castle with its tower and the Trinity Chapel (see: pp. 56-61). Further beyond the Castle there is a city district known as Kalinowszczyzna and the St. Agnes' Church (see: pp. 203-204). The area of today's Kalinowszczyzna used to be a private town, which had its own market square called Słomiany Rynek. Looking down the Castle, there is a the St. Adalbert's Church and St. Lazarus' Hospital (see: pp. 77-78).

Walking down the Po Farze Square we enter Grodzka Street, once the centre of the Old Town founded on the slope of the loess hill. The historic Old Town was surrounded by defensive banks and a palisade running along the hill over Podwale. Opposite the Dominican Church one could see the lines of the defensive banks over the ravine in the place of the present streets, namely: Złota, Rybna and Rynek. The banks reached as far as to the valley of the Czechówka and further back along the slope into the Old Town gate. The Old Town Square occupied the widening of Grodzka Street, opposite the parish church. The historic marketplace in Gdansk had identical location (the widening of Długi Targ). There was a cemetery in the square as well.

THE HOUSES AT GRODZKA STREET

Greater number of buildings at Grodzka Street, forming the old northern frontage of the Old Town Square, date back to the 16th and 17th century. They were rebuilt in the 19th century. The façades underwent the thorough restoration in 1954. The houses served as a permanent residence to the member of the Tribunal jury.

We are going to start with the house at *16 Grodzka Street*, on the corner of Ku Farze Street. According to historical documents, on the night of May 7, 1575 the fire broke out, which destroyed almost entire Old Town. In 1968 a water intake – element of the old water supply system was found in the courtyard of the house at 16 Grodzka Street. The water, transported through wooden pipes from the spring in Wrotków, had several intake points: at Rynek and at Rybny Square where it supplied the local bath. The water system supplied the house at 16 Grodzka Street.

The Medallion Portrait of Józef Ignacy Kraszewski at 24 Grodzka Street

TU·MIESZKAŁ·W·LATACH 1826-1827
JAKO·UCZEŃ·SZKOŁY·WOJEWÓDZKIEJ
JÓZEF·IGNACY·KRASZEWSKI

The House at 23 Grodzka Street

Among the houses at Grodzka Street the most worthy of note is the House *No 24*. In the years 1826-1827, it was the house of the former student of Governmental School and the later famous Polish historian – Józef Ignacy Kraszewski.

After his coming to Lublin, the young graduate of school in Biała Radziwiłłowska stayed with his maths professor – Franciszek Ostrowski. Seweryn Liniewski wrote in his diary: "in order to get to the apartment of the professor, one had to climb up the stairs and then turn left into the nice corridor".

In the corner of the Po Farze Square, there is a huge Building No 11. When the church collegiate was opened in 1574, the house was into the building register as the clergy house. At first, the head of the parish church was an archdeacon of Lublin. His 16th century residence was located at 11 Grodzka Street. According to the historical description it was "a house made of bricks, built in the lot belonging to the head parish, inhabited by the parish and the jury bishop. The post of the head parish priest was performed by the collegiate priest known as a prepository. The house at 11 Grodzka Street was burnt by the fire in 1575. The restoration works had been going on for years until the contemporary bishop issued a decree that a new priest residence be built. The registers of 1803 contain the written description of the new house raised ex muro solido. After transferring the main collegiate to Lublin, the local one was closed down. In 1819, the parish house was turned into the residence of Bishop Wojakowski. Between 1869-1870, the Tsarist authorities confiscated the entire property of St. Nicolas' Church, and the surrounding complex of buildings at Grodzka Street. Since that time, it was the state property. The building was handed over to the Jewish community and transformed into an orphanage. On May 9, 1941 the Jewish "shelter" (see: p. 174) ceased to exist. The Nazi murdered all children and took over the building. The inscribed tablet placed on the building facade commemorates the tragic events of May 1941. After the war, the building became the seat of the local magistrate. Later it was turned into the house for the senile. After that it housed an orphanage. Ever since 1970, it has been a cultural centre for the young people known as The House "Pod Akacją". The only remainder of acacia bush that once grew here is the name of the place where young people come to spend their free time.

The old tenement houses stand on both sides of Grodzka Street. The house *No 13* standing behind the Youth Cultural Centre, dates back to the Renaissance. The house maintained its rustic front and the characteristic features of the great order used by an Italian architect – Andrea Palladio. The house is finished with the classical bracketed cornice. The neighbouring house of the Bielewicz Family having added 19th century superstructure was built in 1785.

At the end of Grodzka Street there is a gate known as the Grodzka Gate.

Classical Frontispiece of Brama Grodzka

THE GRODZKA GATE

Built along the main axis of the Medieval town and leading towards the Krakowska Gate, the Grodzka Gate was built on the point of land jutting toward the Castle Hill. The wooden gate became a part of the defensive banks finished with the sharp bends. After the Tartar invasion in 1341, the town was reconstructed. Kazimierz Wielki surrounded the town with a ring of walls. At his order the two main gates: Krakowska and Grodzka were built as defensive structures. The Grodzka Gate had a square base of 12 m, a fore-gate and a sharply – bent entrance gate. Over the latter, there was a shooting gallery for the local guards. The top was covered with the high roof and the palisades. The gate had a drawbridge, which linked it with the Castle building. In 16th century an additional element was added. It was the chamber of the man who collected fares for opening and closing the gate. In 1572, the drawbridge was replaced with a regular bridge of bricks. Two decades later it was totally destroyed and the Gate was damaged. Until the mid 17th century, the Gate and the bridge suffered numerous damages and were reconstructed. The invasions of the Cossacks, the Russians and the Swedes left major trails of destruction. In 1778, the Gate was about to collapse. The Good Order Council decided that the Gate should be thoroughly rebuilt. The rebuilding works started in 1785. The author of the project was Dominik Merlini, the court architect of King Stanisław Poniatowski. This time, the gate was given the Classical character. The frontispiece was decorated with the royal initials and the two vases on both sides. The Gate was no longer the element of a defensive structure and it turned into house. In place of the bridge that once joined the Gate with the Castle, appeared a new embankment. After the next destruction in 1866, the Gate was put for auction and seven years later it was purchased by a Jewish merchant who built additional storeys and joined the Gate with the neighbouring houses. During World War II the roof was burnt. After the war, between 1947 – 48, the Gate was rebuilt for the last time. Again, it was given fresh, Classical – looking character. Today, the Gate houses the "NN Theatre".

Passing through the Grodzka Gate, we are heading toward the Castle.

The view of Grodzka Gate from the Castle (phot. – CZH)

The Royal Castle and the Castle Square

THE ROYAL CASTLE

Among the remains of the original castle buildings are the following: the tower known as Donjon, the Trinity Chapel and the fragments of the former Jewish Tower. Other buildings date back to later periods. The origins are not known but the old tourist guides mention that around 1000, during the reign of Bolesław Chrobry, it was a wooden look-out-tower. The old castle was inhabited by the royal delegates. The first of them, known as Wojciech, is mentioned in the register of 1224. He commanded the local army, collected taxes and decided cases in the name of his sovereign. In the second half of the 12th century, Lublin was the centre of the eastern Polish frontier. In the 13th century, the rebuilt and the enlarged Castle fought the invasions of the Russian armies: the Dukes Daniel and Roman as well as the Eastern Slavs and the Lithuanians. In the mid 13th century, for the purpose of better protection, a new late Romanian cylindrical – shaped tower was built within the ring of the defensive banks. It had a diameter of 15 m and 4 m thick walls equalling the level of the courtyard. The tower was the last building, which resisted invasions. In the later centuries, the tower served as a prison. The 14th century abounded in foreign invasions.

After the Tartar invasion of 1341, the wooden fortification was rebuilt. The new Gothic castle of brick and stones was erected here. The new castle took the rectangular shape. Other defensive elements added at that time were: the defensive walls, the gate, the housing part and the four sided tower to the north. The tower was later

The Trinity Chapel and the Donjon

called the Jewish Tower. The castle had two storeys and the Gothic arch interiors. The upper storey had a huge conference hall supported by the central column. Here is where the conferences and the legal trials took place.

Until 1358 King Kazimierz Wielki paid regular visits to the castle. During the Jagiellonian rule, the sovereigns liked to come and visit the place. King Władysław Jagiełło and his wife Jadwiga were one of them. Here is also where Jan Długosz – the famous Polish historian – raised and educated the sons of Kazimierz Jagiellończyk. Around the year 1520, during the reign of King Zygmunt Stary, the Castle was rebuilt in accordance with the standards of the Renaissance style. The works were ordered by the contemporary Mayors – Stanisław and Jan Tęczyński – and supervised by the outstanding Italian architect – Bartomeo Berecci – who rebuilt the Wawel Royal Castle in Krakow. A new tower and a mansion was built in the southern wing of the Castle. The upper storey was enlarged by a superstructure – an impressive apartment for the royal court members. In the mid 16th century, one more element was added – a new building housing the municipal office and serving as an apartment of the local administrator. During that time, the place served as a debate room for the parliament.

In the 17th century, Lublin suffered numerous invasions by the Cossacks, the army of Moscow, the Swedes and the Hungarians. During the invasions the Castle was

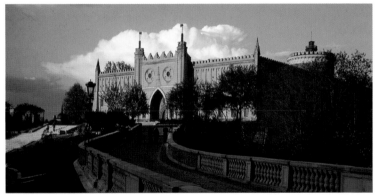

The View of the Castle from Grodzka Street

The Castle Courtyard

seriously destroyed. In the first half of the 18th century, the authorities took the effort of a general rebuilding. It was conducted by the local mason – Jan Cangerle. Eventually, the government decided to turn the castle into a prison. Within three years, starting from 1823, the team of workers transformed the place into the prison for up to 300 people. The huge Neo-Gothic building with the Renaissance elements was built by Jacob Hempel. The author of the building project was Jan Strompf. Among the prisoners at Zamek were the participants of the January Insurrection in 1863. The castle served as a prison for 130 years. During World War II many Polish patriots were executed here. On the 22nd of July 1944, shortly before their withdrawal, the Nazi murdered about 300 prisoners. Ten years after the war, during the post war Soviet Regime, many anti – communist and underground activists were killed here by the NKWD (the Soviet State Police) and the UB (the Polish State Police). In 1954, the prison was closed down. Since 1957, it has been housing the local community, played the role of the arts and social centre, and was the seat of the Local Museum. Today, the whole castle complex functions as the Museum of Lublin (see: pp. 156-161).

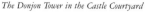
The Donjon Tower in the Castle Courtyard

The Arch Window of the Donjon Tower

The most outstanding architectural monument of the Castle complex, unequalled anywhere else in the region, is the Trinity Chapel.

THE TRINITY CHAPEL

The oldest written records date back to the first half of the 14th century. The chapel is known to have been built earlier than that. It is assumed that its history dates back to the 13th century. During the reign of Kazimierz Wielki, the south-eastern corner already had a polygonal presbytery which was the element of the defensive walls. The chapel extended beyond the line of fortification. Its upper storey consisted

The Holy Trinity Chapel and the Donjon

The Fresco "The Heavenly Glory of God"

The Fresco: The act of the founding of the Chapel

Christ the Pancrator

The Presbytery with Gothic Vault

of a presbytery with double severy bay and a nave with quadruple (fourfold) severy bay supported by an eight – sided pillar in the centre.

At the end of the 15th century the lower part of the building began to serve as the crypt for the clergy and the high royal dignitaries. Decorated with the wall paintings the Chapel is a perfect combination of Latin West European Gothic and the Eastern Orthodox religious polychrome. The Chapel has been enrolled in the worldly list of the humanity's cultural heritage.

Especially unique are the 15th century Russian – Byzantine frescoes – one of the rarest and the most beautiful in Poland. They are attributed to the Russia – born painter Andrzej and his workers. The lower nave and the presbytery display spread curtain. Above, there is a frieze decorated with the palmettos and the medallion portraits. The upper walls have been decorated with Biblical scenes on a mountainous background. The leading theme is the painted image of Christ the Pancrator with the apprentices (he is crowned with an almond – shaped halo, sits on the throne and holds an opened Gospel), which covers the vault.

The arch of the stairs shows the portrait of Mary and the Child sitting on the throne and surrounded by holy saints. An old man, having a narrow triangle-shaped face,

The Nave and the Eight – sided Pillar in the Centre

wearing a fur coat kneels at her feet with a great humility. The old man is said to be the image of King Jagiełło. The restoration was completed on the 14th of August 1418. This date has been preserved in the form of the signature by the Master Andrew.

The unique frescoes at the Trinity Chapel in Lublin are the perfect example of merging of the western and the eastern cultures.

The damages of the 17th century wars seriously affected the Chapel. When the Castle was turned into a prison in 1823 to1826, one of the chapel walls were plastered. A lot of priceless polychromes got wasted. Around 1857, the paintings were partly uncovered by Adam Lerue. He thought that the frescoes were of no real value. They were fully appreciated by the painter Józef Smoliński in the late 19th century. Since then, the frescoes remained the main interest to the Russian authorities and the contemporary Polish scientists. The chapel was first renovated during the I World War. The project was realised with the help of the art historians from Lublin. In later periods the chapel was renovated several times by various groups of conservators. The last renovation was done between 1972-1997.

Having left the castle complex we are turning right. On the castle slope we can see the remains of the old Jewish Tower made of white stone. Around the tower there

The Castle Square

The Monument – the Symbol of Lvov

The Castle Square (phot. – JM)

are the remains of the huge defensive slopes. On the right side of wide stairs, which lead down to the square there is a monument symbolising the city of Lvov. This is a copy of the original monument belonging to the famous Pantheon of Glory. The monument was made by an artist sculptor – Witold Marcewicz in 1993. The animal is meant to remind the people of the strong historic links of Lvov with Poland and with the city of Lublin, in particular. The building complex situated at the foot of the Castle near the valley of the Czechówka, used to be a part of the Jewish district known as the Podzamcze (see: p. 175).

The View of the Old Town seen from the Castle Square

From the Castle Square, we are continuing our walk in the northern direction approaching Ruska Street. On our way, we are passing the Coach Terminal and the market at Tysiąclecie Avenue.

In the old times Ruska Street was a part of the main trade route, which led from Russia, passed round the marshes of the Bystrzyca valley, Świętoduska Street, the Kraków Gate to end up in the Old Town. From here you can admire the spectacular view of the Russian Orthodox Church located at the foot of the Czwartek Hill.

THE RUSSIAN ORTHODOX CHURCH

In the 15th century, the place of today's temple was occupied by a wooden Russian Orthodox Church of the Holy Transfiguration. Around 1588, the temple was reconstructed. Instead, at the order of King Zygmunt III, a new Greek Catholic monastery was built. It was the residence of the Bazillions. Today's Russian Orthodox Church appeared in the place of the former one, which was destroyed by the fire in 1607. After its completion, the new temple was consecrated by the contemporary Archbishop of Kiev – Piotr Mohił. In the 17th century, the church belonged to two different Christian communities: the Orthodox and the Greek Catholics. Since 1875, it was the orthodox temple. The building has one nave and high heavy tower supported by sloping. The building has the Renaissance features i.e.: decorative architectural details at the presbytery, which bring to mind the vault decoration at the Dominican Basilica. This might suggest that the two buildings were designed by the same architect. The vaults have been supported by two pillars. In the centre, there is a beautiful, later Renaissance three piece barrier – golden,

The Orthodox Church of Holy Transfiguration

The Later Renaissance Decorative Iconostas in the Interior

richly decorated with icons – which separates the nave from the altar (iconostas). The ornamental barrier is filled with the icons arranged in a traditional way. The icons are separated from one another with the ornamental, Renaissance columns.

The central part of the barrier is richly decorated with "the Paradise Gates" that lead to the part that was used by the priest. The existence of the orthodox church, located near the heart of the city, points out to the ecumenical role of Lublin as the city that has always been on the borderline of western and eastern cultural and religious tradition.

Continuing our walk along Ruska Street we are reaching Szkolna Street (former Kościelna) and Czwartek. The latter was one of the oldest settlements, which started up the history of the city. At the turn of the 6th and the 7th century there was a regular marketplace situated at the foot of the hill, near the crossing point of the River Czechówka. The market was open on Thursdays (Czwartek = Thursday). Turning right into Krzywa we are approaching the steep entrance to the St. Nicolas' Church.

St. Stanislavs Kostka School at Krzywa Street (the former Bishop School)

St. Nicolas' Church. The Sculptured Figure of St. Nicolas Situated in the High Altar

SAINT NICOLAS' CHURCH

According to tradition, the church of St. Nicolas was erected in 986 at the order of Mieszko I – the first Polish King. However, the archives mention the year 1424. The present temple dates back to the late 16th century. By that time the church had a school, since 1593 it had a printing house owned by Pawel Konrad. The reconstruction of the church building was initiated in 1630. The complex was given a Renaissance character. After the project was completed in 1644, the church was consecrated.

Charity organisation known as "the society of musicians playing various instruments", formed in the mid 17th century. Its main objective was that of guarding moral rules during private and public meetings. The society of St. Nicolas was a charity organisation that offered financial help to the widows and orphans.

The Interior and One Nave *The Holy Heart of Jesus*

The Pulpit and the Font made at the special order at the local Scale Factory owned by Wilhelm Hess (the Beginning of the 20th c.)

Its members collected dowry for young girls who came from poor homes. In the second half of the 17th century, the priest Walenty Turobojski, ordered the church to be rebuilt. The new parish church was built at that time and in 1781 the altar was changed. Since then, the Church of St. Nicolas underwent many ups and downs. It was burnt and rebuilt time after time. Today, it has a simple shape and a very simple decoration.

Czwartek Hill gives one of the most impressive views of the Old Town, the Castle and the Town Centre.

Walking down Szkolna, Ruska and Lubartowska Streets we are slowly approaching the Town Centre.

The View of the Old Town

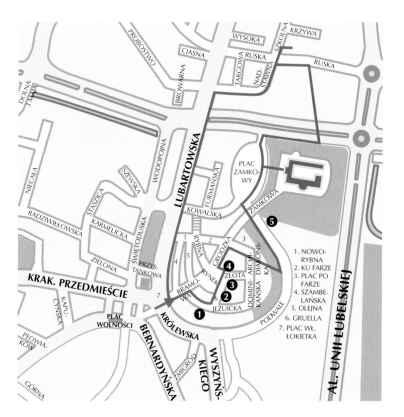

THE OLD TOWN ROUTE II

The Władysław Łokietek Square – the Kraków Gate – Jezuicka Street
– the Trynity Tower – Teodor F. Gretz-Gruell Street – the Market Square
– the Rybna Gate – Rybna Street – the Rybny Square – Ku Farze Street
– Grodzka Street – the Po Farze Square – Podwale Street – Zamkowa Street
– the Castle Hill – the Castle Square – Nadstawna Street – Szkolna Street
– the Czwartek Hill – the Castle Square – Kowalska Street
– Lubartowska Street – the Władysław Łokietek Square

Major objects:

1. *The Trynity Tower*
2. *The Konopnica House*
3. *The House under the Lions*
4. *The House of the Lubomelskis*
5. *St. Adalbert's Church*

The House at Jezuicka Street

We begin our walk from Władysław Łokietek Square (see: p. 30). To the north, the Łokietek Square is closed by the New Town Hall (see: p. 31). We enter the Old Town after passing through the Kraków Gate (see: p. 32). The main entrance to the Old Town was protected by the additional fore-gate. The fore-gate had a separate gate of its own. Before the invaders managed to get to the main gate, they were bombarded with the shooting arrows and heavy stones. Another defensive element was an iron gate that was lowered by the guides fixed inside the base. The gate guarded entrance to the Old Town. Right above the arch of the fore-gate there is a portrait of Mary. The portrait, painted by Janusz Świeży, has been hanging here for ages. On the opposite side of the tower, facing the Old Town, there is a huge portrait of St. Anthony of Padua.

Having passed through the gate, we are turning right to see one of the oldest watching towers – a defensive element of the walls surrounding the historic old town. Their height ranged from 4 to 12 meters. The walls were about 2 m thick. The defensive system was supported by the towers jutting out the main body of the walls. The semicircular tower is to be seen in Jezuicka Street.

We are coming back to Bramowa Street and turning right into Jezuicka. The street was given its name after the residential houses of the Jesuits offered by the contemporary Mayor of Kraków – Andrzej Tęczyński. The houses, located on the right side of the street, represent the architectural style of the provincial Baroque of the late 17th century. It is undoubtedly the oldest part of the Jesuit monastery (see: p. 42). Having passed the former collegiate building, we are approaching the Trinity Gate.

THE TRINITY TOWER

This Neo-Gothic building is the most dominant architectural element of the present Old Town. Once a modest monastery gate, the Trinity Tower was rebuilt by Antonio Corazzi in 1819. The former look of the gate is shown in the painting at the Dominican Church – *The Fire of Lublin in 1719.*

The tower was named after the monastery of the Trinitarians. Having left the monastery at Rybny Square, they moved into the buildings that once belonged to the Jesuits. Today, the Trinity Tower houses the Archdiocesan Religious Art. Museum (see: pp. 152-153).

Behind the Tower, the are two monastery buildings, which comprise the second wing of the former Jesuit complex. They are joined with the arcade gallery cathedral. Burnt during World War II, rebuilt soon after, the buildings house the State Local Archives. The façade rising from Jezuicka Street maintained the features of the mid 17th century Baroque. From the courtyard (between the Trinity Tower and the Cathedral) you can admire the remains of the former galleries and the two Baroque portals.

Continuing down Teodor F. Gretz--Gruell Street we are re-entering Rynek. This time, we will take a close look at the houses on the right.

The Trinity Tower (in the foreground)

The House of Rzemieślnicy (first to the left, 11 Rynek)
The House of Konopnica (12 Rynek)
The House of Students (13 Rynek)

THE HOUSES OF RYNEK

The building **No 13** is called **the House of Students**. Next to it, there was a way to the Jesuit collegiate located near the Cathedral. The house is decorated by the portraits of the former collegiate students. Many decorative paintings include scenes from their school life. Among the paintings you can notice the inscription attributed to Biernat of Lublin: „Boć mądrzy nie umierają, jako szaleni mniemają, a po śmierci prawie żywią, ludzi rządząc nauką swą" ("Wisemen do not die, as do think the crazy ones, but they live ever after and teach the living"). The building has the decorative coat-of--arms: a jumping deer having a crown around its neck. All the decorative paintings date back to 1954. They are attributed to Gałysz, Sarnecki and Łukawski.

*The Konopnica House with the Characteristic
Decorative Window Frames, at 12 Rynek*

The most beautiful building at Rynek is the richly embellished **Konopnica House No 12**. Around 1512, the house was owned by Andrzej Sadurek – the former Mayor. The next owner was the merchant and the Mayor – Jan Domarat. At the end of the 16th century, it was purchased by the Kretko Family. Katarzyna Kretkówna offered the house as her dowry to Sebastian Konopnica – the owner of the local farms and Konopnica (the tiny country village near Lublin). In the 17th century, the house had another owner – the Armenian family of Kieremowicze from Zamość. The present house owes its present looks to Sebastian Konopnica who rebuilt it after the fire in 1575. The frontage was given the mannerist style. It is decorated with the limestone carvings combined with the Renaissance features of the Italian and North European (the Netherlands) architecture. The decoration was made in one of the artistic workshops in Pińczów and modelled on the greatest works by Santi Gucci. Above the windows of the first floor there are the portraits of Sebastian Konopnica and his wife Katarzyna. Right above there is a family coat-of-arms and the initials of Katarzyna – "KK" who was in charge of the rebuilding project after her husband's death. The works were finished under her supervision in 1608. The façade is richly decorated with the elements including the cartouches with the rolled corners at window jambs, stone masks, rosettes and heads of the fairy – dragons. The impressive first storey interiors have been finished with the beam – framed floors. One of the beams bears the initials of Sebastian Konopnica and the date 1579. The window pillars with the fluted columns have been given the finials of caps surrounded by the stone sculptures of little angels. In the second half of the 19th century, the house was deprived of the third storey and the attic. The missing elements were added in 1938-1939, according to the project by Czesław Doria-Dernałowicz. The works were finished in 1954.

The neighbouring house **No 11** draws attention to the wall paintings by Wollenberg and Brodziak. They display the scenes from the lives of the local craftsmen: coopers, tailors and clockmakers. The paintings contrast with the frieze of the floral ornament and the symbolic pictures of the local guilds. Another fascinating element is the attic with delicately shaped edges. The later Gothic portal with the inscription of the former owner is the proof of the Medieval origins of the building.

The house **No 10** is dedicated to Andrzej Frycz-Modrzewski – the great Renaissance poet, a gifted lawyer and a theologian. The only remain of the 20th century decoration, made by the Strzałecki Family exist in the form of a popular Renaissance embellishment displaying flowers, animals and birds.

The house *No 9* standing at the corner of Złota Street is called *the House Under the Lions*. In 1521, it was owned by Jan Organista. During the fire of 1575, it belonged to Katarzyna Lubomelska-Zaborowska whose family owned the neighbouring house No 8. In 1582, the house was purchased by Piotr Cholewa – a member of the contemporary Town Council. At that time, it was a two storey building with a vestibule located on the main aisle. The building was entered from Rynek. Decorative interiors of the first floor were richly appointed: the tapestry – covered ceilings, numerous portraits and paintings. The house was called *the Chociszewski House* after its successive owner. The Renaissance building was restored at the turn of the 16th century. Ever since it presented high aesthetic standards. The gorgeous attic was decorated with three sculptured lions.

At the beginning of the 17th century, the house was handed over to the Dominicans as a gift from the Cholewa Family. They sold it to a Mayor and a member of the Town Council – Adam Przytycki. Next owners were the Cieszkowski Family. Since 1641 its new owner was a tailor and the city Mayor – Jan Reklowski. He decided to give the building a new appearance and ordered to enlarge the window frames and – according to some information sources – to richly decorate the attic. At the end of the 17th century, the legal proprietors were the monks of St. Augustine Order. The one who gave the building its classical character was Józef Potocki with the Prussian coat-of--arms. The almost devastated attic was demolished and the two sculptured lions were placed on the cornice, right above the ground floor. During the World War I the house was purchased by Ludwik Księżycki. The upper floor parlour served as a meeting place for the men of letters as well as an exhibition room for the works of the local painters. One of the two lions became the logo of the local publishing house – the Lublin Book Admirers' Society). Having suffered extensive damages during World War II, the house was rebuilt and redecorated by the pair of artists – Maria and Lech Grześkiewicz.

Having left Rynek right behind us, we are entering into Złota Street, former Dominikańska Street. in the past, the street was known for numerous goldsmith and jeweller shops. The house *No 2* has the walls dating back to the 16th century. Here is where a famous Polish female soldier and a poet – Franciszka Arnsztajnowa (1865--1942, see: pp. 173) lived. Opposite her, in the house *No 3*, lived a custodian of the State Archive – Jan Riabinin (1878-1942) – the writer of the city's history. The miniature building *No 4* is called *the House of Goldsmiths*. Its decoration was designed by the Majchrzak Family and refers to the popular legend associated with the

The House of Goldsmiths, 4 Złota Street

The Polychrome Displaying the Legend the Beautiful Daughter of a Goldsmith

The House of the Lubomelskis (in the middle) at 8 Rynek

place (see: p. 185). The neighbouring Gothic building **No 5** is the only example of an Old City house facing the street – a feature typical of the Medieval architectural style.

From the mid 18th century, it was the property of the nuns who ran St. Lazarus' hospital in Podwale. In the corner house **No 6** there is a fragment of an old wall made of heavy, Gothic brick, which dates back to the 15th century.

We are back in Rynek to see the last lineal extend of the old houses. Looking to the right, we see the house **No 8**, which belonged to a noble Middle Class family of the Lubomelskis. In 1540, the old Gothic houses were given a new Renaissance appearance. The proof exists in the form of the fragmentary remains of an old portal with the inscription of a shortened version of the full surname Lubomelski – "Jan Lubom", with the date "1540". The rebuilding was made at the order of Jan Lubomelski – the legal owner since 1522. In 1573, the property was inherited by his son – Erazm Lubomelski. After the devastating fire of 1575, the house was reconstructed and given the Renaissance character. Embellished attic appeared as a new element at the top of the building. After Erazm's death the house was in the hands of the contemporary chief executive official of the Lublin Municipality – Jan Lubomelski. Since the mid 17th century, the property had many different owners. The sophisticated facade decoration was replaced with more simpler classical structure. During the pre-war period the house belonged to the Jewish community. The ground floor housed the seat of charity organisation helping poor young maids.

During the first rebuilding in the 16th century, the owner Jan Lubomelski, opened a wine cellar inside the three-storey Medieval cellar room. The cellar offered only top quality wines. The place was extremely popular during the official meetings, tribunal congresses and fairs.

The place was regularly visited by the dignitaries of the Tribunal, the Nobility and rich merchants. After the reconstruction of the building, devastated by the fire in 1575,

The Royal Castle in Lublin. The Remains of the Polychrome on the Lubomelski House at 8 Rynek (phot. – IRB)

The view of Dominican Church, the Parish Church of St. Michael and the Grodzka Gate. The Polychrome on the Lubomelski House at 8 Rynek (phot. – IRB)

The House of the Chociszewski Family (right) at 6 Rynek

the uppermost cellar storey was decorated with gorgeous wall paintings. The polychrome, attributed to the unknown author, indicates that he must have been German. The outstanding piece of art. that has no equal in the country serves as the example of the secular Renaissance art. The leading theme points out to the high humanistic culture of the contemporary Lublin. The work is an illusionist composition containing allegorical ancient scenes. According to the Renaissance standards the entire work combines the leading theme with floral elements. The cartouches, situated right above the pictures, include Latin and Old Germanic inscriptions. The central motif of the paintings is Venus Marina, which can be seen in the vault. The oval portrait displays a naked woman emerging from the sea and holding a spread sail in her hand. This type of image showing Venus-Aphrodite could only be seen in many European ports and cities connected with the sea trade. Recovered in the 1930s, the paintings were restored until the outbreak of World War II. In 1937, the wine cellar was reopened to visitors. Some time ago, the paintings underwent another restoration. Recently, a new gorgeous polychrome has been uncovered on the first floor of the building. It is located under the Renaissance ceiling on the right side of the room. The painting displays a battle, which takes place outside the walls of old Lublin. You can easily recognise the outlines of the most characteristic architectural elements of the Old Town. Next to it, there is a beautiful image of Madonna. The newly uncovered polychrome will need further examination and careful restoration.

At the corner of Grodzka Street there is one of the oldest houses at Rynek. The house *No 6* appeared as a joining element of two neighbouring Gothic houses. Its Gothic origin can be recognised by looking at the late Gothic portal over the entrance gate. In 1524, it belonged to the local official Adam Doydzwon, since 1546 it was owned by Barbara Skromowska. In 1630, the building was called *the Chociszewska House*. Later owners were the family of Lemkowie. Jerzy Lemka – doctor of law and the author of a written political dispute was the first who published the Lublin Calendar (1636).

Between 1675-1864, the house was in the hands of the Lublin Seminary. In the later period, it was sold on the auction. In the mid 19th century, the attic was gone and the general restoration took place in 1954. A new attic was designed. It was later decorated with sgraffiti designed by Lech and Maria Grześkiewiczowie.

We are passing through the Rybna Gate (see: p. 38), continuing further down the route of an old ravine we are slowly approaching the Rybny Square.

THE RYBNY SQUARE

In place of an old ravine and the former wall fortification, a long downhill run appeared. As the urban sprawl spread, the ravine was gradually filled in and eventually Rybna Street was formed. Until 1524, it was called Łazienna Street. At the King's order in 1317 a bath was built here to serve the needs of the local community. Money collected from the entrance fees supplied the local treasury. Near the Medieval Old Town walls Łazienna Street turned into a square called Psia Górka (Dog's Hill). In the 16th century, there was a wax manufactory here. In the later years, the square was given a new name the Rybny Square where fish trade was flourishing. The 16th century, the street the gate, which closed the street were given the same name. The whole area was the first economically developed part of the old Lublin. In the beginning of the 16th century, it was supplied with water from the municipal sewage system. There was a prostibulum (public house) run by the local decapitator. In 1874, the town authorities ordered a new passage to Kowalska Street to be built. The stairs have been preserved until today.

The Rybny Square

THE PAWĘCZKOWSKI PALACE

A new Trinitarian church and a monastery was built before the mid 18th century. The Trinitarians – the order of the Holy Trinity – was formed at the turn of the 12th century. Their mission was freeing the hostage Christians from the hands of the Muslims. The Trinitarians came to Poland in the second half of the 12th century. They were brought to Lublin by the royal dignitary – Prince Jerzy Lubomirski. They settled down in the old town around 1728. Prince Lubomirski promised to built them a church and a monastery but failed to keep his promises. In 1746, the high official from Lvov – Mikołaj Łoś Dębno from Grodków took up the task of building the houses for the monks. By 1751, a new monastery had a roof and a church, raising from Lubartowska Street and was given the finishing touches. Unfortunately, the founder died unexpectedly. The construction works stopped. After the liquidation of the Jesuit monastery (today the square in front of the Cathedral) in 1773 the Trinitarians moved there. The post – Jesuit residence was their home until the last members of the Order died.

After 1824, the huge building at Rybna Street was purchased by a hairdresser Jan Pawęczkowski for 4033 zl. The new owner transformed the building into a tenement house. Raised on the old monastery foundations, it looked like a new classical palace. The town guide from 1830 mentions the Palace as one of the finest and largest buildings in town. Until 1848, the building was the seat of the Russian Governor. Its later owners were Rozenblatt and Poraziński.

Leaving the Rybny Square behind, we are walking along one of the most charming Old Town streets – Ku Farze. This tiny Gothic street, a real Medieval relic, has given delight to many architects and art. historians. From here, we are entering Grodzka Street.

THE HOUSES OF GRODZKA STREET

We are passing the House *No 14* (now the National House of the Folk Art.). It is the seat of the Head Office of the Society of the Folk Artists and the Lublin Branch of the Tadeusz Steich Union of the Admirers of the Podhale. Here we reach the corner of the Po Farze Square. There is a large House *No 7*. It a combination of two buildings – the older one form the end of the 15th century and the younger one from the 19th century, located closer to the Square. The house once belonged to Karol Rozenberg, the medical doctor. He was famous for his energy and he served the role of the Provincial Physicist. He organised there the so-called "Institute of the Sanitary Diseases". Many diseases were then caused by antiseptic environment. The building was fully restored in the years 1837-1839 and then the elevations, which a part of it were unified. In effect the house with the rusticated ground floor, the wide hall, the large courtyard with outhouses was created. On April 20, 1807 Wincenty Pol was born in this house. He was a scientist and a poet, the professor of the Jagiellonian University, a participant of the November Insurrection of 1831 decorated with the Virtuti Militari medal, the author of the patriot poems and geographical publications. This outstanding Polish patriot was the sun of a German from the Mazurian District who served the Austrians – Franciszek Ksawery Pohl and the Frenchwoman – Eleonora Longchamps. She came from the polinised family. The house was destroyed during World War II and then rebuilt.

In the adjoining House *No 5a* there is a Chemist Shop – the Museum (see: pp. 154-155). It is the only museum of the kind in the Lublin Region.

St. Adalbert's Church

The Former St. Lazarus Hospital

The Rosary Altar with the Picture of St. Mary's Coronation. Stanisław Janowiecki, 1611, canvas, oil

From Grodzka Street through Po Farze Square (see: pp. 51-52) via the picturesque steps we come to Podwale Street.

SAINT LAZARUS HOSPITAL AND SAINT ADALBERT'S CHURCH

St. Lazarus Hospital was built in the 16th century near the Grodzka Gate but outside the city walls. A wooden church was built near it. At the beginning of the 17th century the hospital was expanded, and Stanisław Garwaski, the Gostyń local governor, founded St. Adalbert's Church nearby. The church was built in 1630. In 1615, at the church the Brotherhood of Mercy founded in 1589 was located. Due to rich contributions the Brotherhood also supported the hospital. In 1730, the hospital with the church went under the auspices of the Sisters of Charity.

The Houses at the Royal Castle Square and the Dominican Basilica

At the beginning of the 19th century the hospital was already to small and the building itself required renovation. Around 1835, the Sisters of Charity were removed together with a hospital to the monastery at Staszic Street left by the Carmelite Nuns. There is still a hospital there.

The hospital building in Podwale was sold on the auction. The hospital and cloister chambers were turned into the residential flats, and the church served as a storage place for iron. After 1920, both the church and the cloister were returned to the Diocese. In the pre-war time there was the Missionary Convent. There was also the cloister of the Canonese Nuns.

St. Adalbert's church is a one-nave building with the semicircular abside with the console mould. The building is an example of the so-called Lublin Renaissance. At the side elevation there are traces of the Renaissance architecture with the flatly modelled pilaster caps of quite a primitive shape that reminds of the folk cutouts. The church maintained the cradle vault decorate with the network of the profiled slats recalling the lacunar vaults from the Enlightenment Period. The old interior of the church from the 19th century was destroyed. The present altar, moved over from the Castle Chapel in 1954 represents the rare Renaissance style. The Church with the monastery complex makes a closed quadrangle with the internal cloister garth.

Walking along Podwale Street on the right hand side we pass by the stylish house standing at Grodzka Gate. It was willingly painted by well-known painters. Via the steps we climb the Czwartek Hill from where we can admire the panorama of Lublin.

Via the Royal Castle Square and Kowalska Street we return to the City Centre, where we pass the steps leading to the Fish Square of the Old City. Leaving Kowalska Street we enter Lubartowska Street. Earlier it was called Nowa Street since it was founded after the city walls were demolished. The Square that is located on our right hand side is the remnants of the gardens that once belonged to the Holy Spirit Hospital (see: pp. 110-111).

We return to the Łokietek Square where we began our journey.

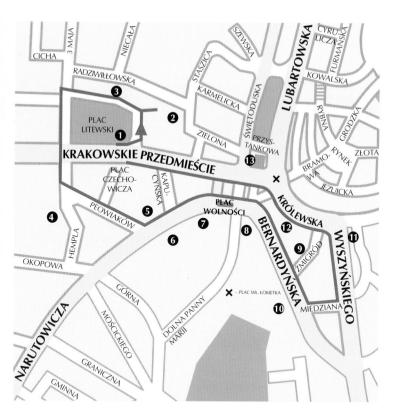

THE TOWN CENTRE ROUTE I

The Litewski Square – Hugo Kołłątaj Street – Peowiaków Street
– Gabriel Narutowicz Street – the Wolności Square – Bernardyńska Street
– Miedziana Street – Stefan Wyszyński Street – the Cathedral Square
– Królewska Street – the Władysław Łokietek Square
– Krakowskie Przedmieście – the Litewski Square

Major objects:

❶ *The Union of Lublin Monument*
❷ *The Czartoryski Palace*
❸ *The Lubomirski Palace*
❹ *The Nuns of the Visitation Monastery*
❺ *The City Theatre*
❻ *The Holy Mary the Victorious Church*
❼ *The Piarist Houses*

❽ *St. Bernard Church and Cloister*
❾ *The Missionaires Church and Cloister*
❿ *The Sobieski Palace*
⓫ *The Bishop's Palace*
⓬ *The Jesuits Church*
⓭ *The Holy Spirit Church*

The Litewski Square with the Governor's Palace at the Background

Visiting the City Centre we begin from the Litewski Square, one (beside the Łokietek Square) of the most representative squares in Lublin.

THE LITEWSKI SQUARE

Its name is directly connected with the events that happened in Lublin in 1569. According to the tradition it was a gathering place for the Lithuanian nobility that came to take part in the parliamentary session that ended with the conclusion of the Polish and Lithuanian Union.

Before the square in it s present form was established (in the 19th century), the Warsaw Tract ran through the Krakow Suburbs surrounded with the loosely standing palaces and cloisters. It was running obliquely to the older section of the present Krakowskie Przedmieście Avenue, at today's "Europa" Hotel, up to 1. Armia WP Street. Along the western side of the Square, near 3 Maj Street there was a church from 1653, a monastery and the Bionifraters Hospital. They were built by the unknown Lubartów architect, perhaps the famous Paweł Fontana. The church, called then the Corpus Christi Church was founded by the Chełm Bishop – Mikołaj Świrski. Since the 16th century there had been a monument commemorating the Union of Lublin and erected probably on King Zygmunt August's orders. It was a quadrilateral obelisk of stone and bricks covered with shingles. In the monument's niche there were figures of Queen Jadwiga and King Jagiełło. The Bonifraters' Church – then ruined – was demolished in the years 1818-1820. At the same time also the Union of Lublin Monument was destroyed. After the road, which is now Krakowskie Przedmieście Avenue was shaped, a new square called Na Rozdrożu was founded between the Warsaw Tract and the newly formed tract. In its western part it was closed by the line of the 17th century defensive walls.

On the orders of General Józef Zajączek, the Military Training Square was organised on the empty grounds were once the Bonifraters' Church stood. The Square was called

The Union of Lublin Monument

Relief – the Symbol of Poland and Lithuania
on the Monument Commemorating the Historic Union

The Monument of the 3 Maj Constitution

the Mars Field. The parades and reviews were organised there. The grounds were covered with gravel and surrounded with a fence and poplar trees. In its eastern part, the first in Lublin public square was established with flowerbeds and lawns. After Czechowska Street (today's 3 Maj Street) was shaped in the years 1823-1824, the final shape of the Litewski Square was established. After the Mars Field was liquidated, the ground was divided into three parts. In the east, the garden was located to be used by the Russian Governor who lived in the nearby palace. The public garden was organised at the eastern side along the 3 Maj Street. In 1874-1876 in its central part the Russian Orthodox Church was erected for the convenience of the Tsarist officials. It was designed by General Chlebnikov, and constructed by the Governor's construction master – Ludwik Szamota. It was a typical Russian Orthodox Church with five cupolas and the tall tower in front. The bell from St. Michael's demolished church was placed on the tower. In the years 1924-1925, as a symbol of the Tsarist oppression it was demolished. The bricks were used to build the Soldiers' House.

In the south-eastern part of the Square, *the Monument of the 3 May Constitution* was situated. At first it was a modest stone located on May 3, 1916 to commemorate the 125th Anniversary of the proclamation of the Constitution. In 1964, on the order of the authorities and while renovating the square, the monument was hidden among the trees at 3 Maj Street. In 1981, the monument returned to its original location. Designed by Edward Kotyłło, it was put on the plinth and decorated with an eagle by Witold Marcewicz. Near the monument, a modest plaque to commemorate the Unknown Soldier was placed in 1916. It was destroyed during the war. A new monument from the red sandstone with the inscriptions commemorating the battles of the Polish Army was erected after World War II according to the design by Jerzy Jarnuszkiewicz.

The new *Monument of the Union of Lublin* is linked to the old monument from the 16th century that was standing in front of the Monastery of the Capuchin Monks. It was erected in 1826 thanks to the efforts of Stanisław Staszic on the artificially created hill. This obelisk put on a plinth was made of iron taken from the Kielce Steelworks owned by Staszic. The monument was decorated with the Classical, gilded relief by Paweł Maliński. It presents the female figures symbolising Poland and Lithuania, and the emblems of the two countries.

The Czartoryski Palace

THE CZARTORYSKI PALACE

In the north-eastern corner of the Square there is the Czartoryski Palace built at the end of the 17th century. It is a typical Baroque building, standing on the design similar to a square with the corner halls and the wide projection going towards the eastern facade. At the turn of the 17th and 18th century, it was a property of Stanisław Herakliusz Lubomirski, the Crown Marshal, the owner of the Końskowola Estate with the centre in Puławy. The famous Flemish architect – Tylman from Gameren, was working for him. The shape of that first Baroque Palace is connected with him. While digging under the Palace the scientists discovered the foundations of the still earlier building, probably the old Czartoryski Palace. In the years 1725-1728 the Palace was restored. It belonged then to the Marshal's daughter Elżbieta nee Lubomirski Sieniawska. The Palace was restored under the supervision of Franciszek Magier from Moravia. Around 1730, the estate with the Palace was inherited by Maria Zofia Sieniawska, Elizabeth and Adam's daughter primo voto Denhoff who married Prince Aleksander Czartoryski, the Governor of Ruthenia. Thus the fortunes of the Lubomirskis, the Denhoffs and the Czartoryskis were united. The Czartoryskis who were linked with Puławy did not live in Lublin; the Palace was taken care of by an administrator. The last owners were Adam Kazimierz and Izabella Czartoryskis. Prince Adam sold the Palace with the estate reaching Krakowskie Przedmieście Avenue in 1805. The owner changed frequently then and the Palace lost its glamour. In the 2nd half of the 19th century it became a tobacco factory. In 1860 it was bought by the well-known Lublin banker – Leopold Kronenberg, and in 1908 it was bought by Wiktoria Michelisowa, the owner of the nearby "Europa" Hotel (see: pp. 115-116).

In 1911 – on the grounds of the former gardens at Radziwiłłowska and Staszic Streets – a skating ring under the name "Lubelski Skating Ring" was organised. A year later, the "Oasis" Cinema was built there, which could accommodate 240 viewers. In that time, the Palace was rebuilt, and the cinema administration was located in it. After World War I the cinema was expanded to 1000 seats and re-named "Corso". The Palace, damaged during World War II was restored according to the project by Czesław Doria-Dernałowicz, and it retained its Baroque appearance. At present it is the seat of the Lublin Scientific Society and the Institute of Central and Eastern Europe.

THE LUBOMIRSKI PALACE

It is also called the post-Radziwiłł Palace. In the 16th century, it belonged to the Firlejs; the family had possessions that stretched from the Vistula to the Wieprz River. It was the Renaissance court then, perhaps the defensive one. It was inherited by the Ostrogskis.

In 1683 – the Lubomirskis came into the possession of the Palace by marriage. Then it belonged to them for several years. It was at that time that it was renovated and turned into the aristocratic Baroque Palace. Tylman von Gameren was the architect. The Palace was a one storey building then with a steep roof and rooms at the corners.

In 1722, the owner of the Palace became Karol Sanguszko, the Marshall of the Grand Duchy of Lithuania. The Snaguszkos who lived in Lubartów did not care much for the Palace. Uninhabited it decayed. In the times of the Bar Confederations it was burned in the Great Fire. Szeptycki owned it in the 80s of the 18th century. They did not restore it. In 1801 the devastated building was purchased on the auction and the Mayor – Benjamin Finke gave it to the State. The renovation began since it was to serve as a military hospital.

In 1810 it acquired a new roof of shingles. It was storage place for straw then. In 1822 on the orders of General Zajączek, the administrator of the Kingdom of Poland it was to become the seat of the Lublin Provincial Government. Jan Stompf, the general inspector of roads and bridges prepared the design. The building received the additional floor, the side pavilions were added, and the Palace acquired more monumental character of the neo-classical style.

After the fire of 1829 the Palace was rebuilt again. This time according to the design of a famous architect – Henryk Marconi. The works were supervised by Ferdynand Konotkiewicz, the head architect of the Province. The building acquired the Classical character with the elements in the central projection of the facade. The original proportions were restored by liquidating the second floor. The side wings were connected with the main corps, and the tall towers were added. That is what the shape of the Palace looks like now. During the Partitions it was the residence of the Russian Governor, and then General Governor of Austria.

In 1918 the Palace was taken over by the Army. It was the seat of the Regional Command, and the residence of the Regional Commander – General Mieczysław Smorawiński. After World War II the building was taken over by the University.

THE PALACE
OF THE PROVINCIAL AUTHORITIES

In the 2nd half of the 19th century, the Lubomirski Palace – the seat of the Lublin Provincial Authorities did not cope with the needs of the expanding Tsarist bureaucracy. On the grounds of the former gardens and near the cemetery of the Bonifraters' monastery, a new building was to be erected, and the preparations for its erection lasted since 1852. In 1859 the design of the Warsaw architect – Julian Ankiewicz – was finally approved. Initially, the new building was to be the exact reflection of the Lubomirski Palace. Finally the convention of the historical styles was approved. It was built in the years 1860-1862 in the eclectic style. After World War I the offices of the Command of the District of the 2nd Corps of the Polish Army and the Provincial Government were located there. After World War II the building deserted by the German authorities was given to the University. At present it also houses Alliance Francaise.

The Provincial Government Palace

Dr Mieczysław Biernacki's Villa   *The Secession Houses at 3 Maj Street*

Along the 3 Maj Street the secession houses were erected at the beginning of the 20th century. The first of them *No 6* was a hotel and a boarding house "Janina". Now it houses the Provincial Educational Inspectorate (see: p. 127). At *No 14*, behind the aforementioned houses there is the villa built in 1880 by Walerian Pliszczyński. Before 1939, it was the house of a famous charity worker, publisher and journalist, the manager of the hospital, Dr Mieczysław Biernacki. Now, it is the seat of the "Kurier Lubelski" newspaper. Several metres further on, at the junction with Chmielna Street, we can see the beautiful palace from the 19th century – that is the eclectic building with the Classical elements (for instance, the column entrance portico). The palace belonged to the Chrzanowski Family. In 1895 it was purchased by Stanisłw Śliwiński, the owner of Antopol and Sadurki, the minister of food in the years 1919-1921. Then the Palace was taken over by the nuns who were educating young maids. At that time there were sheds and pigsties, the vegetable and the flower garden. In 1955 the whole complex was taken over by the Oculist Department of the Lublin Medical Academy under the leadership of Professor Tadeusz Krwawicz, a pioneer of the crio-surgery of the eye. In 1978 a new clinic was built near the old one.

The Old Building of the Lublin Provincial Commission

The Former State Bank

Going towards Krakowskie Przedmieście Avenue, at the corner of 1. Armia WP Street we shall pass the interesting Neo-Gothic building No 4 erected in 1826 on the design of Jan Stompf for the Lublin Provincial Commission. The identical building was standing at 37 Krakowskie Przedmieście, and it housed the Customs and Excise Office. Between them there was a scale. In 1914, on the ground of the Customs House, the State Bank was built on the design of the provincial architect – W. Sołowiew. It is a bank today too, the seat of the Polish Investment Bank (see: p. 134).

THE BUILDING OF THE FORMER SOCIETY OF THE LUBLIN INDUSTRIALISTS

Leaving the 3 Maj Street we come to Kołłątaj Street. At the corner of Krakowskie Przedmieście Avenue we pass by the building erected in the years 1899-1900. It was designed by Gustaw Landau for the Society of the Lublin Industrialists. It was a credit bank with unlimited liability, established in 1884. In the pre-war time, on the ground floor there was the popular cafe of Józef Rutkowski, and nearby "the breakfast rooms" of Władysław Radzymiński with excellent cuisine. The building of the eclectic architectural shape was the monumental accent of the new part of Krakowskie Przedmieście Avenue. On the place where it was erected, once a one floor building stood. It was the house where Klemens Junosza Szaniawski, a writer and a journalist was born.

The Former Building of the Society of the Lublin Industrialist

The Building of the General Post Office

THE BUILDING OF THE GENERAL POST OFFICE

In the 19th century, beside the present building of the Post Office at 52 Krakowskie Przedmieście there was once a small, one-floor building. In 1848 the building that belonged to the chemist Jan Górecki, was purchased by the town. The municipal authorities organised a post office there. The needs of the post office rapidly grew. In 1861 on the neighbouring plot a new, two storey building of the post office was erected. It had 11 windows in front and the entrance in the centre of the facade. At the back there were stables, cart sheds and a smithy that served coaches. The entrance for them was at the left hand side. In 1923 the fire consumed the roof and the second floor. The Post Office was rebuilt in 1924 by Bogdan Kelles-Krauze and Jerzy Siennicki. The third floor was then added, and it was crowned with the attic wall. In the middle a clock was placed and on the wings the emblems of Lublin and the Lublin Province. The author of these reliefs was Anna Trzcińska-Kamińska. The whole was crowned with the sculpture of the eagle destroyed by the Germans in 1940. It was reconstructed in 1995 by Witold Marcewicz according to the design by Zbigniew Kotyłło. Where once the carts were kept, a theatre was organised probably in 1936. It had a stage, a backstage, the curtain and the basic elements of the stage machinery. The theatre was owned by the Polish Military Organisation and amateur theatre performances were organised there.

THE NUNS OF THE VISITATION MONASTERY

Walking Kołłątaj Street we pass a small square closed by the building of the former cloister of the Nuns of the Visitation. The Order was founded in 1610. The Nuns of the Visitation were invited to Poland by Queen Maria Ludwika in 1654. They came to Lublin in 1723. The settled in a wooden cloister and organised the educational boarding house for girls. Their property burnt in 1732. About the 18th century, a new complex of brick buildings was erected in that place. It took the form a quadrangle, with the internal garth and the Baroque church in the middle of the front elevation. The house of the Cloister Chaplain was erected near the monastery, at its western side, in the old cloister gardens. This building is also a good example of the baroque architecture. During the Napoleon campaign of 1809, when the Polish Cavalry under Prince Józef Poniatowski entered Lublin, the cloister was turned into a military hospital, and the Nuns of the Visitation were moved to the Carmelite cloister at Świętoduska Street. During the Russian occupation, *The Chapel with the Sad Christ's Figure*

there was a military hospital there. The remaining part of the building was taken over for the soldiers' quarters. The cloister church was changed in 1837 into the Russian Orthodox church. It played its role until the representative church was built at the Litewski Square. In the pre-war time, the cloister remained in the hands of the Army. Around 1921 the church was divided into two floors and a military canteen was organised there. There was still a hospital there. After World War II the building was occupied for some time by the Army. Then it was taken over by the Medical Academy. Now, there is the Lublin Cultural Centre there. The witness to the building past is the beautiful Baroque chapel from 1767 with the Sad Christ's Figure. Its Baroque character is underlined by the fine, bent endings of the corner pillars and rich moulds.

We are leaving the monastery of the Nuns of the Visitation and turn left into Peowiaków Street. Here we can find the examples of the Lublin secession. It was the style that governed in the years 1905-1913 character of the elevations of the houses erected at the main streets of Lublin. At *No 5* there is the three storey building with the rich stucco of the elevation, the secession crates of the balconies and the interesting gate where the floral ornaments were used as well as linear endings. One can find both Berlin and Munich elements and Viennese elements in the Lublin Secession.

THE CITY THEATRE

At the outlet of Peowiaków Street there is the building of the Lublin Theatre. The Lublin theatrical traditions go back in time to the 17th century. The Lublin students presented religious plays at the Jesuit school theatre at the time. Since the middle of the 18th century, the groups of the wandering actors visited Lublin and they played in various palaces and hastily prepared rooms. The first aim at organising the permanent theatre was the so called Comedy room at Królewska Street, and the next one – the building erected at Jezuicka Street in 1822. When even this one

The Juliusz Osterwa Theatre

proved to be too small, the committee to build a new theatre was founded. The initiators and the main sponsors were Lublin industrialists, brothers Adolf and Julian Frick. The theatre in front of which we are standing at 17 Narutowicza Street was built from the collection of funds from the inhabitants of Lublin. The Society "The Lublin Theatre" was created and the contests to design the building was proclaimed. The building was to be located on the lot in front of the Church of the nuns of the Visitation. There were formerly the Capuchin gardens there between Peowiaków, Narutowicz and Kapucyńska Streets. The winner of the contest was the Warsaw architect Karol Kozłowski, the designer of the Warsaw Philharmonic Opera. The theatre building was being built in the years 1884-1886 under the supervision of Marian Jarzyński. The building acquired the eclectic character, and the facade reflected the variety of styles. At the beginning of the 20th century, on the ground floor there were the offices of the Society of the Bicycle Riders and the Lublin Society of the Horse Races. In 1921 the theatre building was purchased by the city. The thorough renovation was carried out then under the supervision of Ignacy Kędzierski, the architect. In the pre-war time, on the ground floor there was a ball room, the seat of the Musical Society and the Musical School. After World War II the Lublin Philharmonic Theatre was also located there for a long time. Now, the theatre is named after Juliusz Osterwa.

At the square (see: p. 94) opposite the Theatre there is ***Jan Kochanowski Monument***. This outstanding poet of the Renaissance Epoch frequently visited Lublin, especially as a courtier of the Lublin Governor, Jan Firlej. Lublin was also the city where Jan Kochanowski died. The Committee of the Public Library and the Society of the Friends of Sciences initiated the idea of erecting the monument of the poet to mark 400th Anniversary of his birth. It was in 1929. The contests for the design won Franciszek Strynkiewicz. The ceremonious opening of the monument was organised on 27 September 1931. First it was placed in the Old City Market Square, opposite the Tribunal. During the occupation the Germans ordered the Monument to be destroyed. Then, Henryk Zaborowski, the chief of the Department of Buildings in the City Council with Stanisław Lis, the stone mason hid the monument in a trench in the Old City. In 1951, the monument was placed on the square at Narutowicz Street.

Jan Kochanowski Monument and the Relief on the Monument Commemorating the Poet

The Former Stanisław Staszic High School

THE BUILDING
OF THE FORMER PROVINCIAL SCHOOL

Right off the square at 12 Narutowicz Street there is a large building. It was erected in the years 1858-1859 for the educational purpose. It was the seat of the Provincial School, and since 1864 – the men's college. First, the Provincial School was located in the post-Jesuit buildings near the Cathedral, then at Bernardyńska Street. Due to bad technical state of those buildings Józef Skłodowski, the headmaster, and grandfather of Maria Curie managed to collect funds for building the new school. It was erected at Namiestnikowska Street. The school was built by Julian Ankiewicz according to the design of Antoni Sulimowski, the architect of the educational region. In 1866 the graduates of the school were: Aleksander Głowacki (Bolesław Prus), the writer, Aleksander Świętochowski and Julian Ochorowicz, the philosopher and the psychologist. Then the college became a Russian language school, and one of the graduates was Lublin – born Tadeusz Gałecki (Andrzej Strug), the writer and the soldier of Piłsudski's Legions. When Polish returned to school it acquired the name of Stanisław Staszic. The school functioned here till 1934. Then the building was taken over by girls' high school. Now, the building houses the Educational Department of the Lublin University.

HOLY MARY, THE VICTORIOUS CHURCH

On the left hand side of the square there is one of the most precious historical sights of the Gothic and Renaissance in Lublin – the Church of Holy Mary, the Victorious. It was built in the years 1412-1426 as a gift for the victory of King Władysław Jagiełło in the Battle of Grunwald. As the tradition has it, the church was built by the German POWs. At the end of the 14th century, the chapel was erected on the grounds

The Portrait of King Władysław Jagiełło founded to mark the 500th Anniversary of the Battle of Grunwald

The Belfry of the Nuns of the Visitation Church (phot. – CZH)

The Facade of the Holy Mary the Victorious Church

of Wojciecha, the widow. The chapel was funded by Wawrzyniec, the administrator of Lublin. Then King Władysław Jagiełło chose that place to found a church there. After building the church, the King brought St. Brigide's Nuns here. St. Brigide was the Swedish Queen whom Władysław Jagiełło greatly admired. The Lublin Cloister belonged to the oldest cloisters of the Order in Poland. The church that was standing far from the city defensive walls was often attacked and robbed.

The Neo-Gothic Altar from 1903

The Ogival Vault

The Stalls (the 20th c.) with the Paintings by Jan Szretter present-ing the Scenes from the Life of St. Brigide (after 1631, oil, board)

The Door in the Portal, Reconstruction, the Beginning of the 20th c.

It was also often consumed by fires. In spite of that it maintained the features of the original Gothic architecture. Only the loftiness characteristic for this style of a building was lost by raising the ground around the temple within the centuries. The Medieval origin of the church is documented by escarpments of the walls, the vertical rhythm of decorations of its top, and the ogival stone portal hidden behind the belfry. At the attic the interesting murals from the times of Kazimierz Jagiellończyk, the years 1466-1477 have been preserved. The paintings show the royal entourage going to Bethlehem. After the exchange of the flat, wooden vaults into the ogival brick vaults set beneath the frieze, the painting cannot be seen by the faithful.

The Temple's Interior and the Choir

SAINT BRIGIDE MONASTERY

The monastery buildings that adjoin the church close a small garth in a kind of a quadrangle. The monastery was built in stages – since the Middle Ages (1432) up to the late Renaissance (1589-1660). Similar to the church it was a frequent object of attacks by the Tartars and then the Swedes, the Cossacks and the Hungarians of Rakoczy. Its buildings were also consumed by fires. In one of the wings of the monastery there was also the male cloister of the same Order, which was liquidated in the 15th century. In the southern wing, built in the 17th century, in the times of Prioress Dorota Firlej, there is the outstanding example of the architecture of Lublin Renaissance – the monastery refectory with the beautiful, stucco decoration of the vaults supported by the centrally placed pillar. St. Brigide Monastery, which ran the school for girls, was abolished in 1819. The nuns still lived there, until their death i.e. around 1842. In 1838 the monastery was taken over by the Nuns of the Visitation when they left the post--Carmelite buildings at Świętoduska Street. They lived in the Monastery till 1882, when they moved to Warsaw. Then the monastery buildings were taken over by the Russian official institutions, the Russian Orthodox clergy, the school and the boarding house, and – during World War I – the Austrian authorities. In the pre-war period, the expansive building was settled by the "black" St. Ursula Nuns. They continued the educational tradition. After World War II, in the Monastery there was the high school for girls.

The square in front of the monastery buildings, where there is the monument of Jan from Czarnolas (see: p. 89), is the former monastery cemetery, liquidated, as all buildings of the kind, at the end of the 18th century.

Entrance into the Monastery Complex

THE PIARIST HOUSES

Along Narutowicz Street we move on to the Freedom Square. This old Kraków Tract has been called since the 19th century till 1928 – Namiestnikowska Street, to commemorate the Tsar administrator – General Józef Zajączek. Earlier it was Panna Maria Street and the name was taken from the church of this denomination. Behind the monastery gardens, we can see two unimpressive buildings on the right hand side, placed towards the street. These are the so-called the Piarist Houses, built in the 17th century in the Baroque style. The building on the right was called the Sarbiewski building, and the building on the left – the Prażmowski building. Later they were a property of the Niemyski Family. In 1732, Mikołaj Moszyński presented them

The Former Prażmowski House   *The Łopaciński Regional Public Library*

to the Piarist Monks, to organise a foundation for the education of young noblemen and burghers. The efforts of the Monks to deal with the education in Lublin were unsuccessful. Soon, they withdrew from Lublin. The buildings were rented. They were used, among others, by the Marshal of the Lublin Tribunal, Count Filip Olizar. During the renovation of the Tribunal, the Austrian authorities occupied the buildings and then it was the seat of the Credit Land Society. In 1819 the houses were purchased by the city, and since 1830 – there was a Russian military hospital. In 1870, both buildings were purchased by Ignacy Jaworowski. The buildings – then linked with a high wall – with the modelled arch gate, were very impressive.

The Piarist Houses were purchased in 1915 by the Society of the Lublin Museum, established on the initiative of the manager of the Lublin Branch of the Commercial Bank – Tadeusz Piotrowski. The museum exhibits and the library were placed in there. The basis for the library was the collection of Hieronim Łopaciński. It was one of the oldest public library in Poland. Earlier, after the tragic death of Łopaciński in 1906, the Society of the Public Library, bearing his name, was established. The books were first placed in the Dominican building in the Old City, then they were moved to the first floor of the Crown Tribunal. The Library was continuously expanding due to gifts and purchases. The room in the Crown Tribunal soon proved to be too small to accommodate the books. In 1933 the idea to establish the Society of the Cultural Activities was formed and its aim was the co-ordination of the cultural activity in the Region. The Łopaciński Public Library and the Society of the Lublin Museum joined the club. It was decided that the building will be created and it will assume the name of the House of the Cultural Activities. It was to be built on the plot at 4 Narutowicz Street that belonged to the Society of the Lublin Museum. The building was erected according to the design of Stanisław Łukasiewicz and it was funded from the public finances. It was built in the years 1936-1939. 18 cultural societies were to find shelter there. The building was opened on June 4, 1939, and Marshall Śmigły-Rydz participated. On the first days of September 1939, the bombs fell at the Sarbiewski outhouse and they destroyed most of the museum exhibits. On September 9, during the heaviest bombardment, two masterpieces of Jan Matejko – *The Battle of Grunwald* and *The Sermon of Skarga* – were brought to the Cultural Centre from Warsaw. First they were hidden in the building, and then moved to another, safer place, where they survived the occupation. At present, both Baroque houses are occupied by the Łopaciński Regional Public Library and the Bureau of the Artistic Exhibitions.

THE FREEDOM SQUARE

Up to 1838 there was a Targowy Square at the Krakow Tract. It was a market place for food products brought to Lublin by peasants from the nearby villages. In 1851 the market place was moved behind the City Council building at Świętoduska, and the name Targowy Square was changed into Bernardyński Square. In 1899 in the middle of the square the water tower was erected in the Neo-Gothic style. It was erected parallel to the water supply system that was built at the time. This investment was carried out under the supervision of Adolf Weisblat at the end of the 19th century. The tower functioned till the beginning of the 30s, when a new and more modern one was built at Racławickie Avenue. It was damaged in 1944, and demolished after the war.

THE PARYS PALACE

It dominates the houses at plac Wolności. The Palace is limited on both sides by Bernardyńska and Przechodnia Streets. It was built in the Baroque Epoch in the first half of the 17th century. It belonged to the powerful Parys Family. Feliks Parys was in 1674 the Governor of Lublin. At the end of the 18th century, the Palace was called the Grotkowski Palace named after the successive owner. At that time, one could admire the theatrical performances here and in the 19th century there were balls organised there by the Entertainment Department of the Lublin Charity Society founded in 1815. In the 19th century the Palace – then the property of the lawyer, Władysław Karwowski – was meant to be a tenant house. In the 2nd half of that century it was thoroughly rebuilt. The building lost its Baroque features. The second floor was added and the building acquired modern architectural shape. At the beginning of the 20th century, it was the seat of the Invest-Bank in Lublin.

At the background, over the escarpment of the Bystrzyca River, at Dolna Panny Marii Street there is a small building of the Tarłos.

The Parys Palace

THE PALACE OF THE TARŁOS

The Palace situated in the gardens between St. Bernard Monastery and St. Brigide complex was erected on the grounds, which – since the middle of the 16th century – belonged to the Słupecki Family of "Rawicz" coat-of-arms. At the beginning of the 17th century Barbara Słupecka, "the fervent Calvin", organised the protestant masses in the palace, since the Calvin church was destroyed by the Catholics in 1627. The Palace had to be ready at that time. After last of the Słupeckis died, their Lublin property was constantly changing hands. In 1701, they became the possession of Jan Tarło of the "Topór" coat-of-arms. He was the Marshal of the Tribunal, the governor of the Lublin Province and Sandomierz Province, the Under-secretary of the Treasury of the Grand Duchy of Lithuania, and general of the Crown Army. At that time the building began to be called the Tarło Palace. After Jan's death, his wife Zofia married Antoni Lubomirski, the Krakow governor. Franciszek Lubomirski sold the Lublin estate to the Piarist Monks, and they rented the Palace to Count Filip Olizar, the Marshal of the Tribunal. At that time splendid balls and meetings were organised here. They were famous even a century later. Then the Palace lost its glorious appearance. In the 19th century, the Tribunal authorities resided here for some time. Then it was occupied by the management of the Credit Land Society and later there was a military hospital. After the Napoleon Epoch, the Russians used it for the Treasury, military hospital and intendenture. In the 2nd half of the century, there was a boarding house for girls and then the state female academy. After 1970, the old building was given to the Provincial Cultural Centre. Once a beautiful Baroque Palace lost its stylish appearance after many renovations and adaptations.

In front of the Palace of the Tarłos one can see the Gothic building – it is St. Bernard church and cloister.

SAINT BERNARD CHURCH AND CLOISTER

It is the oldest historical sight in this part of the city. It was built in the 2nd half of the 15th century. Jakub Kwanta, the Mayor of Lublin and the inhabitants of the city gave the ground that was located outside the city walls to St. Paul's Church. In spite of efforts of St. Bernard monks, nobody was bold enough to build a cloister

The Figure of the Angel, the stucco sculpture, 1908-1910

St. Bernard Church and Cloister Complex

The Rococo Altar, the 17ᵗʰ c. with the picture
of Częstochowa Madonna, the 19ᵗʰ/20ᵗʰ c; oil, board

The Baroque top of the Cloister Buildings

outside the city walls. It could have been used as fortress by a potential invader. So only a wooden church was built. In 1470-1497 the building of the Gothic church of bricks and stone was undertaken after the permission granted by King Kazimierz Jagiellończyk. The Cloister was ready in 1519 and it was surrounded with a wall in fear of the Tartar invasion. A few years later the church was consumed by fire. It was rebuilt during the reign of Zygmunt III. In 1569, the ceremonial Mass was served here to commemorate the Polish and Lithuanian Union. The successive fire consumed the temple in 1602, and it was restored it he years 1607-1630 by the Italian architects – Rudolf Negroni and Jakub Balin. These were first attempts to transfer to Lublin the Renaissance style. Transformed by the Lublin craftsmen it turned into the Lublin Renaissance, which was adopted by towns from Kalisz to Grodno. The longitudinal, Gothic crowning of the presbytery turned into the semicircular one; the top of the church decorated with the Flemish "frames" was crowned with a silver bell; instead of the Gothic ogival vault turned into the cradle vault with rich decorations. Among others, also the Sobieski Family was among the benefactors of the church. They took care of it and provided rich donations.

The Interior of the Church with the Elements of the
Lublin Renaissance

The High Altar with St. Anthony de Padua,
the Beginning of the 17ᵗʰ c. the unknown author, Lwow

The Sculptures in St. Bernard's Church

Marek Sobieski, the King's grandfather, and the Governor of the Lublin Province was also a benefactor. Jan III Sobieski prayed in the chapel later called the Royal Chapel.

The successive changes in the church architecture came in the 19th century. St. Anne's Chapel was then demolished, and the western top of the church was changed into a vestibule. This, however, has destroyed the balanced, homogenous, Renaissance appearance of the building. In 1864, as repression for the participation of the Bernardine Monks in the January Uprising, the Tsarist authorities closed the church. The monks were removed, the cloister rebuilt, and the layman parish was established at the church.

Andrzej Osmólski's Tomb

Inside the temple there are some tombs giving evidence to the rich past of the place. Among them, there is the Renaissance tomb of Andrzej Osmólski from the 16th century, designed by Hieronim Canavesi workshop. There is a tomb of Jan and Eremian Kochanowski from 1604 from the black marble, the epitaph of Teodor Ustrzycki in Greek, and the Baroque tomb of Wojciech Oczko, an oculist, the outstanding doctor of medicine, the author of medical books and the secretary of three Kings: Zygmunt August, Stefan Batory and Zygmunt III.

99

THE CLOISTER OF SAINT BERNARD NUNS

The Cloister of St. Bernard Nuns was erected in the 17th century opposite St. Bernard's Church. The Lublin flag-bearer Piotr Czerny and cupbearer of Lublin, Marcin Siemieński gave the nuns the house and the plot "on Korce" in 1617. The nuns arrived in Lublin in 1618 and they dealt with knitting the liturgical robes and educating noblemen's daughters. The church and the cloister in the Lublin Renaissance style were erected for them till 1636. The cloister, expanded till the end of the 17th century, was closed in the irregular quadrangle, and linked with the nearby church. The garden stretched over to Żmigród. After the liquidation of the Order in 1864, the buildings began to collapse. The western wing was demolished in 1866 while the narrow Bernardyńska was regulated. At the end of the 19th century, the southern and eastern wings were demolished, together with the adjoining buildings. The Renaissance decorations were retained at its elevation. The Youth Cultural Centre is located there.

THE VETTER SCHOOL

At the beginning of the 20th century, to obtain the ground for new projects, the relics of St. Bernard Nuns' Cloister were removed. In the years 1906-1907, a large, three-storey building of the school of commerce for men was erected.

The building was erected in the spirit of the eclectic architecture with the tops decorated with the Pseudo-Gothic pinnacle. The school was funded by August Karol Vetter and designed by the Warsaw architects – Józef Holewiński and Teofil Wiśniewski. It is worth noting that the Vetter Family had also founded a hospital and gave numerous charity and social donations. August Karol Vetter became the chairman of the School Council. The Lublin School of Commerce, as the first educational institution in the Kingdom of Poland obtained the permission of the Tsarist authorities to teach in Polish. After August's death, his younger brother Juliusz Rudolf became the chairman of the School Board. Now there is the Complex of Economic Schools bearing the name of A. and J. Vetters, there.

The Building of the Old School of Commerce

The Sobieski Palace

THE SOBIESKI PALACE

A little further on, there is the Sobieski Palace from the 2nd half of the 16th century. It belonged to Marek Sobieski, a famous warrior from King Stefan Batory's times. This Baroque building with the characteristic tower crowned with a copula and a lantern, was inherited in 1660 by Jan III Sobieski. It was expanded then. In 1699, the Palace was visited by King's sons. The report from 1704 has it that after August II was removed from the throne, the Swedish King Karol XII visited St. Paul's church. In the 18th century, Radziwiłłs took over the Palace. It was not their residence, however. The neglected palace underwent decay. It turned into ruins when the roof collapsed. In 1811, it was purchased by a Lublin Lawyer, Dominik Boczarski. Before the middle of the century, he restored the tower in order to organise a mill there. It had large, horizontal wings. He spent all his money on the mill. He was not lucky, however, to reap the fruits of his investment. First storm destroyed the mill, and the lawyer went bankrupt. That fact gave vent to the local proverb: "He made business as Boczarski with his mill". The tradition was continued, however, since in 1860 there was a steam mill there. And although the owners frequently changed, they still wanted to make the mill operable in the palace. Finally, in 1884, the Strachociński Brothers purchased the building and changed it into the tenant's house. The Palace was rebuild according to the design of Marian Jarzyński. Now it represented the eclectic style. Then the building belonged to the Vetters. Helena Czarnecka organised the private school for girls there. Now it houses the Technical University of Lublin.

THE VETTER BREWERY

Situated a little further on the former monastery complex was originally in the 17th century the manor house of Halina Sapieha. She gave the palace and the adjoining garden to the Reform Monks. This Order that came to Poland at the beginning of the 17th century dealt with giving sermons and carrying missions. In 1663, the Kamieniec governor, Mikołaj Bieganowski founded a monastery, and in 1666 – the one-nave church that represented the modest, monk architecture. The Reform Monks had stayed there till 1820. Then, the cloister was settled by the Bonifrater Monks that left the monastery at Litewski Square, and then moved to Czechów.

The Buildings of the Vetter Brewery

When the monks left the cloister, the church was divided into floors and was used for the industrial purposes, similar to the adjoining cloister buildings. Only the preserved fragment of the elevation give evidence to the former sacral character of he building. The building destroyed by fires were put on auction as the government property. Karol Vetter, the industrialist from Poznań who came to Lublin in 1835 purchased them for 5000 zlotys. The beginning of the 19th century marked the beginnings of various kind of industry in Lublin. The deserted palaces and monasteries became the seat of these industrial companies. Karol Vetter with his sons August Karol and Juliusz Rudolf had turned the Reform cloister complex into the factory of vodka and liqueur. In 1864, they opened a brewery. In 1892, the energetic brothers commenced – as first in the Lublin Region – the production of malt, selling it not only in the Kingdom of Poland but also in Russia and Manchuria.

Now, at 15 Bernardyńska Street, there is the management and brewery No 2 that belongs to the Perła Browary Lubelskie S.A. – one of the largest companies in the Region. Beer from Bernardyńska was awarded medals for its quality on international contests as early as at the turn of the 19th and the 20th centuries.

MIEDZIANA STREET

At Bernardyńska Street, between Żmigród and Miedziana Streets, in the years 1860--1900 there was the coppersmith workshop of Albert Plage. Various kinds of steam, copper and iron boilers were manufactured there. Due to a huge demand, the plant had soon turned into a factory. It produced the facilities for distilleries, sugar factories, starch-works and breweries. At the end of the 19th century, the enterprise was taken over by Albert's son, Emil, and in the last year of the century he moved the factory to Bronowice. There he turned into – together with Teofil Laśkiewicz – into an aircraft factory. The only reminder of the factory at Bernardyńska is the name of the Street – Miedziana. The boilers were produced from copper and "miedź" means copper in Polish.

The narrow Miedziana Streets takes us to Cardinal Stefan Wyszyński Street. On the opposite hill there is the church of the Missionaries.

The Former Missionaries Cloister Complex

THE MISSIONARIES CHURCH AND CLOISTER

The hill called Żmigród that once played the defensive role was inhabited early. In 1627, the grounds belonged to the Sierakowski Family who gave the buildings that stood there to Benedictine Monks from Sandomierz. Before the estate belonged to Jan Lubieniecki, a protestant, who built a manor house there and organised a cemetery for the Arians. Then the estate belonged to Anna Stanisławska-Zbąska (1651/54-1700), the first Polish female poet, the author of laments written after the death of her third husband. The collection had a title *The Transaction or the Description of the whole Life of One Orphan described by Herself in the form of Bitter Laments in 1685.* In 1696, she gave the Palace with the adjoining grounds in Żmigród, to the foundation of the Missionaries, who preached Good Hope especially among the village people.

The Palace that comes from the beginning of the 17th century makes the oldest, northern wing of the cloister buildings. Its walls are decorated by a flatly sculpted frieze. It is composed of the set of medallions making a sequence of legendary and prehistoric Poland. They are surrounded by decorative tree branches.

The decorations were made probably in the middle of the 18th century, and they were modelled upon the wood engravings of Maciej Miechowita from 1521.

The 18th Century Frieze on the Cloister Building

The Baroque Interior
of the Former Missionaries Church

The High Altar with the picture of the Lord's Transformation
by Szymon Czechowicz, 1737-1740, oil, canvas

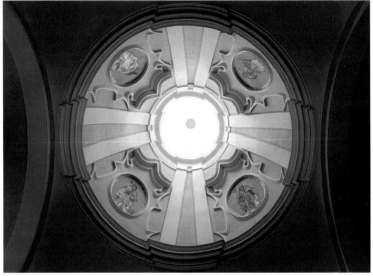

The Cupola of the Lord's Transformation Church

In 1714, the Priests' Seminary was moved to the cloister buildings in Żmigród from the Old City. Due to this fact, in the years 1719-1730, the construction works were being done at the Baroque Lord's Transformation Church. The temple erected on the design of Mikołaj Augustynowicz, Father Missionary, was set on the plan of the Greek Cross with the copula on the intersection of its arms. At present, the Neo-Gothic chapel from the 19th century is close to that church (it was adapted to the needs of the Greek Catholic Seminar that is there now and it was decorated with the contemporary iconostas by Jerzy Nowosielski). The whole complex is surrounded by pseudo-Gothic, 19th century fence. After the Missionary Order was abolished in 1864, the church and the cloister was taken over by the layman clergy.

The Seminary went on functioning. In the years 1907-1908, a monumental wing of the Classic architecture was added according to the design of Władysław Sienicki. During World War I, the buildings were occupied by the Russian and then Austrian authorities. Now there is the Metropolitan Priest's Seminary.

Along Cardinal Stefan Wyszyński Street we go up. On the left-hand side we can see the Wroński Palace.

THE WROŃSKI-HUSSAR PALACE

At the road leading to Zamość there were once the buildings of the brewery that at the beginning of the 17th century belonged to Bartłomiej Helt. The Palace was built there in the same century for the Jesuits who came to Lublin then. It was rected in the Baroque style. It had characteristic arcade arches of the ground floor and of loggia in the first floor, over which there was a corrugated roof. The building deserted by the Jesuits was later taken over by Lubomirskis, and then the Głuski Family. At the beginning of the 19th century the Palace was purchased by Józef Wroński. The successive owners were the Bentkowskis, and from the middle of the 19th century – the Hussars. After 1803 theatrical performance took place in the Palace. The room were small, however, and uncomfortable. In the years 1817-1820, the building stood beneath the level of the street when it was reshaped in order to diminish the slope of Królewska Street. To raise its level, the constructors used the bricks from the demolished Jesuit College at the Cathedral Square. Before World War I, the Palace was inherited by the Paprockis. Twice, new floors were added. First the second floor over the Baroque mouldings, and then the attic. The Palace became an ordinary tenant's house.

THE SEAT OF THE METROPOLITAN CURIA

Opposite to the Wroński Palace, just before the Cathedral, there is a palace complex that adjoins the Podwale and Misjonarska Streets. Right to the entrance gate, there is the Bishop's Palace. Originally it belonged to the Łańcuchowskis. At the beginning of the 19th century – together with the adjoining building that was later the seat of the Bishop's Court – belonged to Colonel of the Polish Army – Zawidzki. Then it was purchased by the Tsarist authorities. They used it first for the government post office, and then for the residence of the military commander of the Lublin Province. At that time it was a house with kitchens and servants' quarters.

The Building of the Metropolitan Curia. The Monument of the Primate Stefan Wyszyński

105

The Bishop's Palace was erected as a brick building in the 2nd half of the 18th century. In 1852 – when it was appointed the seat of the Bishop – it was thoroughly rebuilt. Another renovation took place in 1933. The author of that adaptation was the Lublin architect and conservator, Jerzy Siennicki. The building was restored and remodelled many times since then. The last renovation took place in the years 1988-1989 on the design of Jerzy Żochowski. During these changes, the building has lost many original features.

The building at the back is the Bishop's Court. The first owner of the place was Antoni Miączyński, the Governor of the Lublin Province. Then, it was a property of Colonel Zawidzki who – in 1817 – sold it to the Masonic Lodge. The purchasers were Paweł Wagner and Jan Reinberger. The Lodge "The Freedom Regained", for which the building was bought, functioned till 1822. There were also some conference halls here, and till the middle of the 19th century – the Criminal Court. In 1852, the complex became a property of the Curia. It was the seat of the Bishop's Court. The Palace, as well as the Bishop's residence was erected in the 18th century and it was rebuilt many times since then.

After 1852, under Bishop Jaczewski, a brick chapel was erected between the two buildings. The frescos of Józef Smoliński decorated its vault. They presented the apotheosis of St. Francisco, the Bishop's patron. In the middle of the 19th century, the complex of buildings was surrounded by a brick fence with a stylish gate. Since 1996, the middle of the flowerbed is decorated with sculpture of Marian Pudełko. It depicts the Primate Stefan Wyszyński who was the Bishop of Lublin in 1946-1949, and lived in this palace. The mentioned buildings are now the seat of the Metropolitan Curia.

Now, we turn left into Królewska Street, which goes up towards the Łokietek Square. There are many interesting buildings at Królewska Street.

THE PALACES AT KRÓLEWSKA STREET

At the corner of Żmigród Street under *No 17*, there is *the Pociej Palace*. It was erected in the years 1678-1700 for Ludwig Pociej, the Chief Commander of the Polish Army and the Governor of Lithuania. The Palace was successively owned by the Dłużewskis, the Borzęckis, the Dłuskis, the Lubomirskis and the Makowskis. In 1787, it was purchased by the Lublin merchant Korn. In 1803, the Palace was bought by the owner of Jastków, Adam Umieniecki. After the middle of the 19th century it belonged to the Zawadzkis, and in 1860 to Szaniawskis. In the 19th century, the building changed its architectural shape since one floor was added. The next floors are added in the pre-war time. The stylish architectural traces come from the time of rebuilding at the turn of the 18th and the 19th centuries. The building had then two large rooms with the stucco decoration of walls and the fresco decorated plafonds and four parlours with marble fireplaces. The walls were covered with fine tapestries. The building has lost its stylish proportions due to the successive remodelling. Today, it is a modest tenant's house.

The House *No 13* is the former *Sapieha* and *Jabłonowski Palace* from the turn of the 17th and 18th centuries. Since the end of the 18th century it belonged to Anna Jabłonowska, the pioneer of the peasants' reforms, the owner of Kock and Sławatycze. In 1805, the Palace was purchased by Adam Ratyński, the chairman of the Lublin Tribunal. When Tsar Alexander was passing by Lublin, he spent a night there. The building, which is situated on a steep slope of the ground going towards the Bystrzyca River was built on a pattern of a rectangle. It has two floors in front.

The Pociej Palace, 17 Królewska Street

One goes to yard through a tunnel of a vaulted gate. In the middle of the facade there is a projection crowned with a triangle tympanum. In the years 1847-1875, the building housed the Credit Land Society. After the 2nd floor and the side wings were rebuilt, the Management of the Society had its offices there. The present shape of the Palace is a result of the renovation from 1877 carried out by B. Orłowski, its successive owner. At the end of the 19th century, there was the "Wiedeński" Hotel there, and during World War I, a German theatre performed there.

The Buildings at Królewska Street

The next house *No 11* is *the Jabłonowski Palace*, probably built at the beginning of the 18th century. It was once called the Bishop's Palace, since in the years 1823-1852 the Bishop resided there when the new Curia was established in the Kingdom of Poland. Then the Bishop moved to his residence at Cardinal Stefan Wyszyński Street. Today, the Palace is a residential, two-storey house built on the plan of a quadrangle with the internal courtyard. It is located on a scarp and supported by huge escarpments. Together with other buildings at Królewska Street it was consumed by the fire in 1803, and rebuilt in the middle of the 19th century. Then it lost its once representative architectural appearance but retained the features of the Classicism.

On the opposite side there is the Cathedral Square where till the 19th century the Jesuit College stood. At the back we can see the Cathedral (see: pp. 42-45) and the Trinity Tower (see: pp. 68-69).

We move towards the Łokietek Square. On the left-hand side we find the presbytery of the former church of St. Bernard Nuns.

THE JESUIT CHURCH

In 1617, the Lublin flag bearer Piotr Czerny purchased a plot opposite the Bernardine Church and brought six St. Bernard Nuns from Krakow to live there Next year he founded for them a wooden church under the denomination of St. Peter and Paul, the Apostles. The construction of the church began in 1636 on the foundation of the Lublin cup-bearer Marcin Siennicki. The construction was interrupted by the Swedish Wars and then continued in the years 1681-1684. The temple had to be reconstructed again after the fire of 1769. The works lasted from 1770 to 1778. After St. Bernard

St. Peter and Paul, the Apostles Church

The One-Nave Architecture of the Church

The High Altar with the Picture "Jesus Walking on the Sea" (1st half of the 20th c., oil, canvas) and the statues of St. Clara and St. Francisco of Assisi

The Illusionist Side Altars by Władysław Barwicki

The Crucifixion – the Sculpture, the 18th c.

Assunta, the 1st half of the 17th c., oil, canvas, board

Order had been abolished in 1864, the church left with nobody to care for it decayed. Ten years later, the government initiated yet another renovation. The belfry that threatened to collapse was then demolished. The temple became a branch of the Lublin Cathedral. At the end of the 19th century, the Lublin painter Władysław Barwicki decorated the church interior with pseudo-rococo frescos. In 1919 St. Bernard Nuns withdrew their claims to their Lublin properties and in the next year, Bishop Fulman gave the church and the cloister to Jesuits. Till the fire of 1769, the building possessed the features of the Lublin Renaissance. During the renovation it lost those features and acquired some features of Baroque.

Now we reach the Łokietek Square (see: p. 30), surrounded with the characteristic historical buildings (the New Town Hall, the Krakowska Gate, see: pp. 31-32).

We enter Krakowskie Przedmieście Avenue. It was the main street of the suburb. Here the Krakow Tract ran through. The Lublin inhabitants started to build houses at this street – then called Wielka Street – in the 16th century.

THE HOLY SPIRIT CHURCH AND HOSPITAL

According to the rules that were binding in the Middle Ages, around the 14th century, a hospital was erected outside the city walls. In fact it was a shelter for the poor, the old, the crippled, the sick and the disabled. It was a large brick house with huge rooms, standing on the plot where the Town Hall is standing now. Beside the hospital there were the outhouses and the flats for servants and the surgeon. The Holy Spirit Church that was erected at the beginning of the 15th century was founded at the same time when the hospital was established in 1419. This foundation was approved in 1421 by the Krakow Bishop and it was binding all through the 15th century.

The Gothic temple had a one-nave construction, the presbytery that was beneath the level of the nave and the step top over the western facade. In 1508, the church and the hospital were rented to Mikołaj Czudło, the burgher, and in 1510, the supervision was executed by the City Counsellors. Due to many irregularities in the management of the foundation, Pope Leon X established the function of the prepository – a priest who took care of the hospital. In the middle of the 16th century, in the times of reformation, the Foundation bankrupted. The Medieval church was twice consumed by fires – in 1575 and 1602. It was restored till 1608 under the probable supervision of the Lublin constructor Jan Cangerle. The Gothic building so far acquired then the features of the Lublin Renaissance. Stanisław Licheński founded the new presbytery. The presbytery was covered with the Baroque, elliptic copula and was decorated with the late-Renaissance stucco. St. Stanislaw's Chapel was also similarly decorated and it had the arcades added. At the beginning of the 17th century, the hospital buildings were demolished, and the Carmelite church and cloister were erected instead (now the new Town Hall, see: p. 31). The second, northern nave, initially St. Mary's Chapel was founded in the 2nd half of the 17th century by Stefan Czarnecki, the Under-secretary of the Crown. The successive changes were caused by the fire of 1733. The Baroque top was added with the wavy moulds and the tower was raised. These forms recall the works of the outstanding Baroque architect – Paweł Fontana. In the middle of the 19th century, the tower acquired the neo-Gothic top. The interior of the Church is Baroque. There are many precious pictures ,and among them the miraculous picture of Mary, Mother of God and of Good Advice. In 1642, a student Jakub Lenczowski noticed tears falling

The Holy Spirit Church. The Crucifix in St. Anthony Chapel

The High Altar with the Picture of Mary Mother of Good Advice, the 15ᵗʰ c. and the unknown author

down the cheeks of Madonna and since then the picture has been famous. Many famous people prayed at the picture and were provided graces. Among them there were: Maria Sobieska, Piotr Skarga and Marianna Kościuszko, aunt of Tadeusz Kościuszko.

Beside, there is house *No 3*, which once made a part of the hospital buildings. At the turn of the 16th and 17th centuries, it had Renaissance architectural features. In the years 1858-1863, it was rebuilt and acquires its present classical appearance. In the drug store opened in 1862 by Xavery Russyan, the old historical equipment has been preserved.

The Świętoduska Gate is linked with the church and the hospital complex. It was added directly to the hospital buildings. The tract that led to it ran along Ruska, Lubartowska and Świętoduska Streets, avoiding the riverbeds and the moors at the Bystrzyca River. The gate did not serve the defensive purposes. It provided, however, the control over the trade movement from East to West. The Świętoduska Gate is the rectangular building with a wide, entrance arcade in the middle. There were the residential quarters over the gate, most probably for the city guards. The whole was crowned with the decorative attic. In the 17th century it was provided with the Baroque, wavy top. In the middle of the 19th century, it was no longer needed, so it was neglected. Its ruins, however, made an attractive subject for painters. It was painted by Wojciech Gerson, Aleksander Orłowski, Leon Urmowski, Adam Lerue. Since the ruins were the obstacles for the street traffic, they were demolished in 1858.

THE HOUSES
AT KRAKOWSKIE PRZEDMIEŚCIE AVENUE

The oldest houses built in the 16th century had to represent the Renaissance style. However, the successive renovations changed their appearance. The first one *No 2* has now a classic facade, and the second one, at *No 4* is provided with the original, narrow elevation and covers half of the original plot. The next one, *No 6* was built at the end of the 16th century. In 1836, the house was purchased by Jan Mincel and opened a store there. The description of the store can be found in *Lalka* by Bolesław Prus.

Bolesław Prus (Aleksander Głowacki) was a student of the Commercial School in Lublin in the years 1856-1861. He had to know Jan Mincel and then made him one of the protagonists of his novel. Another real hero of the book was a Lublin clerk Wokulski. He became an inspiration for the main protagonist of *Lalka* and bore the same name.

In the house *No 8*, the Chmielewski Family is having (with some breaks) a famous cafe and a confectionery since 1911.

One should not forget the houses *Nos. 15* and *17*, situated behind the Świętoduska Gate, which is no longer there. In the 19th century they served as an inn. The first post office of the times of coaches was located in house *No 19*, the property of Jan Grundlich, the postmaster and the commissioner of the post. Two adjoining houses *Nos. 21* and *23*, once served as Hotels *"Saski"* and *"Angielski"* and together with "Europa" were counted among the best hotels in town.

On the ground floor of the house No 15 there was the bookshop of Stanisław Arct; there was also a reading room of the Polish and French press and the publishing houses of books and musical notes. In 1887, the company moved to Warsaw but the career of this distinguished firm in the history of Polish culture commenced here in Lublin.

The monogram "W.G." (Wincenty Gałecki) and the number "1826" placed on the balcony of the house *No 25* informed of the date when the building was erected and

The Oldest Part of Krakowskie Przedmieście Avenue – at night... (phot. – CZH), and during the day

113

The Lublin Promenade

The Houses at Krakowskie Przedmieście

The Facade of a House at Krakowskie Przedmieście 24

The Chmielewski House (first on the left)
8 Krakowskie Przedmieście

The Houses at Krakowskie Przedmieście
(Nos. 18, 20, 22, 24)

The House No 25 Krakowskie Przedmieście

of its owner. The Magierski Family had a warehouse of medicines here. Stanisław Magierski was engaged in the Scout Movement and during the Polish-Soviet War of 1920 he fought as a volunteer. After graduating the Pharmacy Department he took over the management of the warehouse as well as the nearby drug store and paint store. He was a great fan of photography so he also sold cameras and photographic equipment. During the Nazi Occupation he was closely linked with the Home Army Resistance Movement and he wrote lyrics to a famous partisan song *I cannot visit you tonight…*

In 1954, the new building of a Savings Bank PKO replaced the houses *Nos. 14* and *16*, which were destroyed during the war.

Tadeusz Wieniawski, a medical doctor and a surgeon, father of world famous musicians: Henryk and Józef lived since 1852 in a luxurious apartment on the first floor of the House *No 20*. In the adjoining Baroque houses there were hotels: *"Warszawski"* under *No 30* with the restaurant, which was at that time regarded the best in Lublin, and *"Rzymski"* under *No 32* with the elegant "Alhambra" restaurant. The house *No 38* is linked with another famous name. It was here that in 1871, Tadeusz Gałecki was born. Later, he published such books as *The Underground People, The History of One Bullet, Marek Świda's Generation, The Yellow Cross* under the pen-name Andrzej Strug. During World War I he fought in the Polish Legions. In 1918, he became the vice-minister of propaganda in the Lublin Government of Ignacy Daszyński. In the house Nor 38 there was also the well-known warehouse of stationary and school equipment. It was run by Jadwiga Cholewińska who also organised the first shop with stamps for the collectors. The Cholewińskis published a lot of guides of Lublin and Kazimierz nad Wisłą.

In 1856, in the house *No 27* built at the beginning of the 19th century on the grounds of the former Czartoryski gardens and called the ZOO, Andrzej Semadeni, a Swiss, opened his confectionery. His son Kasper Semadeni organised poolrooms on the first floor.

After the fire of 1874, the Samadenis bought the whole house. After its reconstruction according to the design of Ludwik Szamota, which covered both wings (from Krakowskie Przemieście and Staszica Street), the house obtained the homogeneous eclectic architectural appearance. The Samadenis opened there an elegant cafe "Semadeni et Comp". On Krakowskie Przemieście Avenue there were the tables outside in Paris style. The porch was later covered with the roof and turned into a glass-surrounded veranda. The cafe functioned till 1946.

Just behind the Semadeni house, there was another hotel in the house *No 29 – "Europa"* built according to the design of Ludwik Szamota as a replica of the "Europejski" Hotel in Warsaw. It was erected on the plot that belonged to the Czartoryskis, and was purchased by Marcin Kobyliński and Chaim Forszteter. The ground were located on the verge of the old Warsaw Tract. The construction materials came from the Zamoyski Estates in Kozłówka. The eclectic building located at the corner of the representative square became its ornament.

Its front part at Krakowskie Przedmieście Avenue was completed in 1866, and the wing at Litewski Square – next year. It was modern building for those times; it had bathrooms, male and female servants, and a restaurant and confectionery on the ground floor. The hotel complex also included the manufacture of gloves, the haberdashery and optical shop. Its owner – Jakub Brilant – brought to Lublin a telephone and here presented its functioning to the public. In 1926, the hotel was taken over by the Lublin Charity Society due to the testament of the owners.

The hotel was twice damaged during the war (in 1939 and 1944). After the war it was nationalised and now it owned by the Polish Tourist Society – PTTK.

The point where Hotel "Europa" stood was gradually becoming a new city centre. From here the horse-drawn carriages transported passengers to the Railway Station. The were subordinated to the times of arrival of seven trains daily.

We are at the Litewski Square again.

THE TOWN CENTRE ROUTE II

The Litewski Square – Stanisław Staszic Street – Zielona Street
– Świętoduska Street – Karmelicka Street – Stanisław Staszic Street
– Radziwiłłowska Street – the Litewski Square

Major object:

1 *The Potocki Palace*
2 *The Carmel Monks' Church and Cloister*
3 *The Church and the Cloister Complex of the Immaculate Virgin*

From the Litewski Square (see: pp. 80-81), beside the Czartoryski Palace (see: p. 82), we reach Staszic Street. At the corner of that street, which was once called Początkowska Street (due to the denomination of the nearby church) and Zielona Street (earlier Kowalska from the smithies that were there) there is the Potocki Palace.

THE POTOCKI PALACE

The Potocki Palace was built in the middle of the 18th century by Grabowiec Governor Jerzy Potocki. It was expanded by his son Eustachy Potocki, the General of the Lithuanian Artillery, the owner of a magnificent residence in Radzyń Podlaski.

The Potocki Palace

The Lublin Potocki Palace was formed like a horseshoe, and was built in the late Baroque style. Its middle corps was elegant, one-storey, tiles-covered, and its two wings were also one-storey, shingle-covered and encompassing the outhouses.

Jan Potocki, Eustachy's son, a historian and an ethnographer, the Brigadier of the National Cavalry, gave the palace in 1790 to the nation. At the beginning of the 19th century, there were still theatre performances presented there. After the Third Partition, the Austrians organised a criminal and re-socialisation prisons there. Since 1835, when the prison in the Royal Castle has also functioned, the former Potocki Palace was left unoccupied. It was traditionally called "the old prison" or "the old arrest house". After the renovation, the office of the Russian Military Commander was organised there. It was also the seat of the Regimental Music School. Then the building was taken over by the Russian police, and since 1892, the chief of the police had a residence and an office there. In the pre-war period, the building housed the State Police. Now it belongs to the Catholic University of Lublin.

Now, we are entering Zielona Street. Its right-hand side was a background of numerous hotels and inns standing at Krakowskie Przedmieście Avenue. At the end of the 18th century, on the plot *No 5* there was a small garden owned by the Targowski Family. It was a recreational place for the inhabitants of Lublin. Among the trees and flowerbeds there were benches and arbours. The shooting place and the poolrooms as well as a nearby wine shop provided entertainment. Behind this – once famous and now neglected – place there is St. Josephat's Church.

SAINT JOSEPHAT'S CHURCH

In 1786, the Greek merchants purchased the manor house that was standing on the place where now the church is situated. With the permission of King Stanisław August they built the Greek Orthodox Church in 1790 from the collected money. This modest building was created by covering two adjoining houses with one roof. Beside, the church cemetery was established, but at the end of the 18th century it was liquidated like all objects of the kind. In 1833, General Hurko decided to turn the church into the Russian Orthodox one. The design was prepared by the Lublin chief architect Ferdynand Konotkiewicz. In the middle of the 19th century the building was rebuilt. Now there is a branch, St. Josephat's Roman Catholic Church.

St. Josephat's Church with the Belfry – now the Chapel of Mary of Ostra Brama

St. Josephat

The Chapel of Holy Mary of Ostra Brama

Zielona Street takes us to Świętoduska Street. On its left-hand side on a modest slope, there is a row of the former inns. The corner building *no 4* is situated on he plot that formerly belonged to Carmel Nuns. Then it was a part of the Greek Orthodox Church at Zielona Street. In 1866, Józef Michnikowski turned the houses that were standing there into *the Nawopolski Inn*. He designed it on the plan of the letter "U" with the passage on the axis. At the end of the 19th century, the complex was changed into a one-storey building with a connection over the gate

The Former Inns at Świętoduska Street

and two outhouses serving as stables. The "Nowopolski" Inn functioned almost to World War II. ***The Staropolski Inn*** (the house *No 6*) was created in 1848 on the plot that belonged to the Treasury of the Kingdom of Poland. In 1867, Józef Poppe erected a brick fence with a gate at the street, and eight years later some outhouses with a stable. In 1912, the building was bought by the Lublin industrialists – Jan and Edward Krausse. The Inn changed its appearance in the pre-war time.

On the plot selected from the Carmel Nuns' gardens and marked with *No 8*, there was a manor house built before 1800. In the first half of the 19th century it was a workshop where coaches were being painted. After the total reconstruction in 1873, the ***Nadwiślański Inn*** was established there. It functioned since 70s of the 19th century till 30s of the 20th century.

The next house *No 10*, was also probably an inn since at the back of the plot there were some umbrella roofs for carts. After the 1832 fire, Ferdynand Konotkiewicz erected an elegant, classical house there. There was a tobacco warehouse there and a hothouse. On the yard, there was a city bus depot.

At the eastern side of the street there is a square – the former Market Place.

The Former Market Butcheries

The gardens of the Holy Spirit Hospital that reached out of the city walls were surrounded by a wall. The cemetery that adjoined the Carmel Monks Cloister (today the New Town Hall) was liquidated at the end of the 18th century. In 1786, the place of former moats and walls was taken by a new street Nowa (today Lubartowska). It was established by the Commission of the Good Order. The former Świętoduskie Gardens were divided into two small gardens that soon were the places of walks of the inhabitants of Lublin. The northern part of the square was devoted in 1851 to the dairy products trading. The Market Place was then moved from the Bernadyński Square (today the Freedom Square). The trading tradition of the place went back in time to 1819, when a butchery was erected there under the supervision of the Lublin constructor, Łukasz Rodakiewicz. There was a city market place here even after World War II. Then it was turned into a city square and in 1963, *the monument commemorating the Jews killed during the war in the Lublin Province* was erected there.

In the pre-war time, the northern part of the square was occupied by the stop of the private buses.

Behind the row of inns at Świętoduska Street, one can see the lofty silhouette of St. Joseph's Church and the Carmel Monks' Cloister.

THE CARMEL MONKS' CHURCH AND CLOISTER

St. Joseph's Church and the Carmel Nuns' Cloister were founded in 1624 by Katarzyna nee Kretka Sanguszko (her portrait is in the presbytery of the church). The church had been erected in the years 1635-1644. The building possesses some features of the Lublin Renaissance. It is a one-nave building with a narrower presbytery and the decoratively cutout top of the facade with some figures of the saints. The cradle vaults characteristic of the Renaissance, decorated with stucco lintels have also been preserved. The Baroque altars are decorated with the column caps that do not support the construction, however. The sacristy and the Neo-Renaissance attic erected in front of the church were designed in 1906 by Stefan Szyller.

The Church and the Cloister of the Carmel Monks

St. Joseph's Church

The cloister building was founded on the former defensive manor house from 1623 that belonged to Rafał Leszczyński, the Governor of Bełz, the owner of a thousand of towns and villages, the proprietor of the castle in Baranów. Rafał Leszczyński had erected that building in Lublin to have his own, comfortable place of living during the Tribunal Sessions. The Manor House projected as a miniature of the Leszczyński palace in Baranów was built by the Lublin constructor of the Italian origin – Jakub Balin who also built the Parish Church in Kazimierz Dolny. The Manor House built outside the city walls was of a defensive character. Four towers at the four corners were strengthened by huge escarpments. While the Manor House was under construction, the Governor Leszczyński – a Calvin himself – had placed there a Calvin praying house. The gossip spread soon among the city population that there was "the synagogue of heretics" there. Students and inhabitants of Lublin started to initiate protests. There were some attempts to burnt the Manor. Well-equipped soldiers of the Governor managed to defend the place, however. After the Governor's death, the Manor House was purchased and adapted by the Carmel Nuns. It was included after 1630 into the complex of the cloister founded by Katarzyna Sanguszko nee Kretka.

St. Joseph with Jesus, the middle of the 19ᵗʰ c. oil, canvas   *St. Kazimierz, 1860, oil, canvas*

The Church Interior with a Band of the Stucco Decorations

The High Altar from the 1st half of the 18th c.

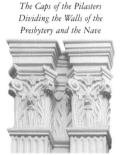

The Caps of the Pilasters Dividing the Walls of the Presbytery and the Nave

The Crucifixion, the Sculpture, the 2nd half of the 17th c.

Pieta, the 18th c., oil, canvas

The Nuns had lived here till 1807. Then they moved to the Cloister at Staszic Street. The building was then occupied for a short time by the Carmel Monks (after their cloister at the Łokietek Square was consumed by fire in 1803). Then the building was taken over by the Nuns of the Visitation, and in the years 1838-1864, it was again a cloister of the Carmel Monks until their Order was cancelled. Then, the cloister was turned into the military barracks. The Carmel Monks returned there in 1919. After World War II the authorities of the People's Republic of Poland organised a prison there. Today, the Carmel Monks are again the hosts of the cloister at Świętoduska Street.

A small street is running between the inns and the cloister wall. It is called Karmelicka Street. It will lead us to Stanisław Staszic Street. Earlier it was called Początkowska Street because of the denomination of the nearby church. It acquired the new name in 1927.

THE CHURCH AND THE CLOISTER COMPLEX OF THE IMMACULATE VIRGIN

After leaving Karmelicka Street and entering Staszic Street we pass the next cloister complex, which is on our right-hand side. This complex was founded by Zofia Daniłowiczowa nee Tęczyńska with her husband Jan Mikołaj Daniłowicz, the Under-secretary of the Treasury. The foundation was also supported by donations from the local gentry and Lublin burghers. In 1646, the founders obtained the permission to build a church and a cloister. The construction lasted almost

The late-Renaissance Head of an Angel in the High Altar (phot. – MK)

123

The Immaculate Virgin Church

The Baroque Pulpit

The Woman in the Nun's
Robes, the sculpture, the turn
of the 17 and 18th c.
(phot. – MK)

The Monk with a Cross,
the sculpture, the turn
of the 17th and the 18th c.
(phot. – MK)

The Capital from the Main Mould
(phot. – MK)

four years. The nave and the presbytery were covered with roofs only in the 18th century. The high altar was also erected at that time. The cloister built in the middle of the 17th century at Staszic Street formed a quadrangle adjoining the church.

In 1807, both fractions of the Carmel Nuns were united. St. Joseph's Nuns moved to the new cloister from the monastery at St. Joseph's Church. The cloister at Staszic Street was soon turned into a hospital. The nuns governed only one fourth of the building. In 1835, after the restoration of the buildings, St. Vincent Nuns were moved here. The church and the cloister became their property. The Charity Sisters also ran the orphanage. In 1865, there were only two Carmel nuns living here. They occupied only w few rooms. The cancellation of the Orders in 1864 shaped the fate of the Charity Sisters as well. Some of them were employed, however, as nurses. They worked as nurses in the hospital after World War II.

The facade of the Church, with no tower but with some features of the Lublin Renaissance shows the traces of the work by a provincial constructor that copied the Renaissance patterns. The Baroque interior of the Church is the effect of the rebuilding of the Church in the 18th century.

From the Immaculate Virgin Church and along Staszica Street we return to Radziwiłłowska Street and reach the Litewski Square.

THE TOWN CENTRE ROUTE III

The Litewski Square – 3 Maj Street – 1. Armii WP Street
– Ogrodowa Street – Spokojna Street – Partyzancka Street
– Wieniawska Street – Stanisław Leszczyński Street – the Saski Park
– Krakowskie Przedmieście – the Litewski Square

Major object:

❶   *The Evangelical Trinity Church*
❷   *The Former Lublin School*
❸   *The Former Seat of the Land Credit Association*

The Former "Janina" Boarding House   *The Secession House at 3 Maj Street*

From the Litewski Square (see: pp. 80-81) we move west towards 3 Maj Street. It was once called Czechowska Street. In 1916, during the celebrations of the 125th Anniversary of the proclamation of May 3 Constitution, it obtain its present name. The houses standing along it represent the Secession style. The House *no 12* was built in 1911 by Stanisław Sokołowski. Faithful to the Secession pattern, the building is asymmetric and ornamented with the geometrical decoration underlying the perpendicular, straight lines and squares. The House is topped with the wavy, Secession top apartments with the characteristic soft lines, and the pseudo-column is supporting the corner. Also the balconies have the Secession decorations – the flower and geometrical patterns. The well preserved, wooden gate at Cicha Street is boasting the excellent flower decoration. In the hall we can see the decorative tiles with the rustic scenes and the murals damaged by time with the mysterious figures of women. From the majestic staircase we can see the sculpted decorations of the doors leading to apartments.

The elevation of the House *No 10* was composed flatly and was added the top apartment with a wavy contour. The most striking elements of the facade are balcony balustrades with the geometric decoration of rectangles, flowers and garlands.

The Secession Decoration of a House at 3 Maj Street

The House *No 8* was built according to the design by Włodzimierz Sołowiow. The elevation is crowned with a garret of a flattened arch wrapped at the corners by volutes. It is topped with a head of a ram – the symbol of vitality and the forces of nature. In the perpendicular row of ornaments on the elevation, which are decorated with wreaths, we can find monsters, female heads and the vases that crown the buildings. In the entrance gate one can find barrel-like, cast-iron protectors against the damages that might be done by the passing by carts. Perhaps once, the statues stood in the empty now niches.

The Seat of the Former Municipal Credit Society   *"Manor House" at 4 Ogrodowa Street*

The vault is supported by the volute consoles. The stylish woodwork in the staircase has also been preserved. In the apartments one will find the stylish stoves with metal doors.

The House *No 6*, which is now the seat of the Department of Education, has lost its stylish features after many adaptations and restorations. Only – different at each floor – balcony balustrades have been preserved. They express the abstract and flower motives, either in a geometrical or natural forms. One can find, for instance, the familiar, sunflowers on the balcony of the 1st floor.

At the side of that house we turn right into 1. Armii WP Street (earlier Powiatowa Street, and in the pre-war time – Pieracki Street). On the right-hand side, at the corner of Ogrodowa Street, under *No 7*, we can see the richly decorated house built for *the Municipal Credit Society*. The construction of the eclectic building was probably commenced at the end of the 19th century, and it was completed in the years 1902-1904. The building was designed by Władysław Sienicki. The building was from the very beginning meant as the seat of the Municipal Credit Society. On the ground floor there were the offices and the cash-box of the Society, and on the floors and in the basements there were the employees' apartments. In the main axis of the house one can notice the traces of the so-called Great Order, from the Renaissance time, which was introduced by the outstanding architect – Andrea Palladi. They are underlined by the pilasters placed on high platforms. They are as high as the building itself. They have fluted cores and composite caps. The entrance to the house is ornamented with columns and covered with the semicircular arch--volute. The prodded projections are crowned with the triangle tops. The corner of the top floor is decorated with a terrace with the stone balustrade of banister.

When we enter Ogrodowa Street, we shall notice two villas that resemble Manor Houses. They bear the *Nos 4* and 6 and are situated on the left-hand side and in the gardens. They come from the beginning of the 20th century when the Polish architects were looking for the national form. This kind of architecture based on the gentry manor houses was promoted by Jan Witkiewicz-Koszczyc, the nephew of Stanisław Witkiewicz.

We return to 1. Armii WP Street. On the left-hand side we can see the Evangelical Church sitting among the trees.

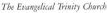

The Evangelical Trinity Church　　　　　*The Tomb at the Churchyard*

THE EVANGELICAL HOLY TRINITY CHURCH

In the 16th century, Lublin was a place where reformation trends collided. There were the Arian Brothers, the Lutherans, the Calvinists, Zwingle and Socyn followers there. The Counterreformation that got strength at the turn of the 16th and the 17th centuries led to the weakening of these religious centres. In 1631, the Lublin Protestant Prayer House was demolished. The Evangelicals prayed in Piaski, which were given the nickname the Protestant Piaski at that time. Before 1784, however, they purchased the manor house with a plot situated outside the city walls from Adam Łaskarzewski. The place complied with the contemporary rules that demanded the non-Catholic church to be situated no less than 500 metres from the city walls, and no less than 100 metres from the nearest Roman-Catholic Church. The Protestants were also given the permission to build a hospital and a school near the manor. The church was founded by the merchants and craftsmen of Lublin. The construction works had been carried out in the years 1785-1788 according to the design by August Zylhert. In effect, a modest, one-nave temple was built in the Classical Style with the Rococo interior (brought in from Piaski), a font, a pulpit and St. Thomas statue. In the brick, Classical altar there is the Baroque, two-storey picture by an unknown painter from 1628. In its lower part there is the Last Supper depicted, the upper one is devoted to the Crucifixion. On the right-hand side from the picture there is King Stanisław August Poniatowski's portrait, which is the expression of gratitude for the permission to build the church. In the nave walls there are commemorative plaques devoted to the Lublin Protestant priests, and the outstanding members of the community. On the staircase leading from the vestibule to the gallery and to the tower there are mourning epitaphs – the largest collection in Poland and one of the largest in Europe. They are made of iron, copper or brass. The names of the dead are written on the plaques and surrounded with flowers, laurel garlands or angles' heads. The Evangelic families that settled and assimilated in Lublin founded schools, hospitals, and during the Partitions fought for the Polish school. Hence the names of the renowned charity founders, social workers and industrialists like Vetter, Krausse, Dubois, Plage. There is a cemetery close to the church, which functioned in the years 1787-1831 (then moved to Lipowa Street). Out of 34 tombs that were standing there only a few have been preserved.

The Interior of the Church

The Portrait of Stanisław August Poniatowski

"The Crucifixion" in the High Altar

The Epitaph Plaques of August Karol Vetter
and Henryk Krausse

THE BUILDING OF THE FORMER LUBLIN SCHOOL

After the school strikes of 1905, the people started to fight for the Polish School in Lublin. "The Lublin School" was ceremoniously opened on March 6, 1906 at 3 Żmigród Street and 11 Królewska Street. The construction commenced in 1909 after purchasing the plot at 11 1. Armii WP Street. The building was designed by Teofil Wiśniewski in the "manor house" style. It was completed in 1915. In the same year, the Polish Cavalry under General Władysław Belina-Prażmowski, which entered Lublin, were stationed there. After World War II, the building was not returned to the school. The equipment was given to the Catholic University of Lublin. In the school building there were the Army Headquarters, and then the Department of Anatomy and Veterinary of the Lublin University. Now, there is Collegium Anatomicum of the Medical Academy.

The Former Lublin School

THE BUILDING
OF THE LUBLIN CHAMBER OF TREASURY

Now we enter Spokojna Street. In the years 1923-1925, in the house *No 4* a large building designed by Ignacy Kędzierski was erected for the Lublin Chamber of Treasury. During the Nazi Occupation the Poles had to leave Spokojna Street, and the district was cordoned off as the German part of the town. The building was now the seat of the German authorities of the Lublin District of the General Gouvernement. Immediately after the Soviet troops had entered the city in 1944, the building was taken over by the National Council with Bolesław Bierut and the Polish Committee of the National Liberation. On July 30, in the Column Hall, the first meeting of the PCNL took place. Lublin became the capital of Poland before – in February 1945 – the central authorities moved to Warsaw. For many years, the building had been occupied by the offices of the Regional National Council. Now, there is the seat of the Lublin Provincial Office and the Marshal Office.

Leaving Spokojna Street and returning to the Centre of the Town, we are turning right into Partyzancka Street. We cross Wieniawska Street, former Czerwona Street (and earlier Starowieniawska Street), and via Stanisław Leszczyński Street we enter the Saski Park.

THE SASKI PARK

The beginnings of the public park for the inhabitants of Lublin go back in time to the 19th century. The establishment of the Saski Park was one of the investments carried out as a part of the action to put the city in order. The enterprise was promoted by the Provincial Engineer, Feliks Łodzia-Bieczyński

In the City Park (phot. – GF)

– the initiator of the regulation of Lublin streets and squares, the establishment of the district for workers and the park for them in Bronowice, the man who also dealt with the sanitary problems of the city. He was the author of the idea to establish the park on the post-Dominican grounds situated near Wieniawa, at the Warsaw crossroads.

The project started in 1837. From that time there is the monument in the shape of a simple cube with the inscription: "The Epoch of Establishing the Park for Lublin, 1837". Well--shaped, wavy ground of 13 ha area allowed the loose composition of the Park. While the park expanded, new buildings were erected: there was a cafe and a confectionery, the stylish arbour, the sun clock, and at the entrance a barometer and a thermometer were placed. Around 1860, the Park was given the name the Saski Park. It was systematically devastated by the Russian soldiers staying in Świętokrzyski Barracks (now the main building of the Catholic University of Lublin), in 1889 it was surrounded with a high wall. The guards were watching the entrance.

At the main entrance at Aleje Racławickie Avenue there is the Guard's House – a neo-Gothic building erected in the middle of the 19th century. In the western part there is *the Monument called God's Martyrdom*, which commemorates the victims of a plague (Feliks Bieczyński in his brochure on the state of trees

The Monument "God's Martyrdom"

131

57 Krakowskie Przedmieście Avenue

in the Saski Park, which was published in 1854 states that the monument was erected in 1723). The victims of the plagues were usually buried outside the city walls. On the artificial hill a chapel with the statue of Jesus was built on the pattern of a square and the roof was added.

Leaving the Park we enter Aleje Racławickie Avenue. Its extension towards the Town Centre is Krakowskie Przedmieście Avenue. We walk along its left-hand side.

The four-storey house from 1908 built on the old city escarpment bears the *No 59*. From the Park's side it is closed by "the blind wall" crowned with a large arcade with the profiled arch of the arch-volute.

The neighbouring House *No 57*, which has five floors and the eclectic appearance is crowned with two pairs of people dressed in folk costumes of the Kraków District. This element is an aftermath of the popular trends at the beginning of the 20th century to search for the national architecture in the folk buildings. The last storey of the building is decorated with by volutes and festoons. Since 1888, there was the track for the fans of bicycle riding.

At Krótka Street (the next block) there is two-storey house *No 53* built in 1908, ornamented with the front projection, and crowned with a top of pinnacles. Its facades go both into Krakowskie Przedmieście Avenue and Krótka Street. The building has additionally oriels, terraces and balconies.

The Building of the Mutual Credit Society

At the second corner of Krótka Street it is worthwhile noticing the decoration of the House *No 51*; its windows are decorated with sunflowers, and the elevation is decorated with the orange facing brick.

The house *No 49* was erected in 1913, according to the design by Bronisław Kochanowski. The eclectic facade, decorated with jutties, maintained its original style.

THE BUILDING OF THE MUTUAL CREDIT SOCIETY

In 1907, the house at Krakowskie Przedmieście 47, was purchased by the Mutual Credit Society who ordered its enlarging. A decade later, the property was handed over to Bank Związku Spółek Zarobkowych. Since 1991, the restored building was the seat of Commercial Bank S.A. Today, it houses the division of Powszechny Bank Kredytowy S.A. The house bears the features of decorative style known as mannerism. The ground floor is decorated with huge, semicircular windows with ornamental grating.

In the neighbouring square, surrounded with a wall, stands the Evangelic church (see: pp. 128-129). Right behind it raises modern courthouse.

The Landowners' Credit Society Building

THE LANDOWNERS' CREDIT SOCIETY BUILDING

The building at Krakowskie Przedmieście 43, built in the years 1874-1876, according to the architectural design by Julian Ankiewicz, was intended to be the seat of the Landowners' Credit Society. Its classicist appearance makes it one of the most remarkable in town. The top of the building is decorated with the figures of ancient gods and goddesses of which the most noteworthy is the figure of Cerera – the symbol of fertility. In June 1944 the building became the seat of Polish Government representatives. Inside, there is a plaque dedicated to Władysław Cholewa – the chief authority of the post – war Lublin. Arrested by the State Police (NKWD), Cholewa spent a few years in the Soviet camp. He returned to Poland after the war, in 1947. Today, the building is a seat of the Local Court of Law.

The House at Krakowskie Przedmieście 39

The House *No 39*, once a popular inn "Pod Białym Koniem". At the beginning of the century, its signature decoration was the head of white horse hanging above the entrance. To make matters clear, it is worth mentioning that the name of the place translates into English as "White Horse Inn".

The last building on our way back to the Litewski Square is Polski Bank Inwestycyjny S.A. – the example of classicist style with "empire" elements.

THE TOWN CENTRE ROUTE IV

The Litewski Square – Krakowskie Przedmieście – Fryderyk Chopin Street
– Okopowa Street – Gabriel Narutowicz Street – Kapucyńska Street
– the Litewski Square

Major object:

❶ *The Morski Palace*
❷ *The Former Seat of the Commercial Bank*
❸ *The Capuchin Church and Cloister*

From the Litewski Square (see: pp. 80-81) we move to the left-hand side of Krakowskie Przedmieście Avenue. We pass by the "Lublinianka" Hotel (see: p. 86). Further on, under No 62, we can see the one-storey building – the former Morski Palace.

THE MORSKI PALACE

The building once belonged to the Morskis. Hence its name. Then it was a property of a notary – Serafin Konwicki. The successive purchasers of the Palace were: the constructor – Antoni Orłowski and the lawyer – Józef Wołowski who sold it then to the branch of the Łódź Bank. When in 1917, the Chamber of Commerce moved here from the building of the theatre at Narutowicz Street, the Palace became a place of magnificent balls of the Lublin Charity Association. After World War II, it was the seat of the publishing house "Czytelnik", and in 1989 – The Citizens' Committee "Solidarity". At present, there is one of the Departments of Bank Pekao S.A. On the plot No 64, since 1835, there was the factory of agricultural tools owned by a Scotsman, Jan Douglas and Andrzej Kedslie. The factory manufactured threshing machines, chaff-cutters and mills. After that enterprise collapsed in 1845, the other Scotsmen, brothers Bair, opened a plough factory there. Today, there is also a branch of the Bank Pekao S.A.

The Morski Palace

On the neighbouring plot, in the garden called "Tivoli" the elegant and comfortable summer theatre was established at the end of the 19ᵗʰ century.

THE BUILDING OF THE STATE AGRICULTURAL BANK

Leaving Krakowskie Przedmieście Avenue we turn into Chopin Street. It was established at the beginning of the 20ᵗʰ century, and first houses appeared there before the I World War. The houses here represent the eclectic and secession styles.

It was built in the years 1932-1934, on the lot No 6, according to the design by Marian Lalewicz. The bank represents the contemporary architecture. It was built

The Former Building of the State Agricultural Bank

as the seat of the State Agricultural Bank, then belonged to various banks, and now there is the provincial branch of the Polish National Bank.

We reach Okopowa Street. Once it led to the city trenches that were running on the right-hand side along Lipowa Street.

Moving along Chopin Street, we reach the plot *No 27*. In 1937 the construction of a cinema was commenced here as an investment of the Catholic Action. It was designed by Jerzy Siennicki. The building was completed after World War II. The building was adapted for the Library of the Catholic University of Lublin.

The Eclectic and Secession Houses at Chopin Street

The Decorations of the Houses at 11, 7, 9 Chopin Street

We return to Okopowa Street. On the left-hand side there is a band of green. In the pre-war time those were the grounds of the Sports Park with the stadium of KS "Lublinianka". Still earlier the plot was a part of the gardens of the Nuns of Visitation. Now, in its centre, there is the huge building of the Eastern Management of the State Railways built after World War II.

We reach Narutowicz Street. In its initial section it was a part of the old Kraków Tract. Then it was called Panna Maria Street (from the nearby church), and in 1822 it acquired the name Namiestnikowska Street (to honour the Tsar's Governor, General Józef Zajączek). In 1928, it was named Narutowicz Street (to commemorate the first president of Poland).

Opposite Okopowa Street there is Górna Street. Once there was a deep gorge here that led to the marshes near the Bystrzyca River. In the 17th century on the verge of the gorge, the city walls were erected. They made an additional defensive device of the expanding City. They led from the valley of the Czechówka River, near 3 Maja Street, cut across Krakowskie Przedmieście Avenue, and ran behind the building of the Nuns of Visitation (now the Centre of Culture), on the edge of Okopowa Street to Górna Street. Here they went down along a slope.

The House at 22 Narutowicz Street

At Górna Street 2 there is an original house with the Doric half-pillars and the Classical row of columns. The one-storey outhouse that was erected by the owner of the foundry, Adam Karwowski, housed a factory shop offering balustrades and cast-iron products.

We are turning left into Narutowicz Street. We pass the successive houses, the examples of the residential buildings from the end of the 19th century. The houses are standing on the grounds, which once were a property of St. Brigide's Nuns. After the liquidation of the Order, the city authorities leased or sold the grounds to the private owners. Initially, there were only outhouses and stables. Then, the magnificent houses were built.

In the yard of the House *No 19*, at the corner of Peowiaków Street, Edward Hartwig, a renowned photographer had his studio.

We are passing the Osterwa Theatre (see: pp. 88-89), and turning left, we enter Kapucyńska Street. As a communication route it was created on the verge of the gardens of the Capuchin Monks in the middle of the 19th century.

The Former Seat of the Commercial Bank

THE BUILDING OF THE COMMERCIAL BANK

In the 70s of the 19th century, on the lot No 4 at Kapucyńska Street, a brick house was erected. It was then purchased in 1898 by the Lublin Branch of the Commercial Bank. It was an elegant, brick, six-axis and three-storey house with the protruding mould and the transitional gate in the right, extreme axis. After the thorough modernisation, it was adapted to the needs of that institution. The interior was illuminated with the gas lamps, which introduced the element of the European modernity. Tadeusz Szymon Piotrowski, a banker and a great charity worker, became the manager of the Bank. He was also the initiator of the establishment of the Museum of Lublin, a member of the Association of Hieronim Łopaciński Public Library, the Chairman of the Society for the Protection of the Historical Sights and the honorary member of the City Council. In the pre-war time, the building was the seat of the Bank of the National Economy. It took over the house in 1922 when the commercial Bank found a new place at 39 Krakowskie Przedmieście Avenue.

We move towards Krakowskie Przedmieście Avenue.

THE FORMER "VICTORIA" HOTEL

At the eastern tip of the Capuchin property, where now there is the square in front of the drugstore "Galeria Centrum", at the beginning of 1875, the luxurious "Victoria Hotel" was built. It was designed by Józef Orłowski, the Warsaw architect and the member of the Academy of Fine Arts in Petersburg. It was regarded the most elegant hotel in Lublin besides "Europa". The two-storey building – the property of Antoni Bokszański – with the front facing Krakowskie Przedmieście Avenue, had a glass entrance for the guests. On the ground floor there was a hotel restaurant. At the back there were two outhouses and two yards – one belonging to the hotel and another one to the stables. The eclectic facade of the building complied with the style of the neighbouring houses. The building reached far into Kapucyńska Street. In the Fin de Siecle Epoch it was extremely popular, especially among the elite. In March 1891, one of the guests of the hotel was Helena Modrzejewska, who gave two performances in the new theatre at Namiestnikowska Street.

The members of the Provisional People's Government of the Republic of Poland that was created in Lublin on 7/8 November 1918 were speaking from the balcony of the "Victoria" Hotel to the crowds of the inhabitants of Lublin. They informed the people of the just proclaimed "Manifest to the Polish People".

The "Victoria" Hotel burnt among another buildings during the heavy bombing of Lublin on 9 September 1939. In 1945 the ruins were demolished and the cellars filled with earth. In 1956 – when the State Supermarket was built according to the design of Tadeusz Witkowski – the workers found a large deposit of explosives left here by the Germans. The wanted to destroy the centre of the City with them.

THE CAPUCHIN MONKS CHURCH AND CLOISTER

Just behind the square where once the "Victoria" Hotel stood, there is St. Paul and Peter's Church and the Cloister of the Capuchin Monks. Karol Sanguszko, the Marshal of the Grand Duchy of Lithuania and his wife Maria Anna, the owners of the Litewski Square, bought the plot in front of that square from Hieronim Jełowiecki, the regent of the Grand Duchy. They meant to erect a church for the Capuchin Monks. The Capuchin Monks, the begging Order and the branch of the Franciscan Monks, were established in 1525. King Jan III Sobieski invited them to Poland. The church and the cloister were under construction in the years 1726-1733. The complex was designed by Karol Bay, and the project was supervised by his nephew, Jan Bay. The project recalled the facade of the Il Gesu Temple in Rome – the building was meant to be its reflection. The church was built in the modest Baroque style and it has preserved it till today. In the west, the quadrangle of the cloister adjoins the church. There were yards and outhouses there. The rest

The Capuchin Church and Cloister

St. Francis, the 90s of the 20th c.

of the large plot adjoining Narutowicz Street was devoted to the gardens. The whole property was surrounded by a high wall. In 1769, the church was consumed by the fire. At the beginning of the 2nd half of the 19th century, the Neo-gothic Chapel of the Rosary Brotherhood was added. It was designed by Bolesław Podczaszyński and Michał Kamiński. The Chapel of the Immaculate Heart of Virgin Mary was established on the foundation of Jadwiga Bielska and Michał Kamiński. Over the altar, there is the figure of Holy Mary sculpted by Sosnowski. After the January Insurrection, in which also the Capuchin Monks participated, the Order was cancelled in 1864. Except for the church, the plot was taken over by the State and divided into small lots. In 1875, the wall reaching the pavement was destroyed and the old lime trees were cut. After World War I the property returned to its righteous owners.

The shape of the church represents the so-called Toscan Baroque. The facade is crowned with the triangle top. In the centre of the tympanum, the oval hole with the Eye of the Providence was placed. Below there is the painting of St. Francis and the Crucified Christ. On both sides of the fronton there are the figures of the Church patrons – St. Paul and St. Peter. The sculptures were probably made in the workshop of Karol and Jan Bay.

The Capuchin Church and Cloister. The Chapel of the Immaculate Heart of Holy Mary

The High Altar with the Picture depicting the Detention of St. Peter. P. Van Roy, around 1771, oil, canvas

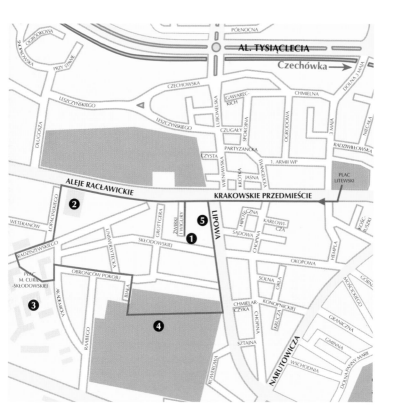

THE TOWN CENTRE ROUTE V

The Litewski Square – Krakowskie Przedmieście – Racławickie Avenue
– Idzi Radziszewski Street – the Maria Curie-Skłodowska Square
– Uniwersytecka Street – Biała Street – Lipowa Street
– Krakowskie Przedmieście – the Litewski Square

Major object:

❶ *The House of the Polish Soldier*
❷ *The former Dominican Monastery, now the Catholic University of Lublin*
❸ *The Maria Curie-Skłodowska University*
❹ *The Cementery at Lipowa Street*
❺ *The Tadeusz Piotrowski Palace*

Walking along Krakowskie Przedmieście Avenue we reach Racławickie Avenue. It obtained its name in 1916, for the 125th Anniversary of the Proclamation of the 3 May Constitution. Once a simple road that was cobbled at the beginning of the 19th century led to the Świętokrzyski Barracks (now the building of the Catholic University of Lublin). The first street on the left is Żwirko and Wigura Street. It was named to honour the Polish pilots who died flying in 1932. This street is closed by the House of the Polish Soldier.

JÓZEF PIŁSUDSKI HOUSE OF THE POLISH SOLDIER

In 1924, on the initiative of the social committee to build the House of a Soldier, the works on the project by Major Mieczysław Dobrzański began. In the course of the construction the bricks from the demolished Russian Orthodox Church from the Litewski Square were used. The works were supervised by engineer Bogdan Kelles-Krausse, the father of the famous opera singer, Beata Artemska. The construction ended in 1933. The house was built in the Neo-classical style and it housed the gym, the concert hall, the lecture halls, the entertainment rooms, the library with the reading room, the rest house and the soldiers' inn. It was also the seat of the educational organisation "The White Cross" and of other veterans' groups from the times of World War I. The House of the Soldier became an important centre of cultural and social life. During the Nazi Occupation it was the seat of the Hitler's Party – NSDAP. After World War II, there was an operetta and the Discussion Film Club.

The square behind Żwirko and Wigura Street is a part of the grounds that stretch along Aleje Racławickie Avenue to Kraśnicka Avenue and were purchased by the city from Teodor Count Rudiger. They were to be given over to the Army (the so-called Western Camp). In the 1st half of the 19th century there was a long, one-storey inn on the square. The present shape of the square comes from after World War II. In 1980, the monument of Henryk Wieniawski was erected here. He was a Lublin born violinist and a composer. The monument was sculpted by J. Pastwa. At the back, behind Grottger Street there is a huge building (under construction) of a new theatre and musical theatre. The street to the left, a part of the Zgoda Avenue planned before World War I, acquired the name of General Gustaw Orlicz-Dreszer after his tragic

The House of the Polish Soldier   *The Lublin Musical Theatre*

death. In the 90s its name was changed into Idzi Radziszewski Street to commemorate the first rector of the Catholic University of Lublin. At this fragment of the street there is another square. In the 19th century it was a training ground for the Russian soldiers that stayed at the Świętokrzyski Barracks. One should pay attention to the plaque devoted to the Resistance Fighters from World War II.

We pass by the Unia Hotel and stop in front of the Catholic University of Lublin.

THE DOMINICAN MONASTERY

At the old tract (now I. Radziszewski Street) that led to Bełżyce, a wooden church was built in 1434. It is said that it was erected by a Gdańsk merchant as a votive offering for the robbery of the Holy Cross from the Dominican Church (see: p. 186). In the years 1603-1623, on the initiative of the Bracław official Jacek Rawski and due to the gifts of the Lublin burghers, the wooden church was replaced by the brick one. In 1607, the church was given to the Dominican Friars (those who strictly obeyed the primeval monk rules). In the 18th century, the small monastery was expanded. The three-storey building was erected then on the pattern of a horseshoe. The last wing was added in the 19th century. The Dominican Friars stayed here up to the cancellation of the Order in 1800. In the deserted building the Austrians organised first a military hospital, and in 1809, the Government of the Warsaw Principality organised the military barracks. In the times of the Kingdom of Poland they were called the Świętokrzyski Barracks (from the name of the Russian Orthodox Church functioning nearby at the time). The Cossacks and the Regiment of the Riazan Infantry stayed there. At the beginning of the 20th century there was a military hospital again, and after World War I, the City Epidemic Hospital.

In 1918, the building was given over to the Priests Seminar that was organised at the time at today's Cardinal Stefan Wyszyński Street. In fact it became a property of the Catholic University of Lublin. Marian Lalewicz was the one who in the years 1921-1939 adapted the buildings and unified their architectural style. Later the facade of the building was reconstructed. The Holy Cross Church was destroyed during World War I, and then became a university chapel. It lost then the features of the Lublin Renaissance style.

The former Dominican Monastery, now the Catholic University of Lublin

*The Courtyard of the Catholic University of Lublin with the Monument of Pope John Paul II
and Cardinal Stefan Wyszyński*

Pope John Paul II Visiting the Catholic University of Lublin on 9 June 1987 (phot. – JM)

*The Sculpture of Christ on the Throne
in the Presbytery of the Holy Cross Church*

*The Organs and the Stained Glass Window
of the Częstochowa Madonna*

On the university courtyard there is the monument of Pope John Paul II and Cardinal Stefan Wyszyński, the Primate of the Millennium.

A little further behind the building of the CUL and in the western direction, there is *the Immaculate Conception of Holy Mary, Mother of God Church*. It was built in 1904 as a Russian Orthodox Church. In the years 1928-1929, it became the Roman Catholic Church. It was adapted for this purpose by Władysław Wojciechowski, and it played the role of the Garrison Church. In the 1929, Karol Frycz painted the murals.

Now we move into Idzi Radziszewski Street. In the cellars of the building at the corner of Uniwersytecka Street there is the Museum of Martyrdom "Under the Clock" (see: p. 164).

Now we move towards *the University Campus*. Its oldest part was erected in 1949 according to the design of Czesław Gawdzik. The social and residential part was designed by A. Górska and K. Różycka from Zakopane. Today, around the Maria Curie--Skłodowska Square there are the buildings of the Mathematical, Physical and Chemical Department, the new building of the Department of Chemistry, the Human Science, the Law Department and the Administration Building. The Monument of the University Patron – Maria Curie-Skłodowska – occupies the centre of the expansive square. It was designed by Marian Konieczny. On the opposite side to Radziszewski Street there is the building of the Main Library of the University. It was designed by Tadeusz Witkowski. After the junction of Radziszewski Street and Sowiński Street there is *the Students' Hut* – the University Cultural Centre – built according to the design of K. Różycka. Further on, there are students' dormitories.

From the University Campus we return towards the City Centre. At Radziszewski Street we turn into Akademicka Street and then into Obrońców Pokoju Street. We pass by Raabe Street – named so in the honour of the first rector of the University. At the street there the TV Tower, and the building of the Lublin TV recalling the style of the 19th century and completed in 1998. Behind the Lublin Radio Station we turn into Biała Street and we reach the military cemetery.

The Maria Curie-Skłodowska Monument   *The University Campus*

THE CEMETERY AT LIPOWA STREET

The gate with the inscription "Peace to the Heroes" leads to the cemetery of the Austrian and Hungarian soldiers that died during World War I. The cemetery was founded in 1916. The graves of the soldiers of the Piłsudski Legions are situated around the monument that commemorates their struggle. It was built in 1934 and designed by Tadeusz Witkowski. There we shall also find the graves of those that were killed during the war with the Bolsheviks in 1920. There are also graves of the soldiers of 1939 and the Home Army soldiers that died while liberating the city in 1944. In the opposite corner there is the symbolic Katyń Grave. Left to the main avenue there are graves of the civilians who lost their lives in Lublin in 1939. Among them there is the grave of the Lublin poet – Józef Czechowicz.

We are passing the main avenue and through the successive gate we enter the Catholic cemetery. It is one of the oldest and most precious of the Polish necropolis. Since the Rome Synod (1059) till the end of the 18th century, the cemeteries were created around the churches. The development of the cities and the growing number of their inhabitants – which characterised the 18th century – made the churchyards inadequate. New cemeteries, the so-called field cemeteries were founded outside the city limits. The history of the Lublin cemetery goes back in time to 1794. The oldest tombstone is on the grave of Marcin Szybicher from 1800, and it was probably transferred here from one of the churchyards. Among them are the tombstones sculpted by Antoni Kurzawa, Konstanty Laszczka, Ludwik Pyrowicz, Andrzej Pruszyński and Bolesław Syrewicz. The others are worth mentioning due to the historical reasons; there are buried the people meritorious to the city and the country. Father Piotr Ściegienny – the exiled peasants' activist, the author of the *Golden Book*; General Cyprian Zdzitowiecki, Jan Baranowski, the astronomer, Hieronim Łopaciński,

The Cemetery Gate

*The Russian Orthodox Church
at the Russian Orthodox Cemetery*

*Symbolic Tomb Commemorating
the Massacre in Katyń*

The Tombstones from the turn of the 19ᵗʰ and the 20ᵗʰ c.

the librarian and a scientist, Feliks Bieczyński, Klemens Szaniawski, Łukasz Rodakiewicz, the constructor of the Winter Theatre, Henryk Wiercieński, Tadeusz Mokrski, the navigator of the "Orzeł" submarine, Leon Głowacki, Bolesław Prus' brother; Stanisław Magierski, the composer of the famous partisan song *I cannot visit you tonight*, Konstanty Kietlicz-Rayski, the painter, the ethnographer and the actor, and Jan Mincel, the owner of the house and a shop at Krakowskie Przedmieście 6, the prototype of the protagonist of *The Doll* by Bolesław Prus. There are also collective graves of the soldiers of 1863 Insurrection with Leon Frankowski and Kazimierz Bogdanowicz; those of the prisoners of the Castle Prison and the Children of Zamość.

The northern part of the necropolis is occupied by the Evangelical cemetery with the graves of the industrialists meritorious to the city: the Vetter Family, Emil Plage; and the Russian Orthodox Cemetery with the Church. It was founded by the Chairman of the Treasury, Andrzej Dejkun in the years 1901-1904 as two-storey building.

Leaving the cemetery we enter Lipowa Street, once called Smentarna Street. Here was the last line of the defensive city walls. We are going left towards Krakowskie Przedmieście Avenue. At Lipowa Street there is a house *No 5* in the cellars of which

149

The Tadeusz Piotrowski Palace at 5 Lipowa Street

there are the relics of the bastion from the 16th century, which made a part of the above mentioned city walls. In 1904, the railway engineer, Tadeusz Piotrowski built a house of his own project on the plot, which belonged to the stonemason Adolf Timme. Piotrowski was working on the construction of the Trans-Siberian Railway. The facade of the house – or to be more precise, of the palace of eclectic style – is decorated with classic tympanum, the plant decorations under the windows, the label mould with a woman's head placed in the keystone of the Roman arch, and the Baroque bent balustrades of the balconies of the flower and geometrical motifs. In the cellars of the house, Tadeusz Piotrowski organised the mead brewery offering the drinking mead. His wife – Marianna – opened up in 1905 together with her sisters the private school, where the reigning language was Polish. The school was situated at 5 Lipowa Street. The elite Jan Kochanowski School continued these traditions till 1935. After World War II the school was liquidated. First, there was a kindergarten there and then – since the renovation of 1993 – the Insurance Agency "Życie".

Inside the building the interesting murals have been preserved, as well as the Neo--Baroque staircase with the balustrade of the rolled banisters. When we look at the staircase from above we have the impression that we look at the far, misty landscape watched from the manor house terrace. On the ceiling, at the background of the fragment of the blue sky there is a small angel playing a large drum. The plafond is surrounded with bunches of roses and poppies. In the rooms of the first floor one can admire the unique stucco decorations of the facets and plafonds. The intertwined patterns of the typically Polish flowers and herbs (nasturtium, field roses, camomile, heads of corn, cornflowers, clematis, lilies of the valley, waterlilies and nenuphars) placed on the frieze and plafonds are the expressions of the 20th century trend to look for Polish form in architecture and art. In the parlour, the faces of the Slavic wives are surrounded with thistle and sow-whistle. One should also pay attention to the Secession doors and the green stove.

From Lipowa Street and via Krakowskie Przedmieście Avenue we return to the Litewski Square.

THE MUSEUM ROUTE

The Władysław Łokietek Square – Jezuicka Street
– Teodor F. Greutz-Gruell Street – Grodzka Street – Zamkowa Street
– Tysiąclecie Avenue – Lwowska Street – Kalinowszczyzna Street
– Podzamcze Street – Unia Lubelska Avenue
– Droga Męczenników Majdanka – Wolska Street – Władysław Kunicki Street
– Józef Piłsudski Avenue – Lipowa Street – Maria Curie-Skłodowska Street
– Uniwersytecka Street – Sowiński Street – Racławickie Avenue
– Warszawska Avenue – the Władysław Łokietek Square

THE MUSEUM OF THE HISTORY OF LUBLIN

The Museum was established in 1965 in the restored and adapted Kraków Gate (see: p. 32). First it was known as the Historical Section, and in 1979 it was renamed the Museum of the History of Lublin, a Branch of the Museum of Lublin.

In the historical rooms of the Krakow Gate, the presented exhibition is devoted to the history of Lublin from the times of the oldest settlements (6th / 7th century) to 1944. Among the exhibits one should pay attention to: the objects coming from the archaeological excavations carried out on the city grounds (horseshoes, axes, ornaments), the clock bell from 1585 made by Aleksy Stanfusor, the "hangman's" sword, stove tiles and pottery. There are also the water pipes from the 16th century, and the exhibits closer to our times (the emblem of Stefan Gąsiorowski's factory of coaches and carriages, the travelling trunk from "Materko i Spoczyński" Factory, prints, photographs, portraits of the people linked with the city or those that contributed much to its prosperity.

In the Museum there are also some temporary exhibitions organised and those are devoted to particular important historical events or people connected with Lublin.

From the last octagonal floor of the Gate one can see the panorama of the city.

The Museum of the History of Lublin – the Fragment of the Permanent Exhibition

THE ARCHDIOCESE MUSEUM OF THE RELIGIOUS ART

The Museum was established in 1975, and besides collecting and exposing the collections it takes care of the objects of the sacral art. in the Lublin Diocese. It is the dominating activity of the Museum thus making it its speciality. The offices and the labs of the Museum are at 7 Filaretów Street, the elements of the sacral art. mostly from the 18th and 19th centuries are exhibited in the Trinity Tower (see: pp. 68-69) at the Cathedral Square. On the few floors in the original interior of the Tower, in the moody half-shades with the Gregorian Chants at the background, the figures of the saints are exhibited and the objects of the sacral art. attain special expression. The visitors – besides the knowledge that they get – are also charmed with the unique "microclimate" of the sacrum. The temporary exhibitions take place in the so-called White Room. From the sightseeing terrace of the Trinity Tower one can enjoy the spacious panorama of Lublin.

The Figures of the Holy Apostles Peter and Paul, the whole sculpture, the 18ᵗʰ c., Tomaszów Lubelski

*The Figures of the Moaning Women,
the whole sculptures, the 19ᵗʰ c.*

The Annunciation, the bas-relief, the 17ᵗʰ c.

Icons: Jesus, Mary, Mother of God, the 19ᵗʰ / 20ᵗʰ c., the unknown author

The Museum of the Town Hall and the Crown Tribunal – the Fragment of the Permanent Exhibition

THE MUSEUM OF THE HISTORY OF THE TOWN HALL AND THE CROWN TRIBUNAL

The Museum was established in 1990 after the renovation and restoration works in the Town Hall – the Crown Tribunal (see: pp. 34-35) had been completed. It is the branch of the Museum of Lublin. The exposition presents the history of the seat of the city authorities and the highest appeal court for the nobility of Little Poland, which held sessions in the Lublin Town Hall since 1578. The Museum is situated in the cellars of the building. One can see here the copies of documents and fragments of iconography. One can also see the recreation of "tortures".

THE DRUGSTORE – MUSEUM

The Museum was first located at Bramowa Street. In 1988 it was moved to its present place at 5a Grodzka Street. It is managed by the State Pharmaceutical Enterprise "Cefarm" and the branch of the Polish Pharmaceutical society.

In the vaulted room of the Old Town house one can see the historical, stylish drugstore furniture from the 19th century collected in the Lublin drugstores as well

The Drugstore-Museum – the Fragment of the Permanent Exhibition

as drugstores of Izbica and Krasnystaw. There is also the unique glass, china, scales (among them the 18th century scale made of animal horns). One will also find there bamboo boxes, Kipp's apparatus, the equipment to roll pills and other curious objects. There are also documents connected with the Lublin drugstores, old pharmacological books, photographs and diplomas of the famous Lublin pharmacists. The exhibitions of herbs are organised as temporary exhibitions.

Jan Matejko, The Union of Lublin. 1869, oil, canvas – The Gallery of the Polish Paintings

THE MUSEUM OF LUBLIN

The Museum in Lublin was created in 1906 on the initiative of the Lublin Agricultural Society. Its first seat were the halls in the Post-Dominican building. The cores of the collection were the exhibits presented at the Exhibition of the Artistic and Ancient Objects. It was organised in 1901 on the initiative of Hieronim Łopaciński, the teacher, the historian, the ethnographer and the librarian. Later the collection of the Hygienic Society was added and in 1911 – the collection of the Museum Section of the Lublin Branch of the Polish Tourist Association. In 1914, the Society of the Museum of Lublin started to operate and it became the owner of the collection. The greatest animators of the Society were Szymon Tadeusz Piotrowski, Juliusz Vetter and Antoni Rostworowski. The Museum was located in the old cloister at Namiestnikowska Street (now Narutowicza 4). The collection started to be catalogued and various exhibitions organised. The reorganisation of the exposition was carried out by Marian Trzciński, the painter. Since 1923 he was the temporary custodian of the Museum. In the pre-war period the collection consisted of a few thousand exhibits, which mostly came in as gifts. Among he most precious and numerous were those offered by Dr Wacław Lasocki, the organiser of the Museum of Nałęczów. Many exhibits were purchased from Dr Stefan Monasterski. Among them were the works of the Dutch masters. The collection was taken care of by volunteers and members of the intellectual elite of the city – Ludwik Grajewski, Ksawery Piwocki, Józef Dutkiewicz, Maria Żywirska. In 1934, the Museum became a part of the Union of the Cultural Work. The Institution acquired the new building that connected the former cloister outhouses (now the complex seats H. Łopaciński Regional Library). In June 1939, the Lublin Institute commenced its functioning, and it supervised many cultural institutions and among them, the Museum of Lublin.

World War II caused great damage to the collection. The most precious exhibits were seized by the Nazis. The Natural and Palaeonthological Departments ceased to exist. The Museum resumed its functions in September 1944. In 1950 it was nationalised. In 1956, the Museum was moved to some rooms in the Royal Castle (see: pp. 56-58). Then – in 1970 – the Museum became the sole proprietor of the Castle itself. The Museum of Lublin is divided into six theme departments (archaeology, ethnography, art., drawings, coin collection, military objects). It has five local branches and five branches outside Lublin.

Besides the permanent exposition, there are also occasional exhibitions organised here too. The Holy Trinity Chapel is a part of the Museum.

THE PERMANENT EXHIBITIONS: THE GALLERY OF THE POLISH PAINTING – 17ᵀᴴ-19ᵀᴴ CENTURIES

The most precious art. objects that are kept in the Museum are exhibited here. The exposition was organised in 1997 and it starts with the coffin and Old Polish portraits, and the examples of the paintings from the Enlightenment Period with the impressive portrait of King Stanisław August Poniatowski by Marcello Bacciarelli. The greatest collection represents the paintings from the 19ᵗʰ century. There are works by Artur Grottger, Piotr Michałowski, Wojciech Gerson, Józef Chełmoński, Juliusz and Wojciech Kossak, Stanisław Wyspiański, Józef Mehoffer, Jacek Malczewski, Olga Boznańska, Teodor Axentowicz and – of course – Jan Matejko. His *The Union of Lublin* (a depository from the National Museum in Warsaw) is the major picture in the Gallery.

Józef Chełmoński,
The Road in a Forest,
oil, canvas, 1905

Stanisław Wyspiański,
Nasturtium, pastel, 1903

Stanisław Ignacy Witkiewicz, The Portrait
of Róża Duchowa, pastel, 1934

Teodor Axentowicz,
The Portrait of Countess T.,
pastel, c. 1910

POLISH HISTORICAL AND MILITARY PAINTINGS

The exposition presents works of the Polish painters, and among them: M. Stachowicz, K. Alchimowicz, W. Kossak, J. Suchodolski. The pictures show the kings, chiefs, national heroes, historical events, battles (like the fragment of the Byczyna Panorama). Most of the paintings were created in the period of time from the 17th to the 20th centuries.

Wojciech Gerson, Queen Jadwiga and Dymitr from Goraj, oil, canvas, 1869

THE GALLERY OF THE FOREIGN PAINTINGS – 17TH-19TH CENTURIES

The Gallery is dominated by the Dutch paintings. Among them the most precious is *Pilatus Washing his Hands* by Hendrick Ter Brugghen. Other precious pictures were painted by Abraham Hondius, Jan Philip van Thielen, Jan Baptist Weenix, Louis de Silvester and Hendrick van Heemskerck.

Hendrick Ter Brugghen, Pilatus Washing His Hands, oil, canvas, 1617

The Furniture in Louis Philippe style, the 2ⁿᵈ half of the 19ᵗʰ c.

The China, Meissen, the 18ᵗʰ c.

The Furniture in Biedermeier Style, 1ˢᵗ half of the 19ᵗʰ c.

The Shepherd with the Shepherdess.
The China Figurine. Meissen,
the middle of he 19ᵗʰ c.

THE ORNAMENT POLISH AND FOREIGN ART 14ᵀᴴ-20ᵀᴴ CENTURIES

This Department covers chronologically, territorially and thematically wide range of the collection. Among the presented exhibits the most precious are European silver products, and among them also Polish and Lublin silverware from the workshops of Karol Rotkiel, Jan Gałecki and Karol Malcz; also the pottery (faience, majolica, and china from the most famous European manufactures); the Polish and foreign glass and portrait miniatures, furniture and cloth, as well as the utility objects.

THE POLISH AND FOREIGN MILITARY OBJECTS 14ᵀᴴ-20ᵀᴴ CENTURIES

The Exhibition presents the examples of the offensive and defensive weapons from the Middle Ages to the 20ᵗʰ century. There are swords, stirrups, armours, hussar breast plates, manual firing weapon, long and short, the wooden weapon, sabres and Polish bayonets or sabres and bayonets used in Poland. The most striking is the collection of the Eastern weaponry, especially the Japanese swords and the Turkish rifles.

The exhibits collected in this Department place the Museum of Lublin among the leading centres in Poland. The oldest exhibits come from the 18th century. A great part of the Collection is the folk art of the Region. The most interesting elements of the Collection are: the interior fishing, plaiting, sieve making, pottery making, smithing, weaving, customs, sculpture, painting and the folk clothes of the Lublin Province.

The Figures in the Re-creation of the Scenes from Jesus' Life by Feliks Dutkiewicz, 1934, Stara Wieś (Lublin)

The Krzczonów Folk Attire

The Weeping Christ, the unknown author, 1906, the Lublin Province

The Weeping Christ, the unknown author, the 19th c., near Kraśnik

ARCHEOLOGY

The Collection illustrates the oldest history of the Lublin Region from the Paleolithic Era to the Middle Ages. The exhibits come from the epoch of the culture of the rounded amphora, the funnel-shaped cups, and the string ceramics. The unique exhibit is e.g. the clay handle in the shape of a pair of oxen in bondage that comes from Krężnica Jara. The most precious exhibits from the Bronze Age belong to the Strzyżowce culture with the treasure of the faience beads. Among those historically and aesthetically important are also the bronze ornaments from Wakijów, the cult pots from Łuków, the treasury from Podlodów, the Roman and Arab coins and the amber beads from Basonia.

The Relics of the Culture of the Funnel-Shaped Cups, Neolithic Era, Lublin – Sławinek

The Relics from the Burial Place of the Przeworsk Culture, the Epoch of the Roman Influences, Podlodów

The Pots from the Culture of the Rounded Amphora, Neolithic Epoch, Lublin

The Amber Treasure from Basonia, the 5th c.

NUMISMATICS

It is the most numerous group of exhibits in the Museum of Lublin. The coin collection includes the Polish coins from the first Piast Kings to the contemporary times, and among them the treasures from the 15th–18th centuries. There are also foreign and ancient coins in the Collection. In the Department of Medals, most of the exhibits are the Polish medals – those given by monarchs, occasional and personal from the Renaissance till the contemporary times. The banknote collection covers the time span from the end of the 18th century till the contemporary times.

In the Collection there are also seals and seal pistons from the 14th to the 20th centuries.

The Treasure of the Arab Coins, the 8th c.

161

WINCENTY POL MANOR HOUSE

One of the branches of the Lublin Museum is the wooden manor house from the 18th century, which – at the beginning of the 19th century – belonged to Wincenty Pol's father. Initially, the house was standing in the Firlejowszczyzna District. In 1969 it was moved to Kalinowszczyzna and was to become the museum devoted to Lublin-born Wincenty Pol.

The exposition in the adapted interior shows Wincenty Pol as a poet, ethnographer, geographer, professor of the Jagiellonian University, the participants of the November Insurrection, the man who knew most of the prominent historical figures of the 19th century.

In July 1999, the exhibitions from the Literary Museum of Józef Czechowicz were temporarily moved to the Manor. The Literary Museum is also a branch of the Museum of Lublin.

Wincenty Pol Manor House

Wincenty Pol Museum – the Fragment of the Permanent Exposition

*Wincenty Pol
(from the Collection of the Museum
of History of Lublin)*

162

THE STATE MUSEUM IN MAJDANEK

The Museum was established in November 1944, on the grounds of the former extermination camp in Majdanek (organised by the Nazis on the fields of the village Majdan Tatarski in the years 1941-1942). The Museum is a special way of commemorating the memory and martyrdom of the victims of the Nazi terror.

The permanents camp exposition consists of the post-camp objects: the prison fields surrounded with the barbered wire, the guard towers, the gas chambers and the crematorium with the tomb of those murdered in the camp. In Field III there are some barracks and among them the three preserved living barracks. In three barracks in the utility part of the camp there are about 800 thousand pair of shoes and the prison clothes. In the barracks No 43, 44 and 45, as well as in the educational pavilion there is the permanent exhibition with the exposition entitled "The System of the Concentration Camps". In Barrack No 47 there is a multi-medial artistic installation called "Shrine – the Place of the Anonymous Victim of Majdanek". The prayers are said in several languages at the background of music. This unique sanctuary of a great symbolic depth was organised for the first time in the concentration camp where 235 thousand people from 52 countries from

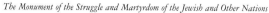
The Monument of the Struggle and Martyrdom of the Jewish and Other Nations

The Fence Around the Majdanek Camp with the Guard Towers

163

The Chimney of the Crematorium and the Copula of the Mausoleum

the occupied Europe were murdered. The special granite obelisk commemorates the execution of 3 November 1943. There is the inscription in Polish and in English there.

The first monument that commemorated the victims of Majdanek was erected in the camp in 1943. The Germans ordered the sculptor-prisoner, Albin Boniecki to make a monument called "The Column of the Three Eagles". It was "to make the camp look nicer". The prisoners inserted the human bones into the base of the monument and thus provided it with the symbolic meaning. Museum covers the original camp area of 90 hectares. It is symbolically encompassed by two monuments – the monument of the Struggle and Martyrdom of the Polish and Other Nations" by Wiktor Tolkin, and the Mausoleum with the inscription written in the frieze: "Our fate should be a warning for you". The Monuments are connected by the Road of Homage. On 9 June 1987, the Holy Father, Pope John Paul II covered that road while visiting Poland and Lublin.

THE MUSEUM OF MARTYRDOM "UNDER THE CLOCK"

The Museum was organised in 1979, in the building that – during the Nazi Occupation – was the seat of the Gestapo. In the cellars, where now there is the museum, at that time was the investigation prison for the detainees of the Royal Castle, the members of the Resistance Movement. Several thousand people were kept in the cells of this third – beside Majdanek and the Royal Castle – centre of the Nazi terror. Many of them did not survive cruel tortures. After the liberation, the place was still used – now by the communist secret police – as the investigative prison. In the preserved cells, the interior was recreated and the permanent exposition was organised to commemorate the prisoners. On the walls one can see the inscriptions made by the detainees.

The Museum collects documents and souvenirs connected with the fate of the prisoners of the Royal Castle and the House "Under the Clock". It also organises occasional exhibitions devoted to these topics. The new permanent exposition is devoted to the young people of Lublin and their struggle against the Nazis.

The "Podhale" Gate designed by Stanisław Witkiewicz

THE LUBLIN FOLK MUSEUM

The Ethnographic Park of 25 ha established in 1976 on the former grounds of the Sławin Estate was divided into sectors representing the villages of the Lublin Upland, Polesie Lubelskie, Podlasie, Powiśle, Roztocze and the Lublin agricultural settlement and a manor house sector. About 100 buildings have been transferred here and among them: the mill from Zygmuntów, the smithy from Urzędów, the households from Urzędów, Żuków, Niemce, Żabno, Tarnogóra, the oil manufacture from Bogucia, the "Podhale gate" from the old manor house in Łańcuchów, the manor house from Żyrzyn, the Greek Orthodox Church from Tarnoszyn.

In the beautiful, full of recreational values landscape one can "feel" the truth of the difficult conditions of living and working on the soil but also the charm of the village custom subordinated to the cycles of nature and the rights of nature. In the Lublin Folk Museum in Sławin there are shows presenting the vanishing village crafts, the customs, the traditional harvest customs and the habits connected with the calendar of the traditional Polish holidays in the aspect of the local, Lublin tradition.

The Dutch Windmill from Zygmuntów

The Pole Chapel

Spinning Well in the Village of Błażek

Cottage House in the Village Niemce

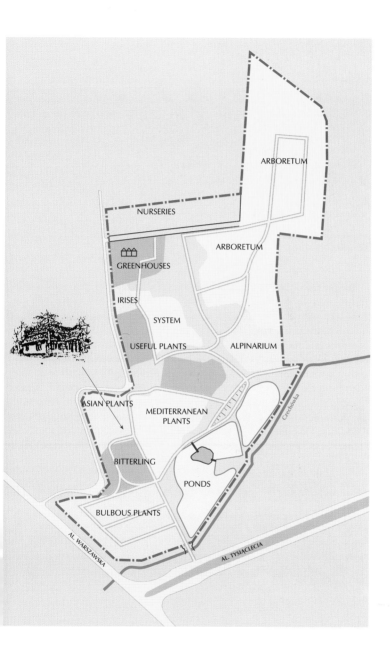

ARBORETUM

NURSERIES

ARBORETUM

GREENHOUSES

IRISES

SYSTEM

USEFUL PLANTS

ALPINARIUM

ASIAN PLANTS

MEDITERRANEAN
PLANTS

Czechówka

BITTERLING

PONDS

BULBOUS PLANTS

AL. WARSZAWSKA

AL. TYSIACLECIA

THE BOTANICAL GARDEN

The Department of the Onion Plants (phot. – PM)

The Botanical Garden is situated in Sławinek at the road to Warsaw. It is one of the five university botanical gardens in Poland and the only one on the right bank of the Vistula River. The Lublin Botanical Garden nicely located on the loess hill cut through by natural, deep gorges, was opened for the visitors in 1974. Two centuries earlier the grounds belonged to Jan Nepomucen Kościuszko. A frequent guest here was then his nephew, Tadeusz, later the leader of the Insurrection and the national hero of the United States of America. In the first half of the 19th century up to World War I there was a spa here with baths, residential homes and a restaurant. The historical splendour of the place can be now traced in the restored Kościuszko Manor House, in the historical lime-tree alley and in 200-years-old lime and larch trees. The so-called burning place of the spa was restored to life by opening a cafe with a terrace here. One can watch from there the old and north eastern part of the city.

The Kościuszko Manor House (phot. – PM)

The Lime-Tree Alley (phot. – from the Collection of the Botanical Garden)

Today's garden, which spreads over 23 hectares area is characterised by a great variety of trees, bushes and flowers. There are about 6500 species of them. Among them there are about 300 species of forest, meadow, marsh, steppe and water plants and about 500 species of the mountain plants from the Tatra, the Bieszczady, the Alps, the Pyrenees, the Caucasus and the Balkan Mountains. There are 1400 species of the lignified plants from Europe, Asia and America, and about 600 species of the so-called utility plants with large, colourful patches that sharply contrast with the green lawns of the decorative plants.

There are also hothouses with the tropical and subtropical plants: cacti, creepers, epiphytes and insectivorous plants – about 1500 species altogether. The Botanical Garden, which is run by the Lublin University plays both didactic and recreational functions.

On the Pond (phot. – from the Collection of the Botanical Garden)

White Cedar (phot. – PM)

Peony (phot. – from the Collection of the Botanical Garden)

Pallas Sandgrouse (phot. – from the Collection of the Botanical Garden)

WALKING THE FOOTSTEPS
OF THE JEWS OF LUBLIN

The Kraków Gate – the Market Square – Złota Street – Jezuicka Street
– the Market Square – Rybna Street – Ku Farze Street – Grodzka Street
– the Grodzka Gate – the Royal Castle Square – the Royal Castle Hill
– Tysiąclecie Avenue – Podzamcze Street – Lwowska Street
– Kalinowszyczna Street – Podmiejska Street – Sienna Street
– Białkowska Góra Street – Kalinowszczyzna Street – Podzamcze Street
– Walecznych Street – Unicka Street – Lubartowska Street
– Wodopojna Street – Świętoduska Street – Królewska Street
– Stefan Wyszyński Street – Zamojska Street
– Fabryczna Street – Droga Męczenników Majdanka – Majdanek

Major object:

- *The Grodzka Gate*
- *The Cementery at Kalinowszczyzna Street*
- *The Cementery at Walecznych Street*
- *The Academy of the Wise Men of Lublin*
- *Former Prayer House of Lubartowska Street (now the Hall of Fame)*

Jan Matejko – Jews Brought to Poland in 1096 – oil, canvas, 1887

THE JEWISH COMMUNITY IN LUBLIN

The Jews appeared in the city on the Bystrzyca River probably when the town received the city rights in 1317. King Kazimierz allowed them to settle in one of the Lublin suburbs known as Piaski. In the 16th century the Jews lived on the grounds north and north east of the Castle Hill. They were forbidden, however, to enter the town by the privilege Privilegium de non tolerandis Judaeis. As all other Jewish communities, also the community of Lublin struggled for the best conditions for its members. The Lublin Community appeared in the historical documents in the 2nd half of the 15th century. First privileges were granted the Community in 1523. King Zygmunt Stary granted the Jews living close to the Castle the same rights as the Jews in other regions of Poland had. Partly, it was the initiative of the Governor of Lublin Jan Pilecki who stressed the profits that the Jews provided; they cleaned the rivers, took care of the dykes, leased the customs, and kept the city scale. Still, the economic activity of the Jews was limited by law. In spite of that – in the 16th century, in the Golden Age of the city, the Jewish merchants played the leading role during the famous Lublin Fairs. The merchants from all over Poland came to the Fairs, and the Jews came also from Lithuania, Podolia and Wołyń. They brought more oriental goods than the Christian merchants. They also became more courageous in operating trade in Lublin. They rented rooms for shops and living quarters in monasteries, burghers' houses and palaces of the nobility. Soon the Old Marker Square was full of Jewish stalls and trading posts.

In 1580 – due to the privilege granted by King Stefan Batory, the Jewish Parliament – Waad Arba Aracot – was founded. Besides dealing with taxes (e.g. tax acquisition), it also played the role of self-government for all Jews in Poland. It held its session every year on February 2, and it was also called Waad Gromnic since it was a day of Holy Mary of the Candles. The Parliament of the four provinces: Great Poland, Little Poland, Ruthenia and Lithuania held its sessions mostly in Lublin and Jarosław but also in Bełżyce, Tyszowce, Opole and Łęczna. It solved trade arguments, approved credits, dealt with the printing of Hebrew books and kosher food. It also dealt with the innocent behaviour of women on the street and in the baths while in the company of the unbelievers, the payments for engagements and weddings. The last session of the Parliament of the Four Provinces took place in Lublin in 1725, and the last final meeting took place on 4 October 1764 in Pilica.

In the Golden Age (the 16th c.) of Lublin the first Hebrew prayer books and books started to appear. In 1578, Kolonymos, Mordechaj Jaffe's son, opened the printing house, which remained famous till the end of next century. This splendid tradition was re-activated in the 19th century by Samuel Arct in his printing house, which later on he moved to Warsaw.

THE OLD CITY MARKET SQUARE

We start at the Kraków Gate (see: p. 32), through which we come to the Old Town Market Square. As Majer Bałaban wrote "only here one can understand the sources of that past, awaken the ghosts of great people who once lived and worked here, recall their deeds and suffering and in their company visit street corners, houses and synagogues". In *the House at 17 Rynek* (see: pp. 39-41), Henryk Wieniawski, Tobiasz Pietruszka's son, the composer, and the violin player was born. Tadeusz Pietruszka, a respected physician from Wieniawa converted to Christianity and assumed the name – Tadeusz Wieniawski. In 1844 his son Henryk was also baptised, which is noted in the parish documents that can be seen in the Acoustic Sacristy of the Lublin Cathedral. Henryk's brother, Józef was a famous pianist.

ZŁOTA STREET

Franciszka Arnsztajnowa (1865-1942?) – the Lublin poet, lived and worked in *the House No 2* (see: p. 71). She promoted the Polish schools for Jewish children that began to be organised in Lublin before World War I. She was killed in the Warsaw Ghetto. Her mother was the writer, Małka (Malwina) Meyerson nee Horowitz (1839-1921), and her father was Bernard Meyerson, the merchant, the owner of the wholesale and retail trade of clothes at Krakowskie Przedmieście Avenue, opposite the Holy Spirit Church. Franciszka Arnsztajnowa's brother – Emil Meyerson (1859-1933) was a well-known philosopher, the creator of casualism, the new trend in philosophy. The curious souvenir kept in the Literary Museum in Lublin is connected with him – these are blades of grass, now in a silver frame, that came from the coffin, in which Adam Mickiewicz's body was transported from Istanbul to Paris. The souvenir was given – among other Poles – to Emil Meyerson. He described it in his letter from 1896. It is unclear, however, how the souvenir came to Lublin and to the Museum.

Franciszka nee Meyerson married Marek Arnsztajn, a well-known physician, social worker, Vice-Chairman of the Lublin Doctors' Society. The marriage between Franciszka and Marek was the sign of the growing polonisation of the Jewish intelligentsia that grew on various links between the Poles and the Jews. The Arnsztajns had an open literary parlour at 2 Złota Street.

In 1939, the Old Town was mostly inhabited by the Jews, and the richer of them had also houses in the city centre.

JEZUICKA STREET

In the building of the former *Teatr Stary at No 20* (see: p. 46) which – because of the name of its owner – was also called the Makowski Theatre, the famous Jewish artists performed. Among them there were: Rachela and Ida Kamiński, Zygmunt Turkow, Rudolf Zasławski, Symcha Natan, Dzigan, Szumacher, Morewski, one of the best Jewish actors, Moris Szwarc from the USA and Aleksander Granach – the former director of a theatre in Berlin. Since there was no permanent Jewish theatre in the city, the actors from Warsaw, Vilnius or Łódź performed in the "Panteon" Cinema at 20 Jezuicka Street. Sometimes they were also invited to "Corso" Cinema at Radziwiłłowska and to summer theatres at Niecała and Rusałka where there was a theatre called also "Rusałka". In "Panteon" at Jezuicka Street, in the years 1910- -1917, the amateur theatre of the Cultural Society "Hazomir" with the seat at Złota 5, performed. The group presented - with a great success – such plays as *The People* by Szolem Alejchem, *Gore* by Perec and *Nora* by Ibsen.

NOWORYBNA STREET

We return to the Market Place via the Rybna Gate (see: p. 38). We reach Rybna Street, the Rybny Square (see: p. 75) and Noworybna Street. In the house *No 3* there is the plaque placed here in 1964 with the inscription: "In this house, in 1944, the 1ˢᵗ Jewish Committee in Poland was founded at the National Council by the Jews that survived the Nazi Occupation".

GRODZKA STREET

From the Rybny Square via Ku Farze Street we reach Grodzka Street. Under *No 11* (see: p. 53), in the years 1862-1942 there was an orphanage for children, organised by the Jewish Community. The Curators of the institution were, among others, Józef Goldsztern and Bela Dobrzyńska, a well-known Zionist activist. When the Ghetto was liquidated, the children from the Orphanage were taken to Tatary and on the meadows near today's Odlewnicza Street – murdered.

GRODZKA GATE

The fervent life of the Jewish town – as Majer Bałaban wrote – began at the Grodzka Gate that was sometimes called the Jewish Gate (see: pp. 54-55). In both its wings there were shops with one door leading to the street and one window. They were called "kneeling shops", since in front of them there were kneeling platforms, which enabled to sell products safely through windows with the closed doors. In those shops one could buy everything. The variety of products was great. They provided quite a good profit to the city although the authorities continuously complained on unprofitableness of the Grodzka Gate. An idea appeared – which also applied to the Kraków Gate – to demolish it. The staircases that linked the houses with the Gate were unusual. They made a true labyrinth of stairs leading upstairs, downstairs and elsewhere. Till today – in spite of the renovations – the old architecture of the interiors did not loose these features.

THE CASTLE SQUARE

Via the Grodzka Gate and the staircase at Zamkowa Street we enter the Castle Square. Here, at the foothill of the Castle (see: pp. 56-58) and around it, the Jewish settlement laboriously started in the middle of the 16th century. It was difficult to live here due to the marshy grounds. At the right hand side leading to the Castle there is the plaque with the plan of the former Jewish town, which ceased to exist in the years 1942-1943 when the Ghetto was liquidated. It will be easier to imagine the pattern of streets from the Crown of the Castle Hill. The town had a shape of a triangle. Its top was situated at Kraków Gate, the left arm of the triangle was marked by Nowa and Świętoduska Streets, which at Kowalska Street were linked with Lubartowska Street. Other streets of the region were: Cyrulicza, Ruska and Czwartek as far as the Lubartów Junction. The right arm was marked by: Bramowa, Jezuicka, Szambelańska, Olejna, Rybna, Grodzka, Podzamcze, Krawiecka, Sienna up to Białkowska Mountain. The base of the triangle was made by Unicka and Kalinowszczyzna up to Tatarska. The main street of the town was Szeroka Street off Kowalska Street and reaching Ruska Street.

The Plan of the Former Jewish District   *The Fragment of the Former Jewish District*

The Plaque Commemorating Jakub Icchak Horowitz ("The Man Who Knows from Lublin")
the House at the Castle Square 10 (former Szeroka 28)

175

SYNAGOGUES AND PRAYER HOUSES

The centre of the Jewish town was the prayer square at Jateczna Street. There was a famous synagogue here *Maharszalszul*, called also the Great Synagogue. The place is commemorated by the plaque erected at the foothill of the Castle Hill. There are ruins of the so-called Jewish Tower. Here (see: pp. 56-57), at the lot purchased by Dr Izzak Maj in 1567 "near the pond", that magnificent synagogue was built according to the King's permission. It was named after the first rabbi – Szlomo Lurii. Several years later, on the first floor of the same building another synagogue was built; this one was a smaller one and was called *Maharamszul*, after the Lublin rabbi – ben Gedala. In both synagogues about 3 thousand faithful could pray. In 1854, the building collapsed but it was restored with a great effort of the whole Community. It lost, however, its valuable Renaissance features. The last administrator of the synagogue was Dawid Keller, who also read the fragments of the Torah. He had a powerful voice and the perfect diction. One of the cantors in the synagogue was Israel Mosze Rudnicki who came here from Zamość. His son, Professor Arad, the Director of Yad Vashem Institute in Jerusalem visited Lublin in 1988 and was in his house at 13 Ruska Street. The Synagogue – as the whole Jewish Town – was destroyed by the Nazis in 1943 when they liquidated the Lublin Ghetto. The remnants were removed in the 60s while the construction of W-Z Highway and Coach Station started.

Near the Maharszalszul Synagogue there was the school, which replaced the school organised here in the 16th century. At Jateczna and Nadstawna Street there were most of the cheders – traditional Jewish schools.

In the 30s of the 20th century, the Lublin Jewish District had about 100 prayer houses that belonged to the merchants, craftsmen, and Chassidic Groups from all over the country. Larger and smaller prayer houses were functioning, which belonged to the private people and to the Mourning Brotherhood. It is worthwhile mentioning the famous *prayer house of Rabbi Jakub Icchak Horowitz*, who was called "The Man Who Knows" from Lublin. The prayer house was organised in a wooden, small house standing in the courtyard at Szeroka Street 28. Hundreds of the pious Chassidic people gathered there. They came because they wanted to hear the prophecies of the Rabbi and to enjoy his charming personality. They came from all over the country and from abroad. The Rabbi was a precursor of the Chassidic Movement initiated in Podolia by Israel ben Elizer in the 18th century. That was a mystical religious movement. "The Man who Knows" from Lublin died in 1815 and was buried at the old cemetery in Grodzisko. Up till today the Chassidic groups from many countries of the world visit his grave. They burn candles, place traditional stones and small pieces of paper with prayers to God.

At the non-existing Podzamcze Street there was one of the oldest synagogues called Lejferszul. It belonged to Szmuel Wahl, the Rabbi from Brest, the legendary, one-day king of Poland.

PODWALE

At the Grodzka Gate, which was also called the Jewish Gate, there started the Podwale. In 1611-1630, *St. Adalbert's Church and St. Lazarus' Cloister Hospital* were erected (see: pp. 77-78). It was a shelter for the homeless Jews. One of the rooms of the former cloister was hired by the Charity Organisation "Achizer".

THE GHETTO

The dramatic climax of the existence of the Jewish Town in Lublin was the creation – on 21 March 1941 – of *the Jewish Closed District* – the Ghetto. It covered the right side of Lubartowska Street from Kowalska to Unicka, then along Unicka it led to Podzamcze or former Franciszkańska and then the Castle grounds to Podwale and Kowalska. It was Part A – its inhabitants were to be murdered first. Part B encompassed a part of Kowalska, Rybna and Grodzka Streets. The officials of the Judenrat who lived there and the people employed in German enterprises were to be transported to concentration camps next.

About 32 thousand Jews were closed in the Ghetto. These were permanent residents of the District and the people transferred here from other parts of the City. Many of the Lublin Jews were transferred to other regions of the country. They were jammed in a confined space and the living conditions were awful; people were hungry, uncertain of their future, terrorised. The executions were the common thing in the Ghetto. In spite of this – there was a cheap public kitchen that served meals to the poor and was operated by the well-known Jewish activists: Bela Dobrzyńska and Bela Szapiro. At Cyrulicza Street there was the illegal school.

The liquidation of the Ghetto started at night 16/17 March 1942. The initial selection of the Jews was carried out at the Maharszalszul Synagogue that was standing at the foothill of the Castle. From here the Jews were transported to the railway station behind the City Slaughterhouse in Tatary. About 1400 people daily were sent to the camps. Engineer Henryk Bekket, the Chairman of the Judenrat also shared the fate of the thousands of the Lublin Jews. While the "final solution" was underway, the Germans started to demolish the Ghetto. Some streets vanished for ever: Krawiecka, Jateczna, Szeroka, a part of Ruska, Furmańska, Nadstawna. The new Jewish cemetery at Unicka was devastated more than the old one in Grodzisko. The tombs were used as construction material for the Lubartów Junction and the road leading to the Crematorium at Majdanek.

In April 1942, the Germans organised the transitory ghetto in Majdan Tatarski for about 7 thousand Jews. Soon they started to take them to the Krępiec Forest where they carried out mass executions. On 9 November 1942, the remaining Jews were sent to the Majdanek concentration camp. In 1988, while the construction works were carried out at Majdan Tatarski, the workers discovered the remnants of 190 victims of the execution – the adults and children. Two years later the remnants were buried at the cemetery at Walecznych Street and in 1992 the monument was erected there with the inscription in Polish and Hebrew.

THE CEMETERY AT KALINOWSZCZYZNA STREET

From the Castle Hill we walk down to the Castle Square and along the Tysiąclecie Avenue we go to Kalinowszczyzna Street. Over the buildings of the Franciscan church and cloister (see: pp. 202-203) there is the Grodzisko covered with bushes and trees. Here was the old Jewish Cemetery. The oldest document referring to the place comes from 1555. It is the permission of King Zygmunt August to give to the Lublin Jews the third part of the hill called Grodzisko so they could organise the cemetery there. The inscription on the grave of a famous Talmud reader – Jaakow Kopelman – has a date 1541, which can mean that it was the first grave on the cemetery. There are, however, some graves deep in the ground, which make the historians believe that the cemetery was organised earlier – at the end of the 15th century.

The Jewish cemetery at Grodzisko was devastated many times. After World War II, out of thousands of tombstones only 200 were left, most of them reconstructed. They present various values: religious, historical and artistic. The tombstones solidly carved are typical examples of the traditional vertical pattern of their construction. The oldest of them – from the 1st half of the 16th century – recall the old Medieval forms; the Renaissance ones from the turn of the 16th and 17th centuries take a from of a portal with the inscription on the corps, crowned with various symbolic decorations. Those from the 18th century have ascetic form revoking the oldest ones; those from the 19th century possess some classical elements. First, modest attempts to ornament the tombs were undertaken at the end of the 16th century. In the middle of the next century they became very rich and flamboyant. Very interesting are personified symbols. On the tombstone of Jehuda Lejba ben Szlomo (d. 1646) these are hands blessing the people; on the tombstone of Cwi Hirsz – the deer; on the tombstone of the scientist Cwi Hirsz ben Azriel (d. 1737) it is a crown – with the title of the book *Eteret Cwi*. The special ornamentation may be found at the tombstone of Aeraham ben Chajjim Heilpern (d. 1762), the last but one Marshal of the Parliament of the Four Provinces. It is the figure of an old man that shoots an arrow from a bow. It is even more valuable since such allegories were not necessarily accepted by the rabbis.

At the Lublin Cemetery there are also tombstones of: Rabbi Szalom Szachna, the creator of the Lublin Rabbinical School, the last General Rabbi of Little Poland

The Old Cemetery at Kalinowszczyzna Street

The Tomb of Jakub Icchak Horowitz ("The Man Who Knows" from Lublin)

The Tombstones at the Old Cemetery

(d. 1558); Szlom Luria, called Maharszal (d. 1573), the most famous rector of the Lublin Talmudic Academy, officially appointed by King Zygmunt August; Rabbi Jakub Icchak Horowitz, called "The Man Who Knows" from Lublin (d. 1815). On the ninth day of the Jewish month Aw – i.e. July – August – the tomb is visited by the Chassidic groups from all over the world. They place traditional stones and pieces of paper with prayers on the tombstone and light candles. The tombstone of "The Man Who Knows" from Lublin is supported on both sides by large columns, and it is ornamented with the figure of a lion.

GRODZISKO AND BIAŁKOWSKA GÓRA

Turning from Kalinowszczyzna Street into Podmiejska Street, which runs along the cemetery wall, it is worthy to make a short walk to Sienna Street. Over the street there is Grodzisko Hill, the stone and brick wall that encompasses the old Jewish Cemetery, which was founded probably in the 16th or 17th century. At Sienna Street there are still some *old houses* that remember the times of the Jewish Town. A similar climate may be found at Białkowska Góra Street, which somehow emerges from Sienna Street and goes up among the rich plants of Białkowska Góra towards Kalinowszyzna Street.

TOWAROWA STREET

Walking along Kalinowszczyzna Street we reach the off-street – Towarowa. Here we can find the historical buildings of the 19th century *tannery*. The owner of one of the buildings was Szmul Ajchenbaum. In the years 1919-1945 he also owned the Siedliska estate in Fajsławice Community, where he ran the prosperous distillery. Ajchenbaum founded also profitable tannery at Towarowa Street in Lublin. This industrialist was the second richest man after the Zylber Family who owned the distillery, the brewery and a brickyard. He was one of the most famous Jewish industrialist in the City. He was also the owner of the Trade and Industry House at Królewska Street. Szmul Ajechnbaum was one of the leaders of the Orthodox political group – Agudas Israel. As a representative of that organisation he was a member of the City Council in 1927.

We return to Lwowska Street. At the roundabout we turn into Podzamcze Street. On the right hand side we pass the Isaak Bashevis Singer Square. It was named after the American writer who lived in the years 1904-1991. Singer's grandfather – Mordechaj Zylberman – was a Rabbi in Biłgoraj. The famous Nobel Prize Winner (1978) immortalised Lublin in his novel *The Magician of Lublin*.

THE CEMETERY AT WALECZNYCH STREET

From Podzamcze Street we turn into Walecznych Street. Opposite the Roman Catholic Cemetery a new Jewish Cemetery was founded in 1829. In the 1st half of the 19th century when there was no place at the old cemetery, the Jewish Community was granted ground outside the city to organise a new necropolis. In 1918, in the northern part of the cemetery, Jewish Military Cemetery was founded. The representatives of the powerful, rabbinical families were buried in the new cemetery. Among

179

Ohel – the Monument – Mausoleum

The Mausoleum Commemorating the Jews of Lublin

The Oldest Fragment of the Cemetery
at Walecznych Street

The Monument to the Anonymous
Victims of the Holocaust

The Monument to the
Victims of the Ghetto

them were members of the Eiger Family. In 1933, Rabbi Majer Szapira was buried there. Over his grave, a splendid tent was erected in the form of a brick building. In 1958, the body of the founder and the first rector of the Higher Rabbinical School in Lublin was transferred by his brother to Jerusalem, and buried at the Har Hamnochet Cemetery. The symbolic tent was left in the cemetery at Walecznych Street and it commemorates the place where once rector Szapira was buried.

In 1991, the new, restored Jewish cemetery at Walecznych Street was ceremoniously opened. The synagogue and the Hall of Fame were designed by Stanisław Machnik. The buildings were erected thanks to the foundation of Sara and Manfred Frenkl from Belgium. The cemetery is being taken care of due to the financial support of the Nissenbaum Family.

THE ACADEMY OF THE WISE MEN OF LUBLIN

From Walecznych Street we turn right into Unicka Street and then into Lubartowska Street. On the left hand side we can see the splendid building of the Jeszybot. The commemorating plaque reminds of the short history of that institution. There is an inscription in Polish and Hebrew there. Jesziwat Chachmej Lublin or The Academy of the Wise Men of Lublin was founded on the initiative of Rabbi Jehuda Majer Szapira, the Chairman of the Agudas Israel in Poland, the member of the Parliament in the years 1922-1927. The idea of creating a rabbinical and Talmudic Academy in Lublin, which would educate the most talented Jewish youth was presented by Majer Szapira in 1924 at the World Congress of the Orthodox Jewry in Vienna.

He also persuaded his audience that the school should be erected in Lublin since the tradition of the rabbinical schools in that city went back in time to the 16th century.

Majer Szapira　　　　　*The Former Academy of the Wise Men of Lublin*

The plot for the Jesziwa was offered by Szmul Ajchenbaum, and the construction materials were provided by Hersz Jojna Zylber and Szmul Brodt. In 1924, the five-storey building was designed by Agenor Smoluchowski. The construction began in the same year and it was carried out by Keren Hator's company. The ceremonial opening of the Academy took place on June 26, 1930. The first rector of the Academy became Majer Szapira. Besides the scientific rooms, the Academy had also a boarding house for 200 students, a reading room and a library of 13 thousand Talmudic books. On the ground floor a special model of Jerusalem Temple was erected. It was the unique plastic work made by Weintraub. In the lecture hall, which at the same time was a prayer hall, there was a huge menorah offered to the Academy by the Jewish Community from Przemyśl. This candlestick from the 18th century was crowned with a beautiful Polish eagle.

Jesziwat Chachmej Lublin – in the intention of its founder – was to educate not only rabbis and experts in Talmud but also clever Jewish citizens, scientists, social activists and leaders of public life. In 1934 the first examinations were held and the first diplomas handed to fifty graduates. The diplomas were called Cerwa d'Raban. Majer Szapira did not see this glorious moment since he died unexpectedly in 1933. The last rector of the Lublin Rabbinical Academy was Szlomo Eiger. In the building of the former Jesziwa there is now Collegium Maius of the Medical Academy of Lublin. There is a special room for the Jews who visit the place. They can rest there and pray. In this room, in the wardrobe called Aron ha Kodesz there is the Torah.

LUBARTOWSKA STREET

At 81 Lubartowska Street there are buildings of *the old Jewish hospital* built in 1886. Doctor Dawid Cynberg was its first director and a long-time administrator. Many respected Jewish physicians worked with him there: Dobrucki, Tenenbaum, Zigelwaks, Płotkin, Kagan, Ziper, Prusak, Zajdman, Mandelbaum, Bromberg. During the destruction of the Lublin Ghetto, also the Hospital was liquidated on March 27, 1942 by the Germans. On one day they murdered all patients – about 300 people. The history of the hospital is told in the commemorative plaque. In the expanded building there is now the Clinic of Gynaecology and Obstetrics. Between Lubartowska, Czwartek and Szkolna Streets there is the former *Icchak Lejb Perec*

The Scriptures

*The Books in Hebrew
(From the Collection of the Hall of Fame
at 10 Lubartowska Street)*

Folk House founded by the workers' organisation "Bund" in 1936. There were to be located here: the school, the gym, the library, the theatre. After World War II, the Jews coming back from the Soviet Union found shelter here.

From among 100 synagogues and prayer houses of Lublin, there has only one been preserved till today and that is the one standing at 10 Lubartowska Street. It ceased to play its role when there was no quorum i.e. 10 pious Jews who could pray together. This *Prayer House* was established at the end of the 19th century and it served not only for praying but also for studying the Talmud. It belonged to the Funeral Parlour Chewra Nosim or the Society of those Who Bury Corpses. It was located at the busy street and was visited by numerous Jews who prayed here almost all day. In the evening they listened to the lectures on the Talmud. The lectures were delivered by famous Talmud experts. Among them were Mosze Ajzenberg and Dawid Muszkatblit. His son, grandson and great-grandson visited Lublin in 1987. Dawid Muszkatblit's great-grandson celebrated religious initiation in this Prayer House. Besides the sacral part, there is also the Hall of Memory of the Jews of Lublin there.

ŚWIĘTODUSKA STREET

From Lubartowska Street through Wodopojna Street we reach Świętoduska Street. On the left hand side we can see a spacious square, and a symbolic monument erected in 1963, commemorating the Jews of the Lublin Province that were murdered during the War. The Monument was designed by Janusz Tarabała and Bogumił Zagajewski, the sculptors. *The monument* reminds of a huge tombstone plate and there is the inscription on it: "In each handful of ashes I am looking for my dear ones". This is a quotation from a poem by Icchak Kancenelson.

MAJDANEK

From Świętoduska Street via Królewska, Wyszyńskiego, Zamojska, Fabryczna and Droga Męczenników Majdanka we reach Majdanek, the former concentration camp. From September to November 1942, the transports of the Jews from the Lublin Ghetto came here, and here – in November that year under the code name of "Harvest" – "the final solution of the Jewish problem was carried out". The Jews perished in gas chambers or were shot. After the War in Majdanek a museum (see: pp. 163-164) commemorating the victims of the Holocaust was organised.

FOLLOWING THE FOOTSTEPS OF LUBLIN LEGENDS

The Kraków Gate – Jezuicka Street – the Trinity Tower
– Franciszek Gretz-Gruell Street – the Market Square – Złota Street
– the Market Square – Grodzka Street – Ku Farze Square
– Bramowa Street – the Władysław Łokietek Square – Przechodnia Street
– Bernardyńska Street – the Władysław Łokietek Square

Every town whose history goes back in time to early Middle Ages has its own legends that are handed over from generation to generation. They create special climate and provide events or facts with special emotional meaning. Also Lublin has its legends.

WHERE DOES THE NAME OF THE CITY COME FROM?

The Polish early historian Wincenty Kadłubek was famous for his flamboyant writing about things he liked. He wanted his beloved Piast Dynasty to look as best as possible, so he "married" Julia Piast with... Julius Cesar. The alleged union of Leszek III with Julia caused the establishment of two Polish cities: Juliusz – after Cesar's name, and Julin – after the name of the founder. Unfortunately, the successive wife of Leszek III jealous of the achievements of her predecessor changed the name of the city into Lublin.

Another talented historian Prokosz who wrote in the 10th century claims that the city on the Bystrzyca River was founded about... one thousand years BC. The town had to take its name from its founder. The legendary ruler Lublin was to be a good prince since the inhabitants of Lublin made a special burial mound for him. Is it Grodzisko in Kalinowszczyzna? Or perhaps the Castle Hill?

The origins of the city's name are described not only in the written documents. Older people tell the younger generations that once a Polish Prince with his entourage came to the small settlement on the Bystrzyca and wanted to name it. He said that the first caught fish would provide the name. When the nets were drawn there were pike and tench. Which one was the first one? The pike called the river wolf or the modest tench (lin). The Prince had no doubts: – Your town will be called Lublin. So it was.

THE CITY EMBLEM

The goat was the coat-of-arms of... Julius Cesar. The town established by his sister could not have a different emblem. In the ancient and Slavonic mythology, the goat was a symbol of vitality, fertility and wealth. It became the emblem of the city, which "was generously provided with the blessings of Providence". Since the town wanted to grow and develop, the goat was added a bush of vine – a symbol of Venus. The city is still beautiful, full of various goods and hospitable.

THE CLOCK FROM THE KRAKÓW GATE

The clock from the Kraków Gate (see: p. 32) was famous as early as the 17th century. "Everywhere the clocks make mistakes but nowhere as big as those in Lublin" – that was a poem that circulated in Poland inspiring various jokes and sneers. It is true that people responsible for that could not regulate the clock. In effect, the inhabitants of Lublin were massively late to work and schools. In the 2nd half of the 19th century, the bad reputation of the clock was even strengthened by those who lived in the Krakow Gate. They used to dry their clothes on the clock's arms. Once a Mr Lutowski started a false alarm with the clock's hammer and demolished the clock room. It is said that at night the ghost of Mr Lutowski is walking around the Kraków Gate.

THE COCK FROM THE TRINITY TOWER

There is a tin cock on the noble Trinity Tower (see: pp. 68-69). It shows the way the wind blows. It is worthy to know where the wind blows from but it is not the reason why tourists come to the Cathedral Square. All are curious whether the cock will crow. Has it ever crowed? It is said that it crows always when the Gate is being crossed by a man faithful to his wife.

ON THE BEAUTIFUL AND INDUSTRIOUS DAUGHTER OF A GOLDSMITH

Perhaps it was not unreasonable that the tin cock sat on the top of the Trinity Tower. Only from this height it could see the smallest house at 4 Złota Street (see: p. 71) and look into the windows of the first floor. There a beautiful goldsmith's daughter "entertained her guests". This young lady fully utilised her charms and had many clients. The legend says that she prospered also because two gates were leading to her house. The industrious goldsmith's daughter devoted one gate for those who were leaving and another one for those who were entering. Perhaps that was the first sign of the one-way roads. Be it as it may, she provided her clients with secrecy. Unfortunately, all the procedure was noticed by the cock from the Trinity Tower.

The Beautiful Goldsmith's Daughter,
4 Złota Street

"THE STONE OF MISFORTUNE"

At the junction of Jezuicka and Teodor Franciszek Gretz-Gruell Streets, at the corner house, there is the famous "Stone of Misfortune". It is said to have been transferred from Sławinek. It was wandering around Lublin and wherever it went it brought misfortune to people. It caused the collapse of a soldier from the tower of prayer house who was looking for golden tiles; it caused the city powder storage to explode; it caused the baker to burn alive because he used that stone to build his stove. In the 15th century it served as a trunk, on which the hangman cut people's heads off. It stood at the Bernardyński Square also

known as the Square of Executions. Once the hangman cut off the head of an innocent person. He struck so hard that there is still a deep scar on the stone. "The Stone of Misfortune" is flat, unimpressive but it is better not to touch it.

The Stone of Misfortune

THE HOLY CROSS WOOD

Złota Street is closed by the impressive silhouette of the Dominican Basilica (see: pp. 47-49). Its history is connected with the relics of the Holy Cross Wood brought here from Kiev. They came to Kiev as a part of the dowry of Byzantine Empress Ann who in the 10th century married the Russian Prince Włodzimierz. The Holy Cross Wood was transported to Lublin by the Kiev Bishop – Andrzej. He intended to take the relics to Krakow but – when he stopped near the church with the relics – "the miracles and other events showed clearly that the Holy Cross Wood should remain here". The relics have protected Lublin and its inhabitants for many centuries. There are many stories of the miraculous cures and saving the city against the elements of nature. These stories are depicted on the pictures by great masters in the church's naves. The fact that the city was the right place for the Holy Relics was proved not only by the blessings that the city cherished. After Bishop Andrzej had left Lublin, the Gdańsk merchant, Henryk tried to steal the relics. When he was running away from Lublin with the treasure, the horses did not want to move after they had crossed the city limits. The terrified and ashamed merchant returned the relics, and on the place of the event he founded the Holy Cross Church (see: p. 145). The beautiful and precious reliquary that weighs 18 kilos was stolen from the Basilica in 1991 but none of the inhabitants of Lublin has any doubts that – sooner or later – the Holy Cross Wood will return to its righteous place.

FATHER RUSZEL'S GHOST

Father Ruszel (1593-1658) was a Dominican, the Theology Doctor, and a person famous for his goodness, piety and ascetic way of living. When he died, he was deeply mourned not only by his Dominican Brothers but also by ordinary people. Soon afterwards, the body at which the Dominicans were praying – vanished. People said that God had taken his servants straight to Heaven. In the meantime, in the chapel devoted to Father Ruszel extraordinary things started to happen. The organs played on their own, shadows and ghosts moved along the corridors. Was it Father Ruszel who visited the monastery? The situation lasted for nearly 200 years. When in 1863, the Tsarist troops turned the monastery into the soldiers' barracks, one of the guards noticed the ghost. He started to run away. The second guard shot at the ghost. The special commission created to investigate the incident soon found the human skeleton with the scapular and rosary of Father Ruszel in one of the niches.

The Devil's Paw

THE LEGEND OF THE "DEVIL'S PAW"

For nearly two centuries (since 1759) the nobility of Little Poland had fiercely fought in the courts of the Crown Tribunal (see: pp. 34-35). The King's privilege allowed them to make court appeals there. The prestige of that institution was low because of common corruption and partiality of judges, and even decreased in 1637. It is said that the legendary Devil's Court sat in session then. The Crown Tribunal was investigating the case of a poor widow who was sued by the rich and unscrupulous nobleman who bought witnesses and was certain to win. The Tribunal made a verdict against the poor widow. Then the embittered woman, instead of to the God's justice, which was praised in the court, made a vow to the Devil's justice. The same night a few coaches arrived at the Tribunal. Strange men left the coaches and went into the courtroom. Forcefully brought court writer recognised them as devils. They investigated the widow's case anew. They made a positive verdict for her. At that time Christ on the Crucifix, which was hanging in the courtroom started to cry bloody tears over the human injustice. He turned his head away. The Chairman of the "Devil's Tribunal" put his hand on the table leaving the burnt mark of "the devil's paw", which can still be seen in the Museum of Lublin. "The Devil's Paw" is also the name of one of the cafes at Bramowa Street. Famous cabaret "Czart" performs there. In the Market Square one can look into the cellar "at the Devil's" and on the facade of one of the houses there is a wall-painting from 1954 that recalls that "Devil's Court". The Tribunal Crucifix is placed in the chapel of the Lublin Cathedral.

LESZEK CZARNY'S DREAM

Ku Farze Square (see: pp. 51-52) has also its own legend. It tells of the difficult times for Lublin. The early Slavonic tribes are destroying the town and no one can escape destruction. Prince Leszek Czarny who has his camp on Ku Farze Square falls asleep certain that Lublin will fall. In a deep dream he sees The Archangel Michael who gives him his own sword. This dream must mean encouragement and hope. The Prince and his troops attack the Slavs. After the victorious battle, the Prince founds St. Michael's church, which later will become the Parish church.

"Leszek Czarny's Dream" – a drawing by R. Dhoghe or a bronze by Altomonte, the end of the 17ᵗʰ c., oil, canvas (the Collection of Capuchin Monks)

GOLD FOR BERNARDINES

The impressive church and cloister of the St. Bernard Monks (see: pp. 97-99) is standing outside the city walls on the steep bank of the Bystrzyca Valley. The oldest inhabitants of Lublin say that the erection of that building was opposed by the City Counsellors. They used arguments of the safety of the town and of the empty city treasury. One night a storm with thunders broke over the city. In front of the Town Hall a coach driven by oxen suddenly appeared straight from Heaven. The stunned burghers asked: What coach is it? Where is the driver? The city gates were closed for good at that time… Curiosity overcame fear especially because they could see a large trunk on the coach. The trunk was transported with great difficulty to the Town Hall. When it was opened, the people saw lots of gold and jewels in it. On the top there was a letter addressed to the City Counsellors. Those who read it could not believe their eyes. The whole treasure was to be spent on building the church. Somebody rushed out of the Town Hall to see if there was anything else on the coach, the coach was nowhere to be seen. "It's a miracle! It's a miracle!" the burghers started to shout. And in this way a great temple could soon be built.

188

THE AUTOMOBILE ROUTE

The Castle Square – Unia Lubelska Avenue – Zygmuntowskie Avenue
– Józef Piłsudski Avenue – Narutowicz Street – Nadbystrzycka Street
– Tomasz Zan Street – Bohaterów Monte Cassino Street
– Armia Krajowa Street – Jan Paweł II Street – Krochmalna Street
– Diamentowa Street – Władysław Kunicki Street – Pawia Street
– Droga Męczenników Majdanka – Łęczyńska Street
– Gospodarcza Street – Mełgiewska Street – Tysiąclecie Avenue
– Kalinowszczyzna Street – Władysław Anders Street
– Mieczysław Smorawiński Avenue – Kompozytorzy Polscy Avenue
– Koncertowa Street – Irena Kosmowska Street – Solidarność Avenue
– Warszawska Avenue – Racławickie Avenue

Major obiect:

- *The Holy Family Church*
- *The Former Mechanical Company of E. Plage and T. Leśkiewicz*
- *St. Michael's Church*
- *The Former Factory of Agricurtural Machines and Tools of Mieczysław Wolski*

- *The Old Krause Mills*
- *Wincenty Pol Manor House*
- *The Church of Holy Mary, the Supporter of the Faithful*
- *St. Agnes Church*

From the car park at the Castle Square via Tysiąclecie Avenue we move towards **Unia Lubelska Avenue**.

This highway opened in the 80s commemorates one of the most important historical facts that took place in Lublin in 1569 – the conclusion of the Union of Lublin.

On the right hand side there is the Old Town Hill, and at its foothill – on Podwale – two historical industrial buildings. The first one is *Henryk Kijok Brewery* from the 19th century, in which beer was brewed and malt manufactured. In 1927, the brewery was consumed by fire. After the restoration the mechanical bakery was opened there. Today, in the former malt production hall there is a gym, and in one of the one-storey buildings of the former brewery there is a bakery. The second building, built of red brick, is the former *malt production plant*. It belonged to the once famous brewery empire of the Vetters (see: pp. 101-102).

The malt production plant at 2 Misjonarska Street was built by Karol Rudolf Vetter in 1846. Later, the plant was expanded by a huge drier with a chimney. The malt that was produced here till 1970 was regarded as one of the best in Poland and in the world.

Among the buildings of the successive hill called once "Żmigród", one pays immediate attention to the old Missionary Complex from the 17th century. It was rebuilt in the 20th century and now houses the Metropolitan Priests' Seminar (see: pp. 103-104).

On the opposite side of the Unia Lubelska Avenue one can see scarce buildings that vanish with time. Most of them are wooden houses at Przemysłowa and Kąpielowa Streets. Closer to the roundabout there are remnants of Wacław Moritz Factory of Machines and the Foundry of Cast Iron.

On Zamojska Street both banks of the Bystrzyca River are connected with

Tysiąclecie Avenue

The Old Town seen from the Bystrzyca River

an *old bridge*, one of the first cast iron bridges in Poland. It was constructed in the years 1908-1909 and designed by Marian Lutosławski, an engineer from Warsaw.

We reach Bychawski Square via Zygmuntowskie Avenue. The idea of constructing the New Highway – officially called Jagiellońskie Avenue – appeared at the end of the 19th century after the Vistula Railways started to function.

At the New Highway, close to the bridge on the Bystrzyca the Arthesian wells were dug in the years 1896-1899. With the help of pumps and the pressure power located at Bernardyński Square, the wells provided water to the Town. This water supply system built on the design of Adolf Weisblatt in 1897 was the beginning of the modern water supply system, which started to function in 1929. It was a famous communal investment carried out by the American company Ulen.

After the Bystrzyca had been regulated and the meadows close to it dried, it was possible to organise the sport and recreational grounds along the Piłsudski Avenue. It was done before the war. In the 50s the Folk Park was established. This part of the Town was even more attractive due to the boulevards along the Bystrzyca. The view at the Old Town Panorama is worth walking from the bridge at Piłsudski Avenue to the historical bridge at Zamojska Street.

At the crossroads of Nadbystrzycka Street there is a several-storey building of the "Victoria" Hotel. It was built in the years 1965-1972. Its name recalls the famous hotel that was built by Antoni Bokszański in 1874 at Krakowskie Przedmieście Avenue and was consumed by fire during the war in September 1939.

After the crossroads of Głęboka Street we enter Nadbystrzycka Street that leads us to the Rury District.

Hotel "Victoria"

RURY
NADBYSTRZYCKA STREET

The Rury District takes its name from the wooden water pipes that were laid on old church and cloister grounds according to the agreement concluded in 1506 with Master Jan. They acquired the names of Rury Brygidkowskie, Wizytkowskie, św. Ducha, Jezuickie, Bonifraterskie. Today's Nadbystrzycka Street is the former Road to Rury Jezuickie.

At Nadbystrzycka Street we pass by the didactic, scientific, social and sports buildings of the Technical University of Lublin. It continues the traditions of the Higher Engineering College founded in 1953. In 1964 it was renamed the High Engineering School.

At the crossroads we turn left into Tomasz Zan Street.

St. Joseph's Church

TOMASZ ZAN STREET

It is a long highway that links the districts of the Lublin Housing Co-operative. Near Bolesław Prus District, the Street runs on the highest point of Lublin. On the modest slope going down to the deep gorge the so-called "Globe" there is the sledge track and ski lift. On the bottom there is a skating ring and the archery track. The dominating building in this part of the Town is *St. Joseph's parish church* built according to the design of Stanisław Fijałkowski. This sacral complex houses the studios of the Diocese Museum of the Religious Art (see: pp. 152-153).

From Bohaterów Monte Cassino Street we turn into Armia Krajowa Street.

ARMIA KRAJOWA STREET

The street begins with a beautiful silhouette of *St. Francis' Church*, which reminds us of a sail. Besides the church there is the *Capuchin Monks Monastery*. Both buildings were designed by Marian Makarski and both were erected at the beginning of the 80s. The lower situated grounds form one of the most beautiful Lublin gorges that reach Nadbystrzycka Street. It is known as the Rury Park, although it is partially occupied by small gardening plots. There are walking and bicycle paths in the Park. The monument to the prisoners of the Royal Castle shot in the years 1940-1944 was erected at the high escarpment at Nadbystrzycka Street in 1986. It was designed by Tadeusz Skrzyński and Leszek Dziekoński.

Armia Krajowa Street reaches Jan Paweł II Street.

St. Francis' Church and the Capuchin Monks Monastery

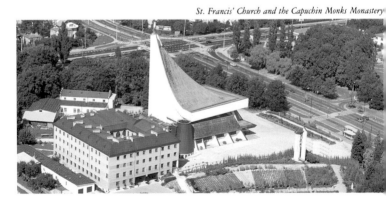

The Holy Family Church

CZUBY
JAN PAWEŁ II STREET

On 9 June 1987, on the grounds of the parish and **Holy Family Church** in construction, Pope John Paul II celebrated the memorable mass. Soon, the former Przełom Street was changed into Jan Paweł II Street. The symbolic relic of the papal visit is the high, azure cross with the figure of Christ designed by Dobrosław Bagiński. The landscape of this part of the Town is limited by the Forest called "Stary Gaj". The "Stasin" Reservation, which is a part of it, protects the rare black birch.

WROTKÓW
KROCHMALNA STREET

We reach the bridge on the Bystrzyca River. Along the River we can see the nicely located grounds of the Lublin Horse Riding Club. Krochmalna Street takes its name from the Factory of the Potato Syrup established here in 1909 by Józef Chuchrowski and Czesław Rodkiewicz. The traditions of the old factory are continued today by the Enterprise of the Potato Industry "Lublin" Ltd., which produces the coveted semolina and potato cubes. Via Krochmalna Street and a short fragment of Gazowa Street we can reach the Railway Station. In the 2nd half

The Sugar Factory

The Old Buildings at the Sugar Factory

of the 19th century this was the main artery of the well-developed industry. Since 1882 there was a gas factory here; since 1895 – a sugar factory; since 1906 the Rectification Plant. At Młyńska Street there were some steam mills working. One could reach from here the fashionable grounds of the Horse Racing Track and the Agricultural Exhibitions, which were organised on the meadows near the Bystrzyca River.

At the roundabout, we turn into Diamentowa Street.

DIAMENTOWA STREET

On the grounds of the southern and western Wrotków, which was incorporated into the Town in 1961, new industrial and storage district began to be organised. Village Wrotków was mentioned in the 15th century documents. The modest estate was owned here by Zofia Nałkowska's grandparents. The author of *The Border*, *The Medallions* and *The Girls from Nowolipki* described the house like that:

The Lord's Mercy Church

The Gas Plant at Diamentowa Street

"Grandparents' house was standing high, and the path to the river, from which we carried water, was steep. From the windows one could see spacious meadows. In the middle of them the river flew, the Bystrzyca, and the landscape ended with the distant forests".

The time of the old Wrotków had passed, however. There were no longer the 19th century water mills and barns at the rover. The most impressive element of the landscape here was now Lord's Mercy Church designed by Andrzej Bołtuć and Waldemar Bezpałka.

From Diamentowa Street we can easily reach the recreational centre "Marina" and Dąbrowa Forest at Zemborzyce Artificial Lake.

We reach Zemborzycka Street and turn left towards the Town. Approaching Kunicki Street we pass by Leon Kruczkowski and Dziesiąta Districts.

DZIESIĄTA

It is the district of residential houses with the pre-war tradition. In 1925, the first housing co-operative in Lublin was established here. The houses hidden in the gardens at the side streets are characterised by various styles and details. Some of them remind us of manor houses, some are wooden houses with azure porches, some have mansard roofs, some have very modern shapes. Once it was a large Royal village, inhabited by the falconers. On the King's orders they dealt with the growing and training of falcons. It was a hard work. The falconers lived in settlements close to the forests full of game. Today, one of the street of the district bears the name Sokolniki (Falconers).

In the 2nd half of the 15th century, King Kazimierz Wielki gave the village Dziesiąta to the Archdean of Lublin. He received one of the houses at the Old Town Market Place instead. In the 16th century, Dziesiąta belonged to a famous Lublin physician and archdean Jakub Montana. He was Jan Kochanowski's friend. Kochanowski dedicated him one of his poems.

WŁADYSŁAW KUNICKI STREET

It is one of the main arteries of this part of the town. Its patron was the owner and the headmaster of the Female Commercial High School. In the 19th century there was a Bychawa Tract here.

In the 80s, the District obtained *a new Parish Church* designed by Mirosław Załuski. It replaced the old wooden church built in 1933 and designed by Tadeusz Witkowski. It was a one-nave neo-Gothic temple with some traces of the Scandinavian architecture. It was built – according to the parishioners' wishes – from the railway sleepers. This wooden church was moved from Dziesiąta to Pilaszkowice in 1985.

Stanisław Konarski High School at Kunicki Street is called the twin school. It was opened in 1926 when two educational institutions were united (primary schools Nos. 1 and 14). The conditions of both schools were so bad that local authorities, the School Council and the Society for Promoting the Construction of the Primary Schools in Lublin decided to build a new building for them. It was designed by Tadeusz Witkowski. It was one of the five educational investments in Lublin before the war. In 1939, it was taken over by the Nazi military occupational forces. In the reading hall and the cloakroom the Germans organised the stable for 40 horses; the lecture rooms were turned into the tailor and shoemaker workshops, and then into a military hospital. The school was restored after the war and it retained the characteristic features of the pre-war modernism.

The industrial buildings at Szańcowa Street come from the 2nd half of the 19th and the beginning of the 20th centuries. These are: the Liberman motor mill in the triangle of the streets Kotlarska, Wyścigowa and Oboźna, and the former Boiler and Mechanical Enterprise of Gniazdowski and Janiszewski.

At 106 Kunicki Street we pass by eight huge 20-metre high rollers, the so-called fermenting tanks where the beer brewed in **Perła Brewery in Lublin** is maturing. In the complex of the buildings close to the brewery there is one of the most modern beer fermenting lines in Europe. In one hour about 36 000 bottles of high quality beer is being produced here. It is filtered by a special method brought to Lublin from the USA.

At Kunicki Street there are some elements of the yeast factory preserved. It was founded in 1910 by Wincenty Barciszewski and Stanisław Wrzodak. Today there is the Branch of the Lublin Enterprise of the Liquor Industry "Polmos".

We are leaving Dziesiąta District, turn left into Pawia Street and via a simple, road bridge we cross the Czerniejówka River into Bronowice.

BRONOWICE
PAWIA STREET

This District situated on the right bank of the Bystrzyca River takes probably its name from the name of its owner – Bronisław. In 1342 the village became a part of the Lublin Community. For many centuries the limestone was excavated here and it was a good material to build houses with. When in 1877, the Railway Line connecting Lublin with Warsaw and Kowel was opened, Bronowice became a suburb and then a district of the town with many important industrial plants localised here.

Today's Bronowice engulfed another district – Kośminek. Those grounds on the Czerniejówka River were purchased in 1860 by a well-known but unlucky Lublin industrialist, Michał Kośmiński. Next year, at Garbarska Street he erected the brick steam mill working in an American system, a tannery and a steam bakery. He also thought of building the whole craftsmen district and a park at the Zamość Tract. Those plans remained unfulfilled due to Kośmiński's bankruptcy.

From Pawia Street we turn into Długa Street and then into Krańcowa Street that leads to Droga Męczenników Majdanka.

DROGA MĘCZENNIKÓW MAJDANKA AVENUE

At the beginning of the Avenue there is **the Holy Cross Church** designed by Antoni Herman. It is the three-nave basilica with the lifted main nave.

At the crossroads of Lotnicza Street and Droga Męczenników Majdanka Avenue there is another **Parish church** of that district. As the Monument of Martyrdom of Saint Maksymilian Kolbe it was built on the pattern of a cross – the sign of

St. Maksymilian Maria Kolbe Church

a sacrifice and devotion of Man. Behind the petrol station, on the right hand side, there is the simple, wooden *Cross of Gratitude* with a figure of a worker tearing off the bondage of a slave. It was erected on 1 July 1981 by the crew of the Lublin Enterprise of Repairing Automobiles.

The inscription says that it is the symbol of a massive protests of the workers in summer of 1980.

We turn into Lotnicza Street and reach Wrońska Street.

WROŃSKA STREET

The Mechanical Company of E. Plage and T. Laśkiewicz established here in 1900 produced first steam boilers for various systems and the complete equipment for distilleries, breweries, rectification plants, starchworks and oil mills. Since 1920, the Factory also produced two-personnel, double wing aeroplanes Ansaldo A-1 "Balilla" and Ansaldo-300, as well as French aeroplanes Potez XV-A-2, Potez XXV-12 and B-2. The factory became famous as the official producer of this kind of machinery when it employed Engineer Jerzy Rudlicki as the chief constructor. The factory initiated then the excellent series of the aeroplanes Lublin R-VIII in 11 varieties. The aeroplanes were designed by Rudlicki. The famous Lublin aeroplanes participated in many international sport events and in 1933 in Madrid they beat the American, British and French construction companies during the international aviation contest. After the Company had been nationalised in 1935 and became the Lublin Manufacture of Aeroplanes, the planes from Lublin were still famous all over the world. At Wrońska Street one can still see three hangars and a few buildings that once formed the Lublin Manufacture of Aeroplanes.

We return to Droga Męczenników Majdanka and reach the crossroads of Wolska, Fabryczna and Łęczyńska Streets.

St. Michael's Church   Fabryczna Street

WOLSKA STREET

At Wolska Street we can see a very photogenic silhouette of *the Archangel Michael Parish Church*. It was built according to the design of Warsaw architect Oskar Sosnowski in the modern – as for the years 1927-1938 – style. In its form it reminds us of the Basilica. The plot for the construction was given by the then owner of Bronowice Estate – Henryk Sachs. He also gave the wooden manor house for the vicarage. Once, there was a small larch wooden church there. Before it appeared in the Bronowice Parish, however, it made a long journey. It was built in 1744 in Pawłów in the Chełm Region. It was founded by Antoni Siła-Nowicki. It was transferred to Bronowice in 1912. When a new brick church had been built, it was moved to Kazimierzówka.

On the right hand side of Wolska Street we can see the beautiful secession gate and the production halls with the preserved architectural detail. The unchanged form of the buildings remind us of the history of *the Factory of Agricultural Machines and Tools*. It was founded in 1874 in Piaski (that was the historical name of this part of the Town). It was founded by the wellknown Lublin industrialist and social worker, Mieczysław Wolski. The traditions of the Company Wolski and S-ka are cultivated now by the Company "SIPMA".

At the crossroads of Zygmuntowskie Avenue and Unia Lubelska Street we turn into Fabryczna Street.

FABRYCZNA STREET

It was marked on the map of Lublin in 1912. There was a vivid sign of *Wacław Moritz Factory of Agricultural Machinery and Foundry of Iron*. This known Lublin industrialist was cultivating the family tradition of industrial activities. The tradition was initiated by his father Robert Moritz and a Scotsman – Douglas Bird. In 1899, Wacław Moritz moved the production of agricultural machinery from Krakowskie Przedmieście Avenue. He located the factory at 2 Fabryczna Street where it remained till 1937. After World War II, the tradition was taken over by the Lublin Factory of the Agricultural Machines "Agromet".

198

BRONOWICKA STREET

Behind the bridge on the Czerniejówka River, in a nice manor house-like style and according to the design by Bohdan Kelles-Krausse, *the Municipal Baths* were erected in 1926. The initiative went back in time to 1811, the first baths were erected at Bronowicka Street. They utilised the mineral sources that sprang into air near the river. On the initiative of a administrator of the Bronowice Estate, Emeryk Chruścielewski, *the Municipal Park* was established in 1869. It was called the Bronowice Park or Foksal. In 1875, the park went under the municipal jurisdiction, and the authorities ordered its planning to the municipal technician, Aleksander Zwierzchowski. The effect of his works was evaluated by "Gazeta Lubelska" writing that Bronowice became one of the most pleasant walking areas in the town. The military bands played here, there were entertainment parks, the sour milk was served, as well as coffee and a very good spring mineral water for one grosch per a glass. The idyll did not last long, however, since in the last years of the 19th century the park lost its splendour due to the erection of the municipal slaughterhouse nearby and to the lack of care from the municipal authorities.

Via Fabryczna Street we return to the crossroads and turn into Łęczyńska Street.

TATARY
ŁĘCZYŃSKA STREET

In the documents from 1464 we can find the information that Tatary as a Lublin village lay in the neighbourhood of Bronowice. In the 19th century it was extracted from the Lublin Community and became a private property. The last owner of Tatary was Kazimierz Graff. That was a rich estate with spacious meadows. In 1839 Emanuel Graff purchased the estate from Adam Ożarowski. Graff was a country gentleman from Strzyżów in Hrubieszów County. Feliksa Chubińska, his wife provided name for the Felin Estate, which was a part of Tatary. Emanuel resided in the Classical Manor House and so did his sons Władysław and Kazimierz (see: p. 240). On the map of Lublin from 1912 the present Łęczyńska Street is marked as the new road to the Cement Factory. In the southern part of Bronowice there were mines of the limestone, provided with numerous privileges. Limestone was used at the construction of the houses built in the suburbs of Lublin.

FIRLEJOWSKA STREET

The limestone from Bronowice was also used for industrial purpose. In 1895, on the border between Bronowice and Tatary a famous *factory Portland-Cement "Firley"* was established in the land that belonged to the Firlej Family. It provided the raw material for many concrete plants that were established in Lublin. Now, the remnants of that factory are the property of the Lublin Scale Factory.

In 1804, Firlejowszczyzna – with a typical Polish manor house – was purchased by Franciszek Ksawery Pohl – Wincenty Pol's father. The family moved to Lvov, however, and the *manor house* often changed owners. In 1860, due to the efforts of the Lublin Bishop Ignacy Baranowski, the manor house was given to Wincenty Pol, the author of a famous *Song on our Land*. Due to the chicanery of the Tsarist authorities, neither the poet nor his daughter visited the place. In 1970, the manor house was transferred to 13 Kalinowszczyzna Street. Today, there is Wincenty Pol Museum there (see: p. 162).

The Church of Mary, the Queen of Poland

GOSPODARCZA STREET

The name evokes the agricultural character of this part of Tatary. In 1991, on the 200 Anniversary of the 3 May Constitution, the Parish Church was consecrated here. It was designed by Stanisław Machnik.

From Gospodarcza Street we turn into Mełgiewska Street.

MEŁGIEWSKA STREET

Once, an important trade route to Russia ran through here. At the end of 1938, the Warsaw Company Lillpop, Rau and Loewenstein commenced at 7/9 Mełgiewska Street the construction of *the automobile factory* – both personnel and lorries – on the licence of the American Corporation General Motors. Since 1951, the prewar traditions were cultivated by the Truck Factory. Today, the owner of the factory is "Daewoo Motor Polska".

Dworek Graffa is situated before the bridge on the Bystrzyca River. It is a manor house built in the middle of the 19th century. Its name comes from the last owners of the Tatary Estate – the Graff Family.

On the right hand side of the roundabout there is one of the few remaining such objects – *the "Budzin" Inn*. It was conveniently situated over the Bystrzyca River and at the major tracts: The Lithuanian – leading via Łęczna and the Ruthenian – running through Mełgiew, Piaski and Krasnystaw. The wooden inn is first mentioned in the 1ˢᵗ half of the 16ᵗʰ century. King Zygmunt Stary ordered that in the Budzin Inn at Tatary only Lublin beer could be served. The fate of the Inn was turbulent. It was consumed by fire and it was restored many times. In 1833, it obtained classical style and was built out of brick. For some time it was the seat of the Communal Court of Peace in Tatary. Since the 30s there is the Factory of Wire and Nails. The factory belonged to the Tuller Brothers.

From Mełgiewska Street we turn into Tysiąclecie Avenue.

The Old Krausse Mills

TYSIĄCLECIA AVENUE

The two historical *tanneries* (see: p. 179) situated at 7 and 9 Towarowa Street come from 1925 and they belonged to the known industrialists: Szmul Sztyk and Pejsach Brykman. Also other people had tanneries here: Lejzor Lidzki, Aleksander Filipowski, Szmul Ajchenbaum, Moszka Silberstein. The tannery traditions are continued in the modernised buildings of the Lublin Tannery Plant.

Opposite the tannery there are historical buildings of Krausse's Mill, now renovated after the fire of 1998. In 1881, Brothers Edward and Henryk Krausse built in the then Tatary Village the mill driven by the largest turbo in the country. The turbine was designed by the Hungarian company Gantz et Company. It could produce up to 120 tons of wheat yearly. Twelve years later the mill had three water turbines and a steam machine of great power. It employed 100 people, and it achieved the turnover of almost one million roubles. Now, there is one of the most modern Polish enterprises making a part of the "Lubella" Corporation. It is worthy mentioning that the first paper mill of Jan Fajfer was built in 1538. It was situated at the "great outflow" of the Royal Pond in Tatary Village. The paper from Fajfer's Mill was provided with its own water sign that presented the coat-of- arms of the Governors of Lublin – the Firlejs.

On Białkowska Góra Street there is a white silhouette of Wincenty Pol's Museum to be seen (see: p. 162).

On the same side of the hill there are still small wooden houses and a few houses of limestone. These are the relics of the old houses of Kalinowszczyzna.

KALINOWSZCZYZNA

It is mentioned in the historical documents from the middle of the 18th century. It was a property of the Governors of Lublin that was not controlled by the municipal authorities. Once it had its own Trading Centre – the Straw Market Place. The Ruthenian Tract cut across Kalinowszczyzna, and it led to Lvov. The whole district was sometimes called the Lvov Suburbs.

The Housing Project in Kalinowszczyzna

The Church of Holy Mary, the Supporter of the Faithful

The Lower Church

The Upper Church

KALINOWSZCZYZNA STREET

Once it was a trading tract, which functioned even before Lublin was founded. Today, the Street runs in a small fragment at the bottom of a gorge that was dug at the beginning of the 20th century. On the slopes and escarpments one can admire the loess plants like hemp or honeysuckle.

The landscape of the initial part of Kalinowszczyzna Street is dominated by the silhouette of *the former Franciscan Church and Cloister*. These buildings are taken care of now by the Salesian Brothers.

The Franciscan Monks came to Lublin in the years 1635-1649 and they built a church. The church was many times restored and in the years 1812-1813 it was turned into the military warehouse. In 1817, after the Franciscan Brothers left the Cloister, the military warehouse and hospital were organised here. Then the build-

St. Agnes Church

The Consoling, the 18th c., board, oil

The Late-Renaissance Presbytery Decoration with the Picture of Mary, Mother of God, the 18th c., oil, board

ings were purchased by the Lublin industrialist Antoni Domański who organised his cloth factory there. In 1855, there was a factory of soap and candles. In 1913, all buildings were purchased by Tadeusz Weisberg. He was a Jew who – after converting into the Roman Catholic faith – gave the buildings and the garden to the Salesian Brothers. It was in 1927. The monks rebuilt the church and reinforced the weak and old walls. They divided the church into two levels. In this way they obtained the three-storey temple. Such construction has been maintained till today in spite of housing offices and stores for so many years.

The Post-Franciscan church and cloister adjoin the Grodzisko Hill with *the old Jewish Cemetery* (see: pp. 177-179). The cemetery was established when King Zygmunt August gave his permission in 1555. At the cemetery's wall there is a plaque commemorating the first massive execution perpetrated by the Germans here on 23 December 1939. They killed 10 members of the Lublin intelligentsia who were detained since November in the Royal Castle.

A little further on, there is *the church and cloister complex* that once belonged to St. Augustin Monks. The beginnings of that foundation go back in time to the 17th century. That was the time when, the burghers from Kalinowszczyzna invited St. Augustine Monks from Krasnystaw. In 1646 the monks started to build the brick and wooden church, and in 1685, when that one was destroyed by the Cossacks and Muscovites, they built a brick one. The church was many times destroyed and demolished and then rebuilt. It managed to maintain the Late-Renaissance features. The belfry that is at the right hand side from the church is a replica of the one demolished in 1885. In front of the church there is the statue of Holy Mary, Mother of God from 1873. In the middle of the churchyard there is the wooden well from 1757. In the years 1866-1902 there was a parish here transferred from St. Nicholas Church at Czwartek.

Via the crossroads at Mełgiewska Street we leave Kalinowszczyzna Street and enter Anders Street.

WŁADYSŁAW ANDERS AVENUE

It cuts across the grounds of two cemeteries: the Jewish one established in 1829 (see: pp. 179-180) with the main entrance at Walecznych Street, and the Roman Catholic one established in 1922 at Unicka Street. From afar one can see *the Cemetery Church* built on design of Aleksander Gruchalski in the years 1934-1935.

Going along the Władysław Anders Avenue we enter the Ponikwoda District. It took its name after the spring that flew here. In 1486, Ponikwoda was a municipal village and its inhabitants were obliged to do various services for the town. Ponikwoda neighbours Bazylianówka with the grounds located between the cemetery at Unicka Street and Spółdzielczości Pracy Avenue, which once belonged to the Basilian monks.

Cutting across Spółdzielczości Pracy Avenue we enter Mieczysław Smorawiński Avenue.

MIECZYSŁAW SMORAWIŃSKI AVENUE

On the left hand side in Lemszczyzna, the former suburban estate, the buildings of Medical Academy were built. In 1964, the Clinical Hospital No 4 was opened.

On the left hand side of he Avenue we are passing by the former Lublin suburb – Bursaki. There are numerous stores and warehouses, trading posts, service workshops, construction sites, printing houses etc.

Via Smorawiński Avenue we reach the Czechów District and Kompozytorów Polskich Avenue.

CZECHÓW

The former suburban grounds located north of the Czechówka River included the oldest settlements like the Probostwo Farne and Bielszczyzna with the 17th century brick manor house, in which the successive owners – the Gorajskis – had a Calvinist chapel. In the Middle Ages there was an important trade tract from Lublin to Mazowsze here and the land was divided into village communities and estates. The manor house was remodelled in the 19th century, was called the Chrznowskis' Manor House.

At the crossroads of Północna Street and Solidarność Avenue there is *a Polish National church* built in 1924.

In the 17th century there was in Czechów a prosperous inn and on the dammed waters of the Czechówka River there was a water mill in the 19th century. There were a lot of brickyards here too.

Czechów means also the famous "Czechów Mounts", the lime hills covered with a thick layer of loess that reach the height of 220 m. They have steep slopes full of gorges and they go down to the Czechówka River that flows through the terrain 171 m high. The gap in the levels of the ground makes the Czechów Mounts the attractive element of the local landscape.

KOMPOZYTORÓW POLSKICH AVENUE

At the crossroads with Koncertowa Street there is a hexagonal frame of *St. Hedwig Church*. Its architecture recalls the royal insignia of the patroness. It was built in 1985 and designed by Roman Orlewski. It was covered with hexagonal cupola in the shape of the Royal Crown topped with a tower encircled with a smaller crown and a cross.

KONCERTOWA STREET

At Koncertowa Street we pass by the villas of the district. Michał Wójtowicz Street reflects the picture of the old, pre-war Czechów – the Czechów Old Town with a few houses – twin houses with wooden tops to keep hay for horses since the inhabitants here were soldiers of the Legion Cavalry. It was one of the districts of the Housing Co-operative of the Union of Legions established in the 20s.

We reach Kosmowska Street by a steep and wavy slope.

IRENA KOSMOWSKA STREET

At the right hand side, on the crossroads of Kosmowska and Północna Streets there is a monument erected in 1996 by the inhabitants of Lublin to commemorate the prisoners of the Royal Castle who were shot in the nearby gorges by the Germans in the years 1940-1944. The monument was designed and made by Jerzy Kierski. Beside the monument there is a wooden cross recalling the memory of the soldiers of the 1863 Insurrection who were shot at the "Czechów Hills".

Via Solidarność Avenue we reach Warszawska Avenue.

WARSZAWSKA AVENUE

On both sides of the Avenue there is Sławinek District. A few, still preserved villas and boarding-houses recall the past of Sławinek as a resort. There is the Botanical Garden there (see: pp. 168-170), and opposite the Garden there is the Ethnographic Park with the Museum of the Lublin Village (see: pp. 165-166).

Via Warszawska Avenue we return towards the Town Centre. Passing the roundabout we enter Racławickie Avenue.

The Last Supper Church

RACŁAWICKIE AVENUE

Out of the buildings that are at this route one should pay attention to an impressive building on the left hand side. It was designed by Ignacy Kędzierski and built in 1925. It was the set of **Bobolanum** – the Mission Institute of Jesuits where future missionaries were educated. Now, there is the military hospital there.

Racławickie Avenue with a row of tall trees form a beautiful panorama entrance to the Centre of Lublin.

The Former Mission Institute of Jesuits "Bobolanum"

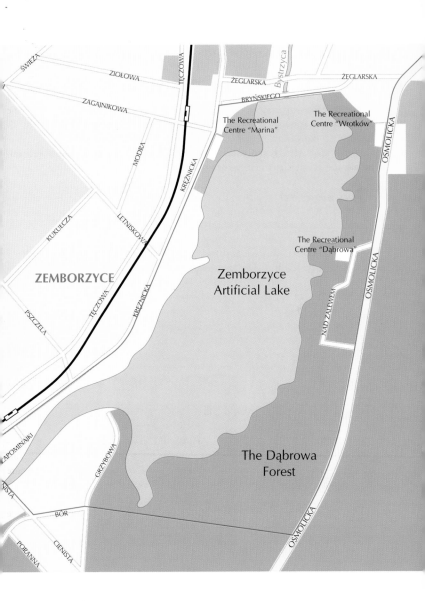

THE SUBURBAN ROUTE I

Bryńskiego Street – Krężnicka Street – Cienista Street – Bór Street
– Grzybowa Street – Cienista Street – Osmolicka Street – Zemborzycka Street

The largest and the most attractive recreational area of Lublin is Zemborzycki Artificial Lake located in the southern part of the City. It was built in 1970-1974 on the wet and peat meadows in the Bystrzyca River Valley located between Dąbrowa Forest and Zemborzyce. Once it was a royal village. In 1364 Kazimierz Wielki appointed the master of Zemborzyce in the person of Grzegorz. His job was to take care of the Bystrzyca Forests full of game. Only Kings could hunt there. In the 15th century the village had 18 fiefs of land, a well prospering mill, eight inns and a trading post on the River. In the 18th century one of the owners of Zemborzyce was Jadwiga Niezabitowska, and in the 2nd half of the 19th century it became a property of General Rudiger. Zemborzyce Parish was created in the years 1371-1429, and it paid tithes to the Bishops of Kraków. In the middle of the 15th century there was *a wooden church*. The new one was erected in 1907 in the fashionable Neo-Gothic style. Inside there are two pictures from the 17th and 18th centuries and the font from the 17th century carved in sandstone. On one of the towers there is a bell made probably in 1539.

Zemborzyce Artificial Lake covers the area of 230 ha. It is 3 850 m long, 1350 m wide and 2,3 to 4 m deep. The bank line of the lake is 12 kilometres long and it runs among the equally attractive landscape. One should add, that the lake is not only a recreational spot but also the retention tank.

The excursion to the "Lublin Sea" we begin with a walk to the dam and weir of the Lake. We go there along Kazimierz Bryński Street, the man who first had an idea of building the lake and the co-founder of the Botanical Garden.

St. Martin Church in Zemborzyce
(phot. – ST)   *The High Bank – the Fragment of the Dąbrowa Forest (phot. – ST)*

The Zemborzyce Artificial Lake seen from the "Marina" Centre (phot. – ST)

On the "Lublin Sea" (phot. – PM)

From the dam one can see a panorama of both of the Lake's banks. The western bank is full of bays and sandy beaches with numerous promontories and peninsulas. There are always some fishermen there who sit either at the boulevard or on the boats. There are various kinds of fish in the Lake. One can catch pikes and eels, carps and crucian carps, tench and grass carps, silver carps, sheat-fish, roaches and bleaks.

Dąbrowa Forest creates the "green wall" of the Lake. There are mostly fir and oak there with a small amount of other trees and bushes. Here there are two recreational centres "Wrotków" and "Dąbrowa". There are car parks, secure beaches and bathing places, entertainment centres, camp and tent sites, seasonal catering posts, sailing platforms and the places where you can rent the swimming equipment. In "Dąbrowa" Centre there is a station of the Lublin Mounted Nature Rangers.

Two tourist trails start in "Dąbrowa" Centre. "The Bystrzyca River Valley" (the yellow trail) leads southward, passes by the Rękaw Bay with the bank densely overgrown with reed, goes into Dąbrowa Forest and reaches Strzyżewice Village. What makes this trail attractive are old wooden water mills and manor houses and palaces like those in Żabia Wola, Osmolice, Piotrowice and Strzyżewice. The Bystrzyca River is here full of trout and grayling. The "Lublin Forests" Trail (green) leads north of Lublin to Podzamcze and Mełgiew. Walking on the east bank

The Western Bank (phot. – ST)

of the Lake we pass by Stara Knieja with the sandy beach and enter Wysoki Brzeg. From this hill we can see the Naked Island situated about 100 m from the bank.

From the dam we start towards the western bank of the Zemborzyce Artificial Lake. On the right hand side we can see the "Marina" Centre" of 28 ha. It was built on the former manor house grounds. Hence the preserved fragments of a park with the monumental trees and a few utility houses.

There is a sailing and canoeing track marked on the Zemborzyce Artificial Lake. It is 2000 m long. The event is being watched from the referee tower and the viewers observe it from the ramp. There is also a small recreational boat that crosses the Lake. The water sports club is located in the "Marina" Centre (the Sea and the River League). Young sailors are trained here.

"Marina" Centre is located on a flat ground. It is situated near the arable lands and huts of the former village Zemborzyce. Today, it is the intensely developing recreational district of Lublin.

Walking along the bank of the Lake we reach the Baza Bay. From here to the opposite promontory in Dąbrowa the distance is only 650 m. It is the narrowest fragment of the Lake. Along its western bank there is a path, which leads to the bridge on the Bystrzyca River at Cienista Street, and then to the road. Once we turn into Bór Street we pass by the former houses and boarding houses and we reach Grzybowa Street. One can return the same way to the Lake. On the left hand side of the beach there is the pump station of the municipal water supply system. The trail that goes right leads to the Rękaw Bay. At its top two trails meet.

THE SUBURBAN ROUTE II

Lublin – the River Ciemięga Valley – Snopków – Jakubowice Konińskie
– Dys – Ciecierzyn – Lublin

The length of the route: 35 km

Jastków (phot. – PM)

From the centre of Lublin we take a local bus to Jastków (see: p. 262). We cross the Ciemięga River Valley to Jastków Północny. We move eastwards along the Valley. The road goes on one side of the River, then on the other. After 6 km we reach Snopków (see. p. 224). In the park there is a monument of nature – an oak with a trunk of 580 cm in diameter. There is also an interesting palace there. Going on the right hand side of the Valley we reach a historical buildings located on the northern part of the River.

JAKUBOWICE KONIŃSKIE

Here we can see the old defensive *manor house* built by the Koniński Family who owned Jakubowice, Krasienin, Wola Konińska (today Końskowola). The village belonged to that family as early as in the 15th century. The manor house was erected on a high hill in the 1st half of the 16th century. It possessed some features of Renaissance and Gothic. At the turn of the 16th and 17th centuries there was an Arian prayer house here. The manor house was rebuilt many times and it lost much of its

The Former Koniński Manor House (phot. – ST)

The Outhouse (phot. – ST)

original architecture. Now, there is a boarding house there. In the older, back part of the manor house there are two cradle vaulted rooms. The front elevation is divided with a mould into two floors. It comes from the turn of the 18th and 19th centuries.

Via the northern part of the Valley we go along the river. We pass by the old riverbeds and springs and reach Dys.

DYS

The village once belonged to the Górkas, Szamotulskis and Sulimierskis. There is *a Parish Church* here erected in 1381 by Gabriel Górka. The church was originally wooden, but since the 16th century it is brick. In the years 1590-1610 it served as a Protestant Prayer House. In 1610, the construction worker Jan Wolff rebuilt the church with the approval of Dobrogost Szamotulski and he provided it with the features of the Lublin Renaissance style. In 1714, Jadwiga Niemyska, the wife of a Lublin judge, gave the parish to the Lublin missionaries. Inside, besides the bea tiful Renaissance details, one can see the Rococo ornamentation as well as the portraits of Jadwiga Niemyska and Anna Zbąska, the benefactors of the Missionaries.

In the nearby Parish Cemetery there are numerous tombstones and monuments from the turn of the 19th and 20th centuries. They are real works of art.

At the southern escarpment of the Ciemięga River Valley there is a Renaissance manor house from 1910. It replaced the family *manor house* of the village chiefs of Dys appointed by the owners of Kozłówka – the Bielińskis. Their Estate stretched as far as the Ciemięga River.

1-3 – The Complex of the Parish Church and the Vicarage (phot. – ST)
4 – The Tombstone from the turn of the 19th and 20th centuries on the Parish Churchyard (phot. – ST)

In the Ciemięga River Valley (Phot. – ST)

CIECIERZYN

It is located 2 km further in a deep valley. The village was mentioned in the documents in the 15th century. In the 1st half of the 17th century it belonged to Jan Zebrzydowski, the Crown Sword-Bearer.

The Ciecierzyn vicinity is of a verified landscape. The ground is cut across by a network of gorges and caves overgrown with a dense vegetation.

From here, by bus or by train, we return to Lublin.

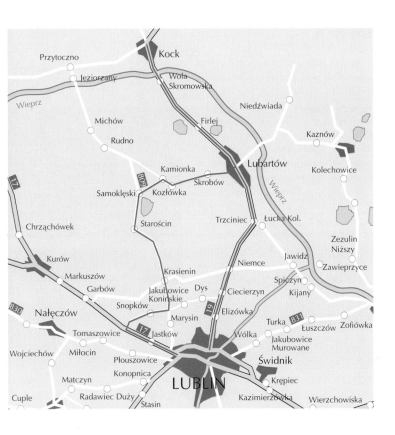

THE SUBURBAN ROUTE III

Lublin – Niemce – Łucka – Lubartów – Skrobów – Kozłówka
– Samoklęski – Krasienin – Snopków – Lublin

The length of the route: 65 km

NIEMCE

13 km from Lublin there is a village Niemce. It was known as Wola Niemiecka. The tradition says that after the Teutonic Knights taken prisoner built the Church of the Victorious Mary, they were settled here. One should pay attention to the Neo-Gothic Church from the years 1907-1909 and the remnants of the manor house park from the 18th century.

Some 10 km further away we pass by the village Łucka, which was established at the beginning of the 15th century. In the 16th century it was a property of the Firlej Family. Stanisław Oczko, father of Wojciech Oczko the famous Lublin physician was born here.

The Parish Church in Niemce (phot. – ST)

LUBARTÓW

We enter Lubartów, the seat of the County authorities, which is situated about 26 km from Lublin. The town was established in 1543 by the Governor of the Lublin Province Piotr Firlej. Initially it was called Lewartów, taking its name from Lewart, the owner's coat-of-arms. At the beginning of the 17th century it was owned by the Sanguszko Family.

St. Ann Parish Church and the Sanguszko Palace (phot. – PM)

St. Ann Parish Church (phot. – JŻ)　　　The High Altar in St. Ann Church (phot. – AC)

Then, its name was changed into Lubartów, from the predecessor of the Family – Lubart. **The Parish St. Anne Church** built in the years of 1733-1737 by Paweł Karol Sanguszko, and designed by Paweł Fontana is one of the examples of the central and longitudinal churches of the Lublin Baroque. In 1741, Paweł Sanguszko founded and Paweł Fontana designed also *the Church and the Cloister of the Capuchin Monks*. These are typical Baroque Capuchin buildings with a modest architecture similar to the church of this order in Lublin. In the temple there are nine pictures by Szymon Czechowicz. The Manor House of the first owner of Lubartów – Piotr Firlej – acquired the palatial character after the renovation in the Sanguszko times and namely in 1693. *The Palace* was designed and its construction was supervised by Tylman from Gameren. The successive renovation of the Palace in the years 1730-1738 was the work of Paweł Fontana. The Palace acquired then its present Baroque appearance.

In the Regional Museum in Lubartów one can see a permanent exhibition on the history of the town. Those who have more time should visit the nearby **Kock**. There is a very interesting **Palace** and a **Park**.

The Sanguszko Palace (phot. – JŻ)

The Knights' Chamber in Sanguszko Palace (phot. – JŻ)

The Church of the Capuchin Monks (phot. – JŻ)

The Regional Museum in Lubartów (phot. – PM)

We return to Lubartów. Opposite the Palace we turn west and direct towards Kozłówka. By the way we pass by **Skrobów**. In the years 1941-1944 there was a Nazi camp for the Soviet POWs. In 1944, the NKWD organised a camp for the soldiers of the Home Army here. Here, under the fire of the Soviet tanks, the 27th Wołyń Division of the Home Army was disarmed by the Soviets. That was the Division that liberated that area.

The Palace and the Park in Kock (phot. – PM)

KOZŁÓWKA

In the 18th century, Kozłówka belonged to the Pepłowski, and then to the Bieliński Family. Around 1742 they built a Palace here designed by Józef Fontana. It was founded by the Governor of the Chełmno Province, Michał Bieliński and his wife Tekla nee Pepłowska. Since 1799, the Estate has belonged to the Zamoyski Family. *The Palace in Kozłówka* with the adjoining buildings and a park was an example of the country residence formed during the reign of the Saxon Dynasty in Poland. One-storey residence made a centre of the complex. It is a solid building, covered with an ornamental, bent roof. Other houses are built in the shape of a horseshoe. These are outhouses, the kitchen, the guardhouse, the chapel, the stables and the coach rooms. Another element of the complex is a park organised in the French style. In 1870, the Kozłówka Estate was taken over by Konstanty Zamoyski. He turned the country palace into a magnificent residence full of the objects of art. (pictures, sculptures, furniture, china, silverware). There were a lot of copies among them but they were cherished equally with the originals since their main function was decorative.

The Palace in Kozłówka is now a Museum of the Zamoyski Family. It possesses a well-kept interiors of the aristocratic residence. Since 1992 there is the largest collection of paintings and sculpture of real socialism (*The Gallery of the Real Socialism Art*). It has 1500 exhibits. The title of the exhibition is "Stalin's Breath".

From Kozłówka we move west towards Samoklęski. We pass by Kamionka founded by the Górkas (it obtained city rights in 1450 and at the turn of the 16th and 17th centuries the Szamotulskis turned the existing church into a Protestant Prayer House.

The Zamoyski Palace Complex (phot. – PM)

The Zamoyski Palace in Kozłówka (phot. – AC)

221

The Manor House in Samoklęski from the 1ˢᵗ half of the 19ᵗʰ c. (phot. – ST)

SAMOKLĘSKI

The village existing since 1533, initially called *Sowoklęski*, since the 17ᵗʰ century had belonged to the Tęczyński Family. Then it was a property of Lubomirski and Sieniawski Families; in 1824, Prince Adam Czartoryski sold the property to General Jan Weysenhoff, and his son, Józef, lost the property playing cards in 1891. In Samoklęski, there is *a Classical Manor House* with the column portico. It was erected in the 1ˢᵗ half of the 19ᵗʰ century and designed by Christian Piotr Aigner. The grounds around Samoklęski have unique natural values. One can meet here the little egret and the black stork and can admire the clean waters of the ponds that stretch on the area of around 200 ha.

Via Starocin we move south to Krasienin, 10 km away from Samoklęski.

KRASIENIN

In the 15ᵗʰ century, the village belonged to the Koniński Family. They built a wooden *Manor House* here. Then the property was inherited by the Czernys (who organised a Calvinist Prayer House here) and then by the Łoś and Morozewicz Families. In 1913, Irena Kosmowska opened an agricultural school for girls in the Classical Manor House from the 1ˢᵗ half of the 19ᵗʰ century. She was arrested in 1942 and died in Berlin in 1945. There is *a church* in Krasienin in the Lublin Renaissance style from the 1st half of the 17ᵗʰ century with *the Baroque Vicarage*.

From Krasienin we move south to Snopków located on the Ciemięga River.

The Parish Church in Krasienin (phot. – ST)

The Manor House in Krasienin from the 1ˢᵗ half of the 19ᵗʰ c. (phot. – ST)

223

The Palace from the 19th c. in Snopków (phot. – ST)

SNOPKÓW

In the 1st half of the 19th century, the village belonged to the Trzciński Family and then to Wiercieńskis and Bobkowskis. They turned the Manor House into *an eclectic Palace*. It is standing in a spacious park with precious trees. In the 20th century, the Estate belonged to the Piaszczyńskis. They even kept Persian lambs here. In the first days of September 1939, the Palace seated the headquarters of the Stuff of Armia "Prusy" with General Stefan Dąb-Biernacki.

From Snopków we return to Lublin, passing by Sławinek between the Botanical Garden and the Museum of the Lublin Village.

The Roadside Chapel (phot. – ST)

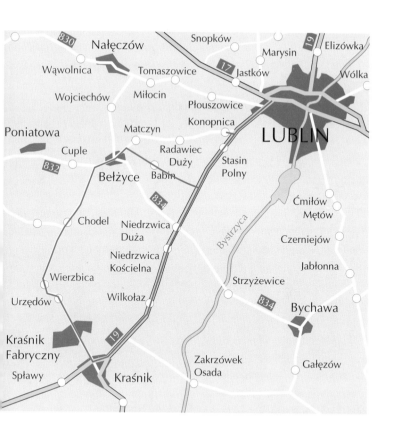

THE SUBURBAN ROUTE IV

Lublin – Konopnica – Niedrzwica Duża i Niedrzwica Kościelna
– Wilkołaz – Kraśnik – Urzędów – Chodel – Bełżyce – Babin – Lublin

The length of the route: 115 km

Via Kraśnicka Avenue we move towards Rzeszów.

KONOPNICA

It is located 9 km from the centre of Lublin. Since 1342 – as a property of the burgher family Konopnica – it was a part of the Lublin Community. The town purchased the estate in 1400. *The Neo-Gothic Parish Church* comes from 1905; there is also *the old vicarage* and the ruins of *the belfry* from the end of the 18th century.

The Parish Church and the Old Vicarage in Konopnica (phot. – ST)

NIEDRZWICA DUŻA AND KOŚCIELNA

14 km further there is Niedrzwica Duża, called Niedrzwica Wielka. It is one of the oldest settlements in this area. It is first mentioned in the historical documents in 1409. 3 km further on, there is Niedrzwica Kościelna with *the Classical Church* from the years 1791-1801 founded by the Lublin Chamberlain, Tomasz Dłucki. Near the church there is *the belfry* from the turn of the 18th and 19th centuries. Nearby there is *an old inn* from the middle of the 19th centuries and *the old vicarage* and the stylish, *wooden chapel*.

The Parish Church and the Old Vicarage in Niedrzwica Kościelna (phot. – ST)

WILKOŁAZ

It is the settlement older than Niedrzwica. The parish was established here in 1325. The Tartars settled in this vicinity. One of the most precious historical sights today is *the Parish Church* built in the middle of the 17th century. It was founded by the owner of these lands, the Governor of Kałusk – Jan Zamoyski. Father Piotr Ściegienny served here as an auxiliary priest; he acted according to the principles described in his *Golden Book*.

KRAŚNIK

There are only 15 km from Wilkołaz to Kraśnik. In the 1st half of the 13th century Kraśnik belonged to the Grajewski Family; then it was a property of the Tęczyńskis, Słuckis and Radziwiłłs. In 1604 the estate was purchased by the Grand Crown Hetman – Jan Zamoyski who incorporated it into his Zamość Estate. In 1877 there was a great fire in Kraśnik, which consumed most of the town. *The Parish Church*

The Church and the Cloister of the Regular Canons in Kraśnik (phot. – ST)

The Hospital Church in Kraśnik (phot. – ST)

The Permanent Exhibition in the Museum of the 24th Regiment of Cavalry (phot. – PM)

comes from the 15th century. Jan Tęczyński rebuilt the Gothic temple into a Renaissance one in 1541. There are some pictures from Tomasz Dolabella's school and precious tombstones: the Renaissance one of Andrzej Kośla by Santi Gucci and the Tęczyńskis – among them that of Jan Tęczyński the Governor of the Lublin Province and his fiancee – Cecylia Waza. These tombstones come from 1604 and are the work of Santi Gucci as well. The architectural complex includes *the church and the cloister built* at the turn of the 15th and 16th centuries. Near the wooden hospital church there is the Baroque, brick *Hospital Church* from the 2nd half of the 18th century. Near the Market Square there are two *synagogues* from the 17th and the 18th century.

In Krasnik one can also visit the Regional Museum presenting the archives connected with the history of the town and the exhibits of archaeology, ethnography, art, industry, craftsmanship and trade. In the Museum of the 24th Regiment of Cavalry one can learn the history of this regiment, which stationed in Kraśnik in the years 1922-1939.

Via Kraśnik Fabryczny we move to Urzędów.

URZĘDÓW

This large settlement divided into many parts was – since 1405 – the trading village, then the town, and then the seat of a County. Urzędów had its Golden Age in the middle of the 16th century. After the Tartars destroyed the town at the beginning of the 16th century, it was rebuilt, surrounded with dykes and a palisade with gates: The Krakow Gate, The Lublin Gate and the Opole Gate. The fragments of the dykes and the old huts have been preserved till today. There is also *the Parish Church* from the 18th century, and the historical *Neo-Gothic vicarage*, the Baroque *Cemetery Chapel* and *the Chapel from 1890* at the spring, which is eagerly visited by pilgrims. In the suburb Bęczyn, the people continue the pottery traditions. In the old stoves they still burn ceramics and original sculptures.

We move towards Bełżyce, stopping for a while in Chodel.

The Cemetery Chapel (phot. – ST)

The Chapel (phot. – ST)

Cezary Gajewski, the potter from Urzędów (phot. – ST)

The Ruins of the Jesuit Church (phot. – PM)

CHODEL

The town established in 1517 by Bernard and Kasper Maciejowski was first called Nowa Kłodnica. In 1582, the co-owners of the town were Jesuits from Lublin. Then, Chodel had many owners, and in 1869 it lost the city rights. Father Piotr Ściegienny was a vicar here in the years 1843-1844. *The Church* founded in 1541 by Bernard Maciejowski is an example of the original Gothic and Renaissance building. Inside, one should pay attention to the few-storey tombstone, probably of the founder and his wife. The ruins of *the Jesuit church* called Loreto, can be seen on the island on the pond in the Chodelka River Valley. It was a late Baroque church similar to the Cathedral of Lublin. Inside one can still detect the murals by Józef Majer. The recreational attraction of Chodel is the picturesque lake.

The Parish Church in Chodel (phot. – PM)

BEŁŻYCE

The town was established in 1417 by the Governor of the Lublin Province, Jan from Tarnów. Since the middle of the 16th century it was a strong centre of Reformation. *The Parish Church* built in the middle of the 17th century retained some features of the Lublin Renaissance (vaults with stucco).

The Parish Church (phot. – ST)   *The Cemetery Gate (phot. – ST)*

BABIN

It is situated 3,5 km east of Bełżyce. In the middle of the 16th century Stanisław Pszonka – the owner of Babin and Piotr Kaszowski – the Lublin judge and the owner of Wysokie – established here the famous "Babin Commonwealth". It was also called "the kingdom of shadows" and "the state upside down". They sneered and joked on the pompous dignitaries. One could become a member of the Babin Commonwealth when he told a joke and drank a special kind of liquor. These conditions were – as the legend says – fulfilled by Mikołaj Rej and Jan Kochanowski. The Babin Commonwealth survived till 1677.

Going east from Babin, at Strzeszkowice we reach the Kraśnik highway and return to Lublin.

The Zalesianka River in Forests (phot. – TB)   *The Kręzniczanka River (phot. – TB)*

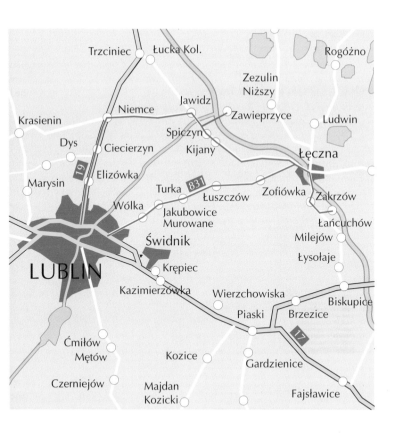

THE SUBURBAN ROUTE V

Lublin – Jakubowice Murowane – Łuszczów – Łęczna – Łańcuchów
– Łęczna – Kijany – Zawieprzyce – Niemce – Lublin

The length of the route: 78 km

Via Turystyczna Street we move north-est direction. In Wólka Lubelska we turn left and we cross the Bystrzyca River.

JAKUBOWICE MUROWANE

Jakubowice Murowane is situated 4 km from Lublin. At the turn of the 16th and the 17th centuries it belonged to the Tęczyński Family. The Tęczyńskis erected a Renaissance Palace here. Then the village belonged to Jakub Sobieski, King Jan's son, and then to the Szeptyckis and Grodzickis. After the destruction made by the Swedish soldiers, the Palace was restored after 1803 by Konstancja Szeptycka. It assumed the appearance of the Pseudo-Renaissance residence. It was destroyed and restored many times, and finally fell into ruins after 1944. Today, one can admire the impressive *Neo-Gothic gate* leading to the Park.

ŁUSZCZÓW

The village situated 10 km further was known as early as the 15th century. There is *the Baroque Church* from the middle of the 18th century founded by the Grand Crown Guard, Józef Potocki. In the nearby Bystrzyca situated on the opposite bank of the river, Jan Wadowski was the vicar at the end of the 19th century. He was a member of the Academy of skills, and a historian of the Lublin churches. From the road we can see the silhouette of the Baroque *Church in Bystrzyca*, which is 1,5 km away.

The Palace Gate in Jakubowice Murowane (phot. – ST)

The Ruins of the Palace from the turn of the 16th and 17th c. in Jakubowice Murowane (phot. – ST)

The Parish Church in Łuszczów (phot. – ST)

ŁĘCZNA

The settlement is located on the Wieprz River and it is the seat of a County. It was known as early as 1350. It belonged to the Gorajski, Tęczyński, Firlej and Noskowski Families. It obtained the city rights in 1457. At the beginning of the 18th century, the horse fairs were moved here from Lublin. They were held in Łęczna till the middle of the 19th century, and they proved to be very profitable.

At that time there were three large market places in Łęczna. *The Parish Church* founded by Adam Noskowski was built in the Lublin Renaissance style in the years 1618-1631. It was designed by Jan Wolff. There is also *the Belfry* from 1827 and *the old Mansion* from the middle of the 17th century, and *the Classical Town Hall*. In the Baroque *Synagogue* from 1648 with the preserved ornamentation of the interior there is the Regional Museum now. It presents a large collection of Judaica, and the exhibits connected with the history of the town and the region. One should also pay attention to the houses at the Market Place and the Jewish houses at Kanałowa Street.

The Parish Church with the Side Altar (phot. – KD)

The Relief on the Facade of the Church (phot. – KD)

The Belfry from 1827 (phot. – KD)

The Former Mansion (phot. – KD)

The Classical Town Hall (phot. – KD)

The Former Synagogue (phot. – KD)

The Old Houses at Kanałowa Street (phot. – KD)

The Interior of the Synagogue in Łęczna (phot. – KD)

Zagłębocze Lake (phot. – KD)

Brzeziczno Lake (phot. – KD)

Brzeziczno Lake (phot. – KD)   *The Reservation "Brzeziczno Lake" (phot. – KD)*

The Wieprz River Valley (phot. – ST)

The Russian Orthodox Church in Dratów. The Dratów Lake (phot. – KD)

Łęczna plays the role of the entrance gate to *the Łęczna and Włodawa Lake District*, which is an area of a very attractive landscape values. There are 67 lakes of the area of 1 ha each. Seven of them have over 100 ha of the area and the deepest – Piaseczno – is about 39 m deep. There is a lot of protected flora and fauna, and we can admire magnificent forest complexes and unique peat bogs. Dratów Lake is situated closest to Łęczna; it is only 9 km away. In *Dratów* Village one can admire *the Russian Orthodox Church* erected in 1880 in the Eclectic Style. Those who have more time may visit other lakes like Piaseczno, Zagłębocze, Krasne and Brzeziczno with the Reservation "Jezioro Brzeziczno".

From Łęczna we move to Łańcuchów via Ciechanki.

ŁAŃCUCHÓW

It is the village of the Kuropatwa Family, and it received the city rights in 1519. Then it belonged to the Orzechowskis, Suffczyńskis, Spinkas, Wołk-Łaniewskis and Steckis. In 1904, Jan Stecki erected an original *manor house* in Łańcuchów in the "Zakopane style". It was designed by Stanisław Witkiewicz.

The Stecki Manor House (phot. – ST)

We return to Łęczna via Kijany and then direct to Zawieprzyce.

KIJANY

In the 16th century Kijany was the family nest of the Kijański Family of the Serokomla coat-of-arms. In the 17th century, the Firlejs built a castle here. In the next century, it belonged to Sanguszko, and in the 19th century to the industrialist – Sonnenbeg. *The Palace* in the park was designed by Tylman from Gameren. The palace was destroyed and reconstructed many times and finally retained the Neo-Renaissance style. It houses the Complex of Agricultural Schools. The Baroque *St. Ann church* was erected before 1783 and founded by Atanazy Miączyński. In *the cemetery* we find the graves of the Skłodowski Family. The nearby Zawieprzyce was visited during summer vacations by Maria Curie- Skłodowska.

St. Anne's Church (phot. – ST)

The Outhouse in Zawieprzyce (phot. – ST)

The Skłodowski Family Grave (phot. – ST)

The palace from the 19th c. (phot. – ST)

The Miączyński Chapel and the Fragment of the Ruins of the Castle in Zawieprzyce (phot. – ST)

ZAWIEPRZYCE

In the middle of the 16th century, it belonged to the Lublin official Andrzej Zawieprski; then, it was the property of the Ciecierskis, Firlejs and Gorayskis, and later of Atanazy Miączyński, the Morskis and the Ostrowskis. In the 1st half of the 16th century, the owners built *the Castle* as an element of the defensive structure of the Firlej Estates. It was destroyed during the Swedish Wars and then reconstructed in the years 1672-1679 by Tylman from Gameren as a Baroque residence. It was consumed by fire in 1838. Today we can only see its ruins. In the Park there is *a chapel* founded by Piotr Miączyński and his wife Anotnina nee Rzewuska. In its cupola one can find the primitive copy of the fresco "the Final Justice" from the Tyszkiewicz Chapel in the Dominican Church in Lublin. Nearby one can see *the old Granary* and a defensive *manor house*. There is also *the Castle Gate* from the turn of the 17th and 18th century. Nearby, there is *the outhouse*, which now houses a school and on a small mound there is the famous *Stone Figure*, crowned with a metal cross.

From Zawieprzyce via Spiczyn and Niemce we return to Lublin.

THE SUBURBAN ROUTE VI

Lublin – Świdnik – Krępiec – Kazimierzówka – Wierzchowiska
– Piaski – Gardzienice – Lublin

The length of the route: 24 km

The Manor House in Felin (phot. − ST)

Via Droga Męczenników Majdanka we enter the Highway No 17 that leads to Zamość. Passing by the complex of the housing projects in Bronowice, on the right hand side we have the former Majdanek Concentration Camp − now the State Museum (see: pp. 163-164). A little further on there is the communal cemetery.

Doświadczalna Street takes us to *Felin* − the housing district built around *the Manor House* and *the Park*. It was the former estate of the Graff Family. It was founded in the years 1850-1856. It takes its name from Felicja Graff. Then, the property belonged to Erazm Plewiński, a country gentleman, social activist who gave the Estate to the Lublin Agricultural Society and thus enabled it to open the agricultural school in Kijany.

The Manor House was rebuilt by the Germans during the Nazi Occupation. Doświadczalna Street derives its name from the Experimental Household of the Agricultural Academy. On the perfect plots, various decorative and medical plant grow together with spices and vegetables. There are also horses and cattle kept here. Famous Felin Ponies come from here. Their population was created by Ewald Sasimowski, a professor of the Agricultural Academy with his crew.

Going east on a highway from Felin we turn left behind Kalinówka and return to the road leading to Świdnik.

ŚWIDNIK

It obtained the city rights late − in 1954. Its beginnings, however, go back in time to the 15th century. There were three villages here at the time: Świdnik Duży − a Royal Village, Świdnik Mały − the nobleman's village and Świdniczek − the Church Village. The place was so divided up to the 19th century. The nearby magnificent forest complexes had a special impact. At the end of the 19th century, one of the

The Old Railway Station in Świdnik (phot. – ST)

settlements – Annopol – turned into a popular resort. In the 30s, the State Authorities got interested in Świdnik and they decided to organise here the training centre of the future pilots. An airport was built here. The Pilot School and the Airport were ceremoniously opened on 4 June 1939. The ceremony was attended by Marshal Rydz-Śmigły and the airport got his name. In 1949 the authorities decided to build in Świdnik the Manufacture of the Communication Equipment. In 1951, the production started. The leading product of the firm is a helicopter "Sokół", the work of the local constructors.

Świdnik was born as a factory district. Now it is a town of 40 thousand inhabitants. The oldest, villa district of the town is Adampol, where one can see the pre-war wooden boarding houses. The oldest social utility building in the town is **the Railway Station** built in the years 1905-1914.

Leaving Świdnik and going in the south-east direction we reach Krępiec after 3 km ride.

KRĘPIEC

The village was founded by King Władysław Jagiełło in 1398. In the middle of the 16th century there were only 22 peasants here who lived in 7 households. There were, however, four inns and at the nearby pond there was a mill. Today, it is a resort with a small artificial lake. Going south from here we reach Highway No 17. In the Krępiec Forest we can see **the Monument** to the Prisoners of Majdanek who were executed here, as well as the prisoners of the Royal Castle and the Jews from the Lublin Ghetto.

On the Highway No 17 we go towards Wierzchowiska and Piaski.

Koźmian Palace in Wierzchowiska (phot. – ST)

WIERZCHOWISKA

Jan Długosz mentioned Wierzchowiska in the 14th century as a nobleman's village. Today, in the Park from the end of the 19th century one can admire the renovated **Palace** and **the adjoining buildings** from the 19th century built by Jan Koźmian. He was a cousin of Kajetan Koźmian, the poet, the author of *The Polish Country Gentleman* and *The Memoirs*. One should also pay attention to **the Castle Guardhouse** with the view at the pond and the park. In the Park there are about 700 trees of 27 species. Some of them have rare natural and historical values.

The Palace Guardhouse (phot. – ST)

The Pond and the Historical Alley in the Park (phot. – ST)

PIASKI

The village similar to the town settlement, the seat of the Community is located at the inflow of the Sierotka River to Giełczew River. Piaski received the city rights in the middle of the 15th century but lost them after the fall of the January Insurrection. As a property of the Orzechowski and Suchodolski Families since the middle of the 16th century it became a famous centre of the Arian Movement (there was here the famous preacher Marcin Krowicki who greatly influenced Mikołaj Rej). Since the middle of the 17th century, Piaski was the centre of the Calvinist Movement. Till 1849, there was *a Calvinist Prayer House* here built on a hill near the pond by Teodor Suchodolski in the years 1783-1785. Its ruins are often visited by tourists. Piaski was often called the Lutheran Piaski. Today's weekly horse and other domestic animals fairs revoke the old trade tradition.

The Parish Church (phot. – ST)

Piaski has retained the characteristic for the small towns and suburbs of Lublin housing pattern; the stone houses of one or two floors. Most of them are

The Stone Mill – the Former Windmill (phot. – ST)

concentrated at Gardzienicka Street. Here one can also see *the stone windmill* from 1898 – now there is the electric mill.

The Parish Church comes from around 1720. It was rebuilt in the years 1945--1948 after the destruction during the war. One should pay special attention to the Belfry from 1866.

Near the highway that leads to Chełm, there was a Suchodolski manor house from the 19th century. During the Nazi Occupation it was a centre of a ghetto established by the Germans for the Jews. The ghetto covered almost half of the town. The Ghetto was the transitory place, from where the Jews from Poland, Germany, Czech Republic and Slovakia were transported to the extermination camp in Bełżec and Sobibór. The Ghetto was liquidated in 1943 and it ended the tragic fate of the Jews of Piaski. In Piaski before the war there were 2030 Jews out of 2773 inhabitants.

At the main road there is *the Monument* commemorating the victims of World War II. On the cemetery there are graves of the soldiers killed in September 1939 and the graves of the partisans, among other, the underground movement "Baony Zemsty". Also the plaque placed at the church's wall commemorates those who lost their lives for Fatherland.

We leave Piaski and going into the direction of Żółkiewka we enter Gardzienice.

The Palace of the Orzechowskis (phot. – ST)

GARDZIENICE

Gardzienice is a village 5 km from Piaski. It was mentioned in 1409 as a property of the Snopkowskis; in the 18ᵗʰ century it belonged to Paweł Orzechowski, then to Wacław Hulewicz, the Bracław Governor, and finally it became a property of Stanisław Czarniecki, the Crown Writer, and a cousin of Hetman Stefan Czarniecki. In the next generation, Gardzienice was inherited by Michał Potocki, the Governor of the Wołyń Province.

The original Orzechowski Manor House was standing on a high escarpment over the Giełczew River Valley. It was built inn 1610. It was destroyed by the Swedes and then restored. The Potockis wanted to turn it into a Baroque Palace at the turn of the 17ᵗʰ and 18ᵗʰ centuries. It was consumed by fire in 1802 and had to be restored again. In the 1ˢᵗ half of the 19ᵗʰ century it was turned into a granary and then into a residence. Now *the Gardzienice Palace* is a one-storey building with the protruding projection in the main corps and the arcades at the sides. In the north there is the oldest ground floor building from 1627 where there was probably a Protestant Prayer House. Near the Palace there are outhouses. The first one-storey building in the east comes from the end of the 17ᵗʰ century, and the adjoining ground-floor building comes from the 1st half of the 18ᵗʰ century.

The Palace and the Adjoining Chapel (phot. – ST)

The Giełczew River Valley (phot. – ST)

After World War II the Gardzienice Palace had many owners and it housed even the People's University. For over 20 years it is the seat of the Theatrical Practice Centre "Gardzienice", the theatrical group famous not only in Poland. The Palace buildings are surrounded by an old, wild park with a modest slope towards the Giełczew River and towards the spacious meadows.

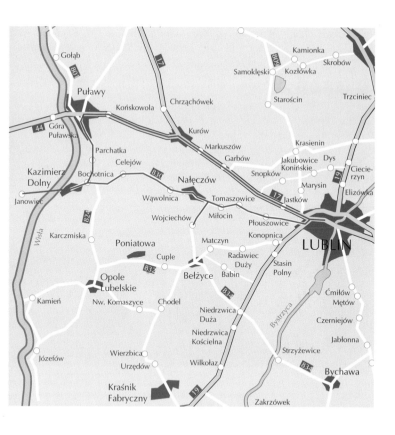

THE SUBURBAN ROUTE VII

Lublin – Dąbrowica – Tomaszowice – Wojciechów – Nałęczów
– Wąwolnica – Celejów – Bochotnica – Kazimierz Dolny – Janowiec
– Parchatka – Włostowice – Puławy – Końskowola – Kurów
– Markuszów – Garbów I and II – Jastków – Lublin

The length of the route: 115 km

From the Centre of Lublin via Racławickie Avenue and Kraśnicka Avenue we enter Nałęczowska Street. 3 km later we turn right and go 1 km further.

DĄBROWICA

King Władysław Łokietek gave it to the Firlejs for the service to the country. They then wrote their name adding "De Dombrovica". They built a residence here. It acquired the perfect shape after the reconstruction made in the years 1610-1630 by Mikołaj Firlej, the Governor of Lublin and the Governor of Sandomierz Province. At the end of the 18th century *the Palace* was in ruins. Only the corner Tower remained with the Renaissance decoration and the fragment of the arcade gallery.

The Turret of the Former Firlej Palace (phot. – ST)

We return to the road that leads to Kazimierz Dolny and we reach Tomaszowice.

TOMASZOWICE

In the 2nd half of the 17th century, it belonged to Stanisław Borowski. Then it often changed hands. In 1864 the old wooden Manor House was replaced by an eclectic, brick *Palace*, in which one can still admire the Classical Hall. Around it there is a park and *the outhouse* from 1854, which later was turned into the Chapel.

We move west. In Miłocin we turn left.

The Palace from the 19th c. and the Chapel (phot. – ST)

WOJCIECHÓW

It is a large eco-tourist centre. There was a parish here in 1328. Since the end of the 15th till the end of the 16th century, the village was a property of the Szczekocki Family. Then it belonged to the Pilecki Family. In the years 1510-1540 they built the residential tower surrounded with a moat called *the Arian tower*. It is the Gothic and Renaissance building constructed on the pattern of a square. The successive owners of Wojciechów were Krzysztof Spinka, Paweł Orzechowski, the Chełm Chamberlain, and his son Paweł who built a Palace nearby. Since that time the Tower began to collapse. In 1910 it was handed over to the Society of Taking

The Arian Tower (phot. — PM). The Roadside Chapel (phot. — ST)

Care of the Historical Sights and it was renovated under the supervision of Jan Koszczyc-Witkiewicz. (Stefan Żeromski described it in his novel *The Conversion of Judas*). After the successive renovations it houses now the Cultural Centre and the Museum of Forging. There is also *the wooden church* in the village founded in 1725 by Teodor Orzechowski.

NAŁĘCZÓW

It was mentioned in the middle of the 14th century as Bochotnica and it belonged to Mikołaj Kazimierski. Then it was a property of the Samborzeckis, and at the beginning of the 17th century it belonged to the Gałęzowski Family who sold it in 1751 to Stanisław Małachowski, the Wąwolnica Administrator. This Family owned it for over 150 years. In the 2nd half of the 18th century, Stanisław Małachowski built a Palace here for his wife Marianna Potocka. The whole residence assumed the name of Nałęczów then. At the beginning of the 19th century, the curing mineral waters were discovered here but they were soon ignored since the owners of Nałęczów did not care. In 1879, however, Nałęczów became a spa when the estate was purchased by Michał Górski who gave it to the physicians co-operative of Fortunat Nowicki, Wacław Lasocki and Konrad Chmielowski.

The most precious historical sights of Nałęczów are in the Park. First of all, it is *the Małachowski Palace*, built in 1772 by Ferdynand Nax with a magnificent

Nałęczów Spa (phot. 1-3 – ST)

The Old Baths (phot. – JM)

Bolesław Prus Museum. The Małachowski Palace – the Concert Hall (phot. – PM)

Żeromski's "Hut" and Adam Żeromski Mausoleum (phot. – PM)

Stefan Żeromski Museum (phot. – PM)

Ballroom, decorated with the Rococo and Classical stucco. In the Palace there is Bolesław Prus Museum since he was the writer closely connected with Nałęczów. Nearby there is *the old manor house of the Gałęzowski Family*. Close by there is Stefan Żeromski Monument made by A. Żurakowski and designed by Jan Koszyc-Witkiewicz. In the Park there are: the sanatorium from 1880 designed by Karol Kozłowski, and built in the Swiss style, *the Neo-Gothic Greek Temple* from the 19th century, *the Bishops' House* from the end of the 19th century, and *the Old Baths* from the 20s.

The Greek Temple (phot. – KD)   *The Villa at Lipowa Street (phot. – KD)*

The Museum of the Co-operative (phot. – KD)   *The Wooden Church (phot. – KD)*

One should walk along the side streets and visit the wooden church built in "the Zakopane style". The same style has also *"the Hut"* of Stefan Żeromski (built by Jan Koszczyc-Witkiewicz), now a museum, near *the Mausoleum* of his son Adam who died in 1918. In Nałęczów there is also the Museum of the Polish Co-operatives. It presents the history of this Movement since 1945 and the exhibits connected with the history of Nałęczów since 1939. The special atmosphere of the place is created by the houses built in the Swiss and Zakopane styles. The Sanatorium with the famous curing mineral waters (lime and iron) and a magnificent micro-climate curing heart functions without interruptions since its foundation.

WĄWOLNICA

It is one of the oldest settlements in the Lublin Province. Once it was the Royal town and in 1448 it received the city rights. It was a seat of the County, and in the 15th century it was the seat of the Lublin Provincial Governor. In the Middle Ages there was a defensive castle there. The Presbytery of the 15th century temple was

The Holy Mary Sanctuary (phot. – KD)

250

The Altar with the Miraculous Figure of Holy Mary Mother of God (phot. – KD)

The Pulpit and the Side Altar (phot. – KD)   *The Ogival Vault of the Side Nave (phot. – KD)*

On the Bystra River (phot. – KD)

turned into *a Chapel* with *a Gothic sculpture of Holy Mary Mother of God* (transferred from the nearby Kębło). The Parish Church was built in the years 1909--1914 and it has some features of Neo-Gothic.

CELEJÓW

In the 15th century it belonged to Jakub Chotecki, then it was owned by the prominent Polish families: the Borkowskis, the Tarłos, the Lubomirskis, the Sapiehas, the Potockis, and in the 19th century – the Czartoryskis. After the Tsar authorities confiscated their estates, Celejów became a property of the Klemensowskis. *The Palace* was erected in the middle of the 18th century. Then it was rebuilt by Anna Potocka at the turn of the 18th and the 19th centuries. Józef Klemensowski rebuilt it after the fire of 1847.

In the Bystrzyca River Valley one will find the picturesque complex of ponds. Near one of them there are ruins of *the paper manufacture* from the 19th century.

The Coat-of-Arms Cartouche on the Palace in Celejów (phot. – ST)

The Potocki Palace (phot. – ST)

The Ruins of the Paper Manufacture erected by the Czartoryskis (phot. – ST)

From Celejów, still driving west, we reach Bochotnica on the Vistula.

BOCHOTNICA

There are remnants of *the Medieval Castle* from the 14th century. It was owned by Ostasz, the precursor of the Firlej Family. At the end of that century the village with the Castle were purchased by the Governor of Sącz, Klemens from Kurów. Then it was a property of the Zbąski, Oleśnicki and Walewski Families. The Castle was ruined even at the end of the 16th century. The legend says that it was a living place of Estera, King Kazimierz Wielki's lover. Over the Vistula River Valley one can

The Ruins of the Castle in Bochotnica (phot. – KD)

The Quarry in Bochotnica (phot. – KD)

see the rocks, where the mountain climbers can train. In the unused quarry one can see the well-preserved fossils, and among them the skeletons of ancient animals.

KAZIMIERZ DOLNY

It derives its name from Kazimierz Sprawiedliwy, who in the 12th century founded a cloister here for the nuns from Krakow. Kazimierz received the city rights in 1406 from King Władysław Jagiełło. At the beginning of the next century *the granaries* were built here and they enabled to sent grain by the Vistula to Gdańsk.

On the Vistula River in Kazimierz Dolny (phot. – ST)

The Market Place and the Parish Church (phot. – PM)

The Market Place (phot. – ST)

The All-Polish Festival of the Folk Singers and Bands (phot. – KD)

The Market Place in Kazimierz and the Parish Church (phot. – KD)

The Attic on the Celej House (phot. – KD)

The Przybyło House (phot. – SC)

The burghers became richer. The town lived through good and bad times according to the historical events. It was destroyed and then rebuilt. During the November Insurrection Colonel Juliusz Małachowski was killed here by the Russians. The ruins of the Castle from the

The Turret and the Castle (phot. – ST)

The Granaries (phot. – ST)

From the Collection of the Silverware in the Museum of the Goldsmithery (phot. – Archive)

14th century are well-preserved. *The Castle* was built by King Kazimierz Wielki; together with a round Bastion from the 13th century these are main tourist attractions of the town. The Gothic *Parish church* was also founded by King Kazimierz Wielki. After the fire of 1561 it acquired a new appearance and became an exemplary building of the Lublin Renaissance. Near the subsidiary *St. Ann Church* there is *the Hospital* with a nicely ornamented top. On the hill behind the Market Place there are *the cloister buildings* form the 17th century and *the church of the Reformati*. At the Market Place and at

The Kuncewicz House (phot. – KD)

The Trench with the Tree Roots (phot. – TC)

Senatorska Street one can see the magnificent Renaissance *houses of Brothers Przybyło* from the 17th century, *the house of the Górskis*, *the White House*, *the Celej House* called the Black House. The landscape of the small market place is even more attractive due to the butchery stalls and there is *an old synagogue* turned into a cinema now.

The local Museum is inviting tourists to see the rich collections. In the Celej House there are presented the exhibits showing the history of the area and the works of modern artists. In the Museum of the Goldsmithery one can see the exhibition of the cult silverware and the jewelry. In the Museum of Nature there are permanent exhibitions entitled *The Kazimierz Landscape Park*, *The Mysteries of the World that Vanished* and *The Middle Fragment of the Vistula River*.

JANOWIEC

One of the tourist attractions is the ferry crossing the Vistula to Janowiec on the opposite bank of the River. The town was founded in 1537 on the grounds of the

The Castle in Janowiec (phot. – PM)

The Entrance to the Castle over the Moat (phot. – ST)

The View from the Castle (phot. – KD)

The Manor House from Moniaki (phot. – KD)

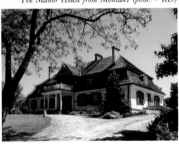

The Parish Church (phot. – KD)

The Ferry from Kazimierz Dolny to Janowiec (phot. – ST)

Serokomla Village by Mikołaj Firlej, the Governor of Kazimierz. One should see here the 14th century **Parish Church**. In the modest interior of the church there is one of the most beautiful Renaissance tombstones in Poland. It was made by Santi Gucci for Barbara and Andrzej Firlej. The dominating element of the landscape is the defensive **Castle of the Firlejs** with a great Bastion that later was turned into a residence. It was built after 1507 and in the 19th century fell into ruins. Now, in the restored fragment there is the Local Museum presenting the history of the Castle. Nearby there is *a manor house* from the 18th century presenting the interior of a typical nobleman's residence and other utility buildings.

We return to Kazimierz and from there to Bochotnica. On the crossroads we turn left towards Puławy. The road goes between the Vistula and the steep escarpment of the Nałęczów Plateau. It is sectioned by numerous gorges. We reach Parchatka. At the turn of the 18th and 19th centuries, Izabella Czartoryska established there a romantic garden.

Via old manor house alley surrounded with large, 200-years-old poplars we move towards Włostowice.

WŁOSTOWICE

Today, it is the suburb of Puławy. We pass by the Parish Church founded by Elżbieta Sieniawska in 1725-1728 according to the design of Franciszek Magier. The interior of the church was provided only in the 18th century, in the Czartoryskis' times. There are many valuable pictures in the Church and one should pay attention to the portraits of St. Teresa and St. Barbara by Kazimierz Woyniakowski who was Marcelo Baciarelli's student. Princesses Maria and Zofia Czartoryski were models for the pictures.

PUŁAWY

Puławy was established in the 17th century as a settlement close to the defensive residence. It belonged to Stanisław Herakliusz Lubomirski. Tylman from Gameren built a Castle for him there. Then it was a property of the Sieniawski Family and then – as a dowry – the Czartoryski Family. Puławy flourished under Adam Kazimierz Czartoryski and his wife – Izabela nee Flemming. Puławy was called in their times "the Athens of the North". Piotr Chrystian Aigner, educated by the Czartoryskis in

The Palace and the Park Complex (phot. – PM)

The Palace Residence (phot. – PM)

The Marynka Palace (phot. – ST)

The Ornaments on the Palace Arcade (phot. – ST)

The Column Cap in the Gothic House (phot. – ST)

The Temple of Sybil (phot. – ST)

The Gothic House (phot. – JM)

The Yellow House (phot. – ST)

The Roman Gate (phot. – ST)

The Grotto in the Park (phot. – ST)

The Rotunda (phot. – KD)

Italy son of a carpenter rebuilt *the Palace*, built *the Gothic Temple* and *the Temple of Sybil*. For Princess Maria Wirtemberska he built *the Marynka Palace*.

In the Gothic House and in the Temple of Sybil Princess Izabela gathered numerous historical souvenirs. The opening of the Gothic House in 1809 is regarded as the beginning of the Polish Museums. (The Collection of Artistic Objects gathered by the Czartoryskis can be seen in the Czartoryski Museum in Krakow. In Puławy there is also the Regional Museum). The so-called Palace settlement in the Park includes: *the Yellow House*, *the China House*, *the English Staircase*, *the Roman Gate*, *the Hothouse* and *the Tombstone* of August and Zofia Czartoryski, who established the power of the family. In the 19th century – after the Czartoryski Estates were confiscated for their participation in the November Uprising of 1831 – the palace was turned into the Boarding House for girls. Then there was the Technical Institute, later the Agriculture and Forestry Institute and then the Institute of Country Economy and Forestry. Now, there is the seat of the Institute of Cultivation, Fertilising and Soil Science (IUNG).

From Puławy we take a return road to Lublin.

KOŃSKOWOLA

Initially it was called Witowska Wola; since the 15th century when it became the property of the Koniński Family it acquired the name of Końskowola. In 1532, Andrzej Tęczyński obtained the permission of the King to receive the city rights. The successive owners of that village serving Puławy were: The Zbaraskis, the Sieniawskis and the Czartoryskis. *The Hospital Church* built in 1613 is another example of the sacral building of the Lublin Renaissance. There is also *the Parish Church*, which was built in stages in the 17th and 18th centuries. Tylman from Gameren and Józef Mayer were engaged in its construction. In front of the church there is *a Monument of Dionizy Kniaźnin*, a poet who died in 1807. It was erected by the local vicar, Fr. Franciszek Zabłocki, the author of the famous dramas. There is also an interesting Granary from the 18th century and *the Neo-Gothic gate* leading to the Parish Cemetery.

The Hospital Church (phot. – ST)

The Parish Church (phot. – ST)

The Vicarage from the 18th c. (phot. – ST)

KURÓW

The oldest information on Kurów comes from 1185. In the 15th century it belonged to the Kurowski Family, then to the Zbąskis, the Szczuka and the Potockis. Ignacy Potocki, the member of the National Educational Committee and the main initiator of the May 3 Constitution resided here. In 1774, he brought in his friend Fr. Grzegorz Piramowicz who became a vicar in Kurów. The construction of *the Parish Church* took some time, since the middle of the 16th century to the 18th century. Then the side naves were added. Inside the Church we can see the tombstone of Stanisław Zbąski who died in 1585. The tombstone was sculpted by Santi Gucci. *The Classical Vicarage* was built in the years 1778-1782 for Fr. Piramowicz. It was designed by Stanisław Kostka Potocki and Stanisław Zawadzki, the architect.

Kurów. The Parish Church (phot. – ST)

Kurów. The Holy Spirit Church (phot. – ST)

MARKUSZÓW

The first information on Markuszów come from the 1st half of the 14th century. It obtained the city rights in the middle of the 16th century due to the efforts of Piotr Firlej, the Governor of the Ruthenian Province, and the owner of Markuszów. There is *the Parish Church* built in the years 1608-1609 in the Lublin Renaissance style by the Italian constructor Piotr Durie. There is also *a Chapel* from the beginning of the 17th century; on its top there are cartouches with Firlej's coat-of-arms – Lewart. In the 2nd half of the 18th century Markuszów was a property of the Governor of the Lublin Province, Kajetan Hryniewiecki who was also the Chairman of a very useful Commission of the Good Order.

Markuszów. The Church of Holy Transfiguration (phot. – PM)

GARBÓW I i II

It is a large village that consists of a factory settlement (sugar factory) and the original settlement in the east. In the factory settlement there is *a Neo-Baroque Palace*.

Garbów as a parish existed in 1326. For three centuries (15th-18th) it was successively owned by the Szczekocki, Iżycki, Czartotryski and Jezierski Families. Jezierskis built *a Classical Manor House* in a small park on the pattern of a letter H. On the hill we can see the shape of *the church* erected before 1678 after the previous one was demolished by the Swedes. This wooden building erected on the pattern of the Greek cross copied the

The Jezierski Manor House (phot. – ST)

The Ruins of the Church from the 17th c. (phot. – ST)

appearance of the brick building. In the 18th century the church was expanded, the brick facade was added and the whole obtained the pattern of the Latin cross. In August 1915, the retreating Russian troops set fire to the church. In the years 1907-1911 a new church was built in Garbów. It was the Neo-Gothic church designed by Józef Pius Dziekoński.

JASTKÓW

The village was probably established in the 13th century. At the beginning of the 15th century Jastków was partially the property of the Jastkowski Family and partially of the Benedictine Monks. There is *the eclectic Palace* from 1894, which replaced the manor house of the previous owners. Nikodem Budny, one of the founders of the Society of the Museum of Lublin resided here. We pass by the wooden *Parish Church* built in 1933 with the belfry. Jastków is a place of a memorable battle, which was fought here at the end of July 1915. The 4th Regiment of the Polish Legions under Colonel Bolesław Roja attacked the reinforced trenches of the Soviets. That was the first battle for the Poles. In heavy fighting 200 soldiers were killed. The Russian troops had to retreat under the Polish pressure. Władysław Broniewski, then a young poet served in the Regiment at that time. The killed soldiers were buried at the cemetery in the middle of the village. In 1931 – to commemorate these events – the brick school designed by Bogdan Kelles-Krausse was built.

The Palace Complex from the 19th c. (phot. – ST)

The Belfry at the Parish Church (phot. – ST)

From Jastków we return to Lublin.

To make this fragment of the road more interesting we can cover it on foot following the Yellow Trail. The route goes through Snopków, Jakubowice Konińskie, Dys and Ciecierzyn. It goes along the Ciemięga River Valley and is 20 km long. The Ciemięga River Valley is located at the edge of the Nałęczów Plateau and the whole Lublin Upland. It boasts the magnificent landscape. It is 20 m deep. In the bottom we have the meandering Ciemięga River, which sometimes gets 4 m in depth. The slopes are sectioned by numerous gorges. There are lots of old riverbeds and water springs. The gorges and the Valley slopes are overgrown with rich vegetation. Among it there are some protected species like spring adonis, some species of scabwort and fescue, stool iris and frutescent cherry. In the forest we find oaks, lime-trees and hornbeam. In its ground moss we shall find rare plants, sometimes of a mountain character like spleenwort, snowdrop or lesser butterfly orchid and greater butterfly orchid.

Bibliography

1. Bortkiewicz Ewa, Santarek Wojciech, Zabiegła Anna, *Zabytki architektury i budownictwa w Polsce*, t. 22: *Województwo lubelskie*, Ośrodek Dokumentacji Zabytków, Warszawa 1995.
2. Buczkowa Irena, *Zamek Lubelski*, Krajowa Agencja Wydawnicza, Lublin 1991.
3. Chmielewski Tadeusz, Dejneka Roman, Kseniak Mieczysław, *Dolina Ciemięgi, mapa z opisem*, Lubelska Fundacja Ochrony Środowiska Naturalnego, Lublin 1994.
4. Cholewiński Witold, *Przewodnik po Lublinie i jego okolicach*, Lublin 1922.
5. Ciświcki Tadeusz, *Najważniejsze pamiątki Lublina*, Lublin 1917.
6. *Cmentarz rzymskokatolicki przy ul. Lipowej w Lublinie*, pr. zbior., Krajowa Agencja Wydawnicza, Lublin 1990.
7. Czajka Wojciech, *Samoloty Firmy Plage-Laśkiewicz*, in: Kalendarz Lubelski, Lublin 1981.
8. Denys Marta, *Mały zakład kotlarski i trzech czeladników*, „Na Przykład", nr 30, Lublin 1995, Stowarzyszenie Popierania Twórczości.
9. Denys Marta, *Zanim powstała SIPMA SA*, „Na Przykład", nr 29, Lublin 1995, Stowarzyszenie Popierania Twórczości.
10. Diecezja Lubelska. *Informator historyczny i administracyjny*, oprac. ks. Marek T. Zahajkiewicz, Wydawnictwo Kurii Lubelskiej, Lublin 1985.
11. Dobrowolska Marianna, *Z dziejów Ratusza i Trybunału Koronnego w Lublinie*, Muzeum Lubelskie, Lublin 1995.
12. Fijałkowski Dominik, Kseniak Mieczysław, *Parki wiejskie Lubelszczyzny*, Państwowe Wydawnictwo Naukowe, Warszawa 1982.
13. Głowacki Ludwik, Sikorski Antoni, *Kampania wrześniowa na Lubelszczyźnie*, t. 12, Wydawnictwo Lubelskie, Lublin 1966.
14. Gawarecki Henryk, Gawdzik Czesław, *Lublin i okolice*, Wydawnictwo Lubelskie, Lublin 1976.
15. Gawarecki Henryk, Marszałek Józef, Szczepaniak Tadeusz, Wójcikowski Włodzimierz, *Lubelszczyzna – Przewodnik*, Wydawnictwo Sport i Turystyka, Warszawa 1979.
16. Gawarecki Henryk, *O dawnym Lublinie*, Wydawnictwo Lubelskie, Lublin 1986.
17. Gawroński Ludwik, *O hejnale i trębaczach w dawnym Lublinie*, Multico, Lublin 1995.
18. Gumowski Marian, *Pieczęcie i herby miejscowości woj. lubelskiego*, Towarzystwo Naukowe KUL, Lublin 1959.
19. Gzella A. Leszek, *Oni bronili Lublina w 1939 r.*, Związek Bojowników o Wolność i Demokrację, Lublin 1989.
20. *Ilustrowany przewodnik po Lublinie*, Polskie Towarzystwo Krajoznawcze, Lublin 1931.
21. Jakimińska Grażyna, *Brama Krakowska, historia*, Muzeum Lubelskie, Lublin 1995.
22. *Katalog zabytków sztuki w Polsce (pow. lubelski)*, Instytut Sztuki Polskiej Akademii Nauk, Warszawa 1967.
23. Kobierzycki Alfred Pomian, *Monografia Lublina*, Lublin 1901.
24. Kruk Stefan, *Życie teatralne Lublina 1782-1918*, Wydawnictwo Lubelskie, Lublin 1982.
25. Kseniak Mieczysław, *Felin jak Feliksa*, „Na Przykład", nr 36, Lublin 1996, Stowarzyszenie Popierania Twórczości.
26. *Lublin – przewodnik turystyczny*, pr. zbior., Wojewódzki Ośrodek Informacji Turystycznej, Lublin 1966.
27. *Lublin w dziejach i kulturze Polski*, pr. zbior. pod red. Tadeusza Radzika i Adama A. Witusika, Polskie Towarzystwo Historyczne Oddział w Lublinie, Krajowa Agencja Wydawnicza, Lublin 1997.
28. *Lublin – Przewodnik*, Polskie Towarzystwo Turystyczno-Krajoznawcze, Spółdzielnia Wydawnicza, Lublin 1959.
29. MAR (Maria Antonina hr. Ronikerowa), *Ilustrowany przewodnik po Lublinie*, Warszawa 1901.
30. Marczuk Józef, *Rada Miejska i Magistrat Lublina. Lublin 1918-1939*, Wydawnictwo Lubelskie, Lublin 1984.
31. Mikulec Bronisław, *Przemysł Lubelszczyzny w latach 1864-1914*, UMCS, Lublin 1989.

32. Molik Andrzej, *Świdnik i okolice*, Wojewódzki Ośrodek Informacji Turystycznej, Lublin 1987.

33. Myjak Józef, Wyszkowski Marek, *Wieś lubelska i tarnobrzeska zaprasza (przew. agroturystyczny)*, Lublin.

34. Myk Sławomir, *Pyasek alias Pyaski, czyli gawęda o dawnych Piaskach*, „Na Przykład”, nr 23, Lublin 1995, Stowarzyszenie Popierania Twórczości.

35. Nowosad Marek, *Szlaki turystyczne okolic Lublina*, Polskie Towarzystwo Turystyczno--Krajoznawcze – Wojewódzki Ośrodek Informacji Turystycznej, Lublin 1989.

36. Panfil Tomasz, *Herb Lublina – geneza, symbolika, funkcje*, Biuro Promocji Miasta, Lublin 1998.

37. *Plan motoryzacyjny „Lublin”*, Wydawnictwo Arkadia, 1997.

38. *Polska mapa campingów 1997*, Polskie Przedsiębiorstwo Wydawnictw Kartograficznych, Warszawa – Wrocław 1997.

39. Radzik Tadeusz, *Uczelnia mędrców Lublina*, UMCS, Lublin 1994.

40. Sierpiński Seweryn Zenon, *Historyczny obraz miasta Lublina*, Warszawa 1843 (reprint).

41. Turski Stanisław, *Na przykład Wierzchowiska*, „Na Przykład”, nr 11, Lublin 1994, Stowarzyszenie Popierania Twórczości.

42. Wadowski Jan Ambroży ks., *Kościoły lubelskie*, Polska Akademia Umiejętności, Kraków 1907.

43. Wojtaszko Tadeusz, *Rzeczpospolita Babińska przez wieki i okupacje*, „Retro”, Lublin 1994.

44. Wojtysiak Władysława, *Dworek Wincentego Pola*, Muzeum Okręgowe w Lublinie, Lublin 1982.

45. Wójcik Robert, *Kościoły Garbowa*, „Rozwój”, Garbów 1997.

46. Wójcikowscy Bogusława i Grzegorz, *Dzielnica „Czechów”*, Krajowa Agencja Wydawnicza, Lublin 1987.

47. Wyszkowski Marek, *Album lubelski, teksty programów TVL*, Lublin 1995-1998

48. Wyszkowski Marek, *Kamienica Lubomelskich w Lublinie*, Polskie Towarzystwo Turystyczno-Krajoznawcze (dalej: PTTK), Lublin 1989.

49. Wyszkowski Marek, *Pałac Tarłów*, PTTK, Lublin 1989.

50. Wyszkowski Marek, *Tradycje związków Lublina z morzem*, PTTK, Lublin 1982.

51. Wzorek Józef, *Drzewo Krzyża Świętego*, Norbertinum, Lublin 1991.

52. Zalewski Ludwik ks., *Katedra i Jezuici w Lublinie*, Towarzystwo Przyjaciół Nauk, 1947.

53. *Zarys dziejów Lublina 1317-1967*, pr. zbior., Wydawnictwo Lubelskie, Lublin 1967.

54. Zieliński Władysław Kornel, *Opis Lublina*, Lublin 1874.

55. Żywicki Jerzy, *Architektura neogotycka na Lubelszczyźnie*, Regionalny Ośrodek Studiów i Ochrony Środowiska Kulturowego w Lublinie, *idea* Media, Lublin 1998.

LUBLIN
AND ITS VICINITY
INFORMATION

PUBLIC OFFICES

THE MARSHALL OFFICE
THE LUBLIN VOIVODSHIP
ul. Spokojna 4
The Secretary's Office, tel. 742 42 77

THE REGIONAL OFFICE
ul. Spokojna 4
The Secretary's Office, tel. 532 45 43

THE TOWN OFFICE
pl. Wł. Łokietka 1, central office: 532 10 11

THE CITY PROMOTION OFFICE
pl. Wł. Łokietka 1, tel. 532 59 66

THE OFFICE OF LOCAL AUTHORITIES
ul. Spokojna 9, tel. 532 21 26

THE PASSPORT OFFICE
ul. Północna 3, tel. 747 64 47

THE REGIONAL CUSTOMS INSPECTORATE
ul. Długa 5, tel. 743 83 94

THE METROPOLITAN CURIA
ul. Wyszyńskiego 2, tel. 532 10 58

EMERGENCY CALLS

POLICE	997
POLICE FIRE	998
AMBULANCE SERVICE	999

BRIGADE AUTOALARM	96 30
POWER ENGINEERING SERVICE	993
BEAK-DOWN TRUCK	981
CRANE-LIFT SERVICE	982
SERVICE HEAT ENGINEERINEG	991
GAS SERVICE	992
TRANSPORT SERVICE	995
SERVICE RESCUE TRUCK	954
WATER&SEWAGE SERVICE	994

THE REGIONAL POLICE OFFICE
ul. Narutowicza 73
tel. 532 01 01

THE REGIONAL FIRE BRIGADE OFFICE
ul. Strażacka 7
tel. 532 10 31

THE CITY GUARD
pl. Wł. Łokietka 1
tel. 532 73 45

HOSPITALS

CHILDREN'S HOSPITAL
ul. Chodźki 2
tel. exchange: 743 03 00

THE RAILWAY HOSPITAL
ul. Kruczkowskiego 21
tel. exchange: 744 26 01

THE STATE CLINICAL HOSPITAL NO 1
ul. Staszica 16
tel. exchange: 532 50 41

THE STATE CLINICAL HOSPITAL NO 4
ul. Jaczewskiego 8
information office: 742 51 49

THE MATERNITY HOSPITAL
ul. Lubartowska 81
tel. 740 83 78

THE MILITARY HOSPITAL
al. Racławickie 23
tel. 533 04 61

THE STATE SPECIAL HOSPITAL
al. Kraśnicka 100
tel. exchange: 525 75 11

The Mental Hospital
ul. Abramowicka 2
tel. 744 30 61

THE JAN BOŻY'S
REGIONAL HOSPITAL
ul. Biernackiego 9
tel. 740 42 74

EMERGENCY AID

THE REGIONAL AMBULANCE SERVICE
al. Kraśnicka 100
emergency phone number: 533 77 90

THE AMBULANCE SERVICE "BRONOWICE",
ul. Topolowa 7
emergency phone number: 741 21 74

THE AMBULANCE SERVICE "CZECHÓW"
al. Kompozytorów Polskich 8
emergency phone number: 741 21 25

THE AMBULANCE SERVICE
"ŚRÓDMIEŚCIE"
ul. Spadochroniarzy 8
emergency phone number: 533 30 92

UNIVERSITIES, INSTITUTES

THE MEDICAL ACADEMY
al. Racławickie 1, tel. 532 00 61

THE AGRICULTURAL ACADEMY
ul. Akademicka 13, tel. 455 50 00

THE RURAL INSTITUTE
ul. Jaczewskiego 2, tel. 747 80 27

THE INSTITUTE OF JOHN PAUL II
al. Racławickie 14, tel. 445 32 17

THE INSTITUTE FOR
CENTRAL AND EASTERN EUROPE
pl. Litewski 2, tel. 532 29 07

THE CATHOLIC UNIVERSITY OF LUBLIN
al. Racławickie 14, tel. 533 80 22

THE SEMINARY COLLEGE
ul. S. Wyszyńskiego 6, tel. 743 65 05

THE LUBLIN POLYTECHNICS
ul. Bernardyńska 13, tel. 538 11 76

THE SEMINARY COLLEGE OF THE ZAMOŚĆ
– LUBACZÓW DIOCESE
ul. Orzechowskiego 10, tel. 744 47 84

THE UNIVERSITY
OF MARIA CURIE-SKŁODOWSKA
pl. M.C. Skłodowskiej 5, tel. 537 51 00

THE INSTITUTE OF CULTIVATION, FERTI-
LISATION AND SOIL SCIENCE
al. Królewska 15, Puławy, tel. 886 43 17

PUBLIC LIBRARIES

THE UNIVERSITY LIBRARY OF UMCS
ul. Radziszewskiego 11
tel. 537 58 35

THE CATHOLIC UNIVERSITY LIBRARY
ul. Chopina 27
tel. 743 73 88

THE I. ŁOPACIŃSKI PUBLIC LIBRARY
ul. Narutowicza 4
tel. 532 07 38

THE PEDAGOGIC LIBRARY
OF THE EDUCATIONAL COMMISSION
ul. 3 Maja 6
tel. 532 69 16

CULTURAL CENTRES

THE CULTURAL CENTRE
ul. Peowiaków 12, tel. 532 32 78

CHATKA ŻAKA
ACADEMIC CULTURAL CCENTRE
ul. Radziszewskiego 16, tel. 533 32 01

THE RAILWAYMAN'S
CULTURAL CENTRE
ul. Kunickiego 35, tel. 534 36 07

THE CULTURAL CENTRE LSM
ul. K. Wallenroda 4a, tel. 743 48 29

THE CULTURAL CENTRE "BRONOWICE"
ul. Krańcowa 106, tel 744 16 38

THE CULTURAL CENTRE "CZECHÓW"
ul. Kiepury 5a, tel. 741 99 11

THE YOUTH CULTURAL CENTRE
ul. Grodzka 11, tel. 525 24 06

THE GRODZKA GATE CENTRE
ul. Grodzka 21, tel. 532 58 67

THE REGIONAL CULTURAL CENTRE
ul. Dolna Panny Marii 3, tel. 532 42 07

THE YOUTH CULTURAL CENTRE
– VETTER
ul. Bernardyńska 14a, tel. 532 08 53

GALLERIES

THE ARTS EXHIBITION CENTRE
ul. Grodzka 5a, tel. 532 59 47
The "Stara" Gallery, ul. Narutowicza 4
The "Grodzka" Gallery, ul. Grodzka 5a
The "Labirynt 2" Gallery, ul. Grodzka 3

THE "POD PODŁOGĄ" GALLERY
Krakowskie Przedmieście 62
tel. 532 68 57

THE ARTISTIC STAGE GALLERY
OF THE CATHOLIC UNIVERSITY
al. Racławickie 14, tel. 533 03 92
Monday – Friday midday – 5pm (during
exhibitions)

THE FINE ART. LOVER'S ASSOCIATION
THE "MAT MAR T" GALLERY
ul. Grodzka 34/ 36, tel. 532 28 31

THEATRES

THE JULIUSZ OSTERWA THEATRE
ul. Narutowicza 17, tel. 532 42 44
Booking office:
10am – 1pm, 4pm – 7pm, except on
Mondays. June to August – theatre closed

THE MUSICAL THEATRE
ul. M. Skłodowskiej-Curie 5

THE RAILWAYMAN'S CULTURAL CENTRE
ul. Kunickiego 35, tel./fax 532 76 13
Monday to Friday 8am – 3pm
June to August – closed

THE JAN CH. ANDERSEN THEATRE
ul. Dominikańska 1, tel 532 16 28
Monday to Friday 8am – 3pm
Sunday 10am – midday
June to August – closed

THE PLASTIC STAGE
OF CATHOLIC UNIVERSITY
al. Racławickie 14, tel./fax 533 03 92
Monday to Friday 10am – 3pm

THE "PROVISORIUM" THEATRE
ul. Peowiaków 12, tel. 532 75 83

THE COMPANY THEATRE
ul. Peowiaków 12, tel./fax 532 75 85

PUBLIC ORCHESTRA
OF HENRYK WIENIAWSKI
ul. M. Skłodowskiej-Curie 5
tel. 532 44 21
Information office: tel. 532 15 22
Booking office:
Monday to Friday 2pm – 6pm
June to mid-August – closed

THE WORKSHOP
PRACTICE CENTRE "GARDZIENICE"
ul. Grodzka 5 a, 2nd floor, tel. 532 96 37

THE SMALL STAGE THEATRE
Dom Kultury LSM, tel. 743 48 29

THE LUBLIN THEATRE
Cultural Centre of Lublin
ul. Peowiaków 12, tel. 532 75 83

STAGE 6
ul. Peowiaków 12, tel. 532 75 83

THE LITERARY
AND MUSICAL THEATRE
ul. Zbożowa 103, tel. 746 65 27

MUSEUMS

LUBLIN

THE LUBLIN MUSEUM
ul. Zamkowa 9
tel. 532 50 01, fax 532 17 43
Wednesday – Saturday 9am – 4pm
Sunday 9am – 5pm
Permanent exhibitions highly recommend-
ed: Historical and war paintings to be seen
at Polish Paintings Gallery, Foreign Paintings Gallery (17th and 18th c.), Regional folk
art, The Holy Trinity Chapel with Russian
– Byzantine frescoes from the early 15th c.

THE HISTORICAL MUSEUM OF LUBLIN
"BRAMA KRAKOWSKA"
pl. Wł. Łokietka 3
tel. 532 60 01
Wednesday – Saturday 9am – 4pm
Sunday 9am – 5pm
Permanent exhibition: *The History
of Lublin* to be seen in the museum locat-
ed within the old defensive walls of the
Kraków Gate

THE TOWN HALL AND THE CROWN
TRIBUNAL MUSEUM
Rynek 1
tel. 532 68 66
Wednesday – Saturday 9am – 4pm
Sunday 9am – 5pm
Permanent exhibition: *The History of the
Town Hall and the Crown Tribunal in
Lublin* at the Lapidarium

THE MARTYROLOGICAL MUSEUM
"UNDER THE CLOCK"
ul. Uniwersytecka 1
tel. 533 36 78
Wednesday – Saturday 9am – 4pm
Saturday 9am – 5pm
Permanent exhibition in the former Nazi
prison cells dedicated to the history
of the Castle prison and the famous
house "Under the Clock". Martyrology
of the youth and the Boy and Girl Scouts
from this region of Poland, who died
in the war. Admission free

THE MANOR HOUSE OF WINCENTY POL
ul. Kalinowszczyzna 13
tel. 747 24 13
Wednesday – Saturday 9am – 4pm
Sunday 9am – 5pm
Permanent exhibition: *The Life and Work
of Wincenty Pol*. Temporary exhibitions
to be seen on the ground floor only.

MUSEUMS

THE MAJDANEK MUSEUM

Droga Męczenników Majdanka 67
tel. 744 19 55
Permanent exhibition: *The Majdanek Concentration Camp* (barracks no 43 and 44) May – September 8am – 6pm, other months 8am – 3pm. From 1 December to 28 January the visitors will have to book in advance at the educational centre office: tel. 744 19 55. The camp compound i.e.: gas chambers, barrack no 45 with small – size mock – up of the camp area, barracks no 52 – 53, field no 3 and crematory. Open all week: October – April 8am – 3 pm May – September 8am – 6pm

THE ARCHDIOCESAN MUSEUM OF RELIGIOUS ART

ul. Filaretów 7, tel. 525 12 01
Monday – Sunday, holidays 10am – 5pm
Permanent exhibition: Religious sculpture, objects of religious cult no longer in use, donated by priests, parishes, and individual persons. Place of exhibition: the Trinity Gate at ul. Królewska 10

THE PHARMACY – MUSEUM

ul. Grodzka 5a
tel. 532 88 20
Tuesday – Friday 11am – 4pm
Permanent exhibition: furniture, lab vessels, pharmacy equipment, professional literature. Once a year – the great exhibition of medical and toxic plants.

THE POLISH FOLKLORE MUSEUM

al. Warszawska 96
tel./fax 533 30 51
1 June – 31 October Monday – Sunday 9am – 5pm including: 1 May – 31 August 9am – 6pm, 2 November – 23 December Friday – Sunday 9am – 3 pm

THE BOTANICAL GARDEN

ul. Sławinkowska 3
tel. 537 55 43 15
April – 31 October workdays 9am – 7pm Saturday, Sunday, holiday 10am –7pm May – July workdays 9am – 8pm Saturday, Sunday, holiday 10am – 20pm

KAZIMIERZ DOLNY

THE VISTULA MUSEUM

ul. Podzamcze 12a
tel. 881 02 88

Divisions: the Silverware Museum, the Celejowski House, the Nature Museum, the Castle in Janowiec

THE CELEJOWSKI HOUSE MUSEUM

ul. Senatorska 11/13
tel. 881 01 04, fax 881 02 77
Tuesday – Sunday 1 October – 30 April 10am – 1pm, 1 May – 30 October 10am – 16 pm. Divisions: The Contemporary Art., The Town History Permanent exhibition: The history of Kazimierz and around from the prehistoric times until today. Paintings, drawings, graphical works of the 19th c. and contemporary artists connected with the place. Temporary exhibitions in the Bell Tower Gallery (ul. Zamkowa 2)

"THE KUNCEWICZ HOUSE"

ul. Małachowskiego
tel. 881 01 02 15
April – 30 September, 10am – 1pm and 3pm – 6pm (except Mondays) Open to visitors during low-season

THE NATURE MUSEUM

ul. Puławska 54
tel. 881 03 26
1 October – 30 April Tuesday – Sunday 10am – 3pm 1 May – 30 September Tuesday – Sunday 10am – 5pm. Permanent exhibition: *The Kazimierz Landscape Park* – geological structure, waters, climate, vegetation cover and fauna. *Mysteries of the extinct world* – life at sea during Cretaceous period 65 million years ago. *Down in the valley of the central part of the Vistula river* – the nature of one of the most spectacular sections of the biggest Polish river

THE SILVERWARE MUSEUM

ul. Senatorska 11/13
tel. 881 01 04
Tuesday – Sunday 1 October – 30 April 10am – 3pm 1 May – 30 September 10am – 4pm. Permanent exhibition: European silverware, Gothic to present day – religious and table silverware, jewellery. Temporary exhibitions: "Bell Tower Gallery" (ul. Zamkowa 2, tel. 881 00 80)

THE CASTLE MUSEUM IN JANOWIEC

ul. Lubelska 20, tel. 881 52 28
1 October – 30 April Tuesday – Sunday 10am – 3pm, 1 May – 30 September 10am – 5pm. Permanent exhibition: *The 16th and*

271

the 18th century Castle, The 18th century mansion, The 19th century granary – ethnographic exhibition, *The 19th century barn, the harness storage room and the carriage room*

KOZŁÓWKA

THE ZAMOYSKI MUSEUM
tel. 852 75 88, 852 70 91
Tuesday, Thursday, Friday 10am – 4pm
Wednesday, Saturday, Sunday 10am
– 5pm. December, January, February.
Permanent exhibition: The palace interior
from the turn of the 19th and 20th century
– the Zamoyski family collection, *Art. and Struggle in Socialism*

KRAŚNIK

THE REGIONAL MUSEUM
ul. Klasztorna 3
tel. 884 34 85
Tuesday – Friday 8am – 3pm, Saturday
– Sunday 10am – 2pm. Archaeological
and ethnographic collections

LUBARTÓW

THE REGIONAL MUSEUM
ul. Kościuszki 2
tel. 855 28 08
Tuesday – Friday 8am – 3pm, Saturday
– Sunday 10am – 3pm. Permanent exhibition: *From the history of Lubartów*

ŁĘCZNA

THE REGIONAL MUSEUM
ul. Bożnicza17
tel. 752 08 69
Monday – Saturday 8am – 4pm, Sunday
9am – 4pm. Permanent exhibitions:
archaeological, geological – paleontological, historical. The Museum is situated
in the monumental synagogue with original mid-17th century interior decoration

NAŁĘCZÓW

THE HISTORY OF CO-OPERATIVE
MOVEMENT MUSEUM
ul. Chmielewskiego 4, tel. 501 41 63

Tuesday – Friday 9am – 3pm, Sunday
10am – 2pm. Divisions: *The History of Polish co-operative Movement*, *The History of Nałęczów*, Permanent exhibition: The history of co-operative movement until the year 1945

THE ŻEROMSKI VILLA MUSEUM
ul. Andriollego 8
tel. 501 47 80 2
May – 31 September Tuesday – Sunday
10am – 4pm, 1 November – 30 April
Tuesday – Sunday 10am – 3pm

THE BOLESŁAW PRUS MUSEUM
al. Małachowskiego 3
tel. 501 45 52
Wednesday – Sunday 9am – 3pm
Permanent exhibition: *Life and Work of Bolesław Prus and His bonds with Nałęczów*

PUŁAWY

THE EDUCATIONAL MUSEUM
ul. Włostowicka 27
tel. 887 71 29
Tuesday – Saturday 8am – 3pm
Multidivisional museum: archives, museum pieces, books, photographs Permanent exhibition: *Education in Puławy between 1811-1939*

THE POLISH TOURISM AND NATURE
LOVERS' ASSOCIATION REGIONAL MUSEUM
ul. Czartoryskich 6a
tel. 887 86 74

THE FORMER ST. CHARLES HOSPITAL
10am – 2pm (except Mondays)

THE GOTHIC HOUSE
Permanent exhibition: *The Czartoryski family*
Friday – Sunday 10am – 2pm, Low-season
1May – 30 October 10am – 4pm

THE TEMPLE OF SYBIL
summer only

WOJCIECHÓW

THE BLACKSMITHER'S MUSEUM
tel. 517 72 10
Monday – Saturday 10am – 5pm,
Sunday (May – September) 10am – 5pm

LUBLIN

MASTERPIECES OF SMALL AUDIENCE MUSIC
The concert series, outstanding performances of most superb musicians and small-audience groups from Poland and abroad.
Temporary exhibitions to be seen during the festival: The Province Gallery Foundation Collection
Organised by: The Province Gallery Foundation, ul. Jezuicka 4, tel. 534 55 47
Place: the Crown Tribunal in the Old Town

BIENNNIAL EVENT CALLED "PUPPETS IN LUBLIN"
The international puppet theatre performances
Organised by: the Jan Ch. Andersen Theatre, tel. 532 16 28. Month: June (held every second year in since 1999)

"THE MUSIC AND ART. TEMPUS PASCHALE"
Festival the Old Polish music originally played during the Lent and Easter.
The integral part of the festival are temporary exhibitions of painting and graphic art.
Organised by: The Pro Musica Antiqua Association, ul. Ułanów 1/ 39, tel. 743 26 30
Month: March/April (Saturday – Sunday)
Place: the Archcathedral and some selected churches, the Crown Tribunal, the Castle

INTERNATIONAL DANCE THEATRE MEETINGS
Individual and group performances, dance workshops conducted by artists.
Organised by: the Cultural Centre of Lublin, Modern Dance Group from the Lublin Polytechnics, tel. 532 45 07
Month: November
Place: the Cultural Centre
ul. Peowiaków 12
The Juliusz Osterwa Theatre
ul. Narutowicza 17

THE INTERNATIONAL THEATRICAL CONFRONTATIONS IN LUBLIN
Held every year, the festival consists of: stage performances presented by the world – famous theatre companies, occasional events (sessions, exhibitions, extra performances).
Organised by: The Festival Office
ul. Peowiaków 12, tel./fax 532 75 83
Month: October

THE INTERNATIONAL NON-STOP GUITAR FESTIVAL
The concerts played all around in the following months: February, April, June, October (the four – day Final).
Organised by:
The Lublin Guitar Music Association
ul. Okopowa 12/6a
tel. 534 92 80
Place: the Crown Tribunal (Old Town), final concerts are held in the Lublin Philharmonics

THE INTERNATIONAL FOLKLORE MEETINGS of Ignacy Wachowiak
Organised by:
The Office of the Song and Dance Group "Lublin", ul. 1 Armii WP 3 tel./fax 532 44 83. Month: 31 June – 5 October
Place: The concert hall in the Saski Garden, E.Leclerc shopping centre, the Zemborzyce Basin, the Local Cultural Centre in Nałęczów

KAZIMIERZ DOLNY

THE FOLK BANDS AND SINGERS FESTIVAL
Competition performances, additional presentations, Folk Art. Fairs
Organised by: the Regional Cultural Centre in Lublin
ul. Dolna Panny Marii3
tel. 532 42 07
Month: second half of June
Place: Town Squares (both)

THE MUSIC FESTIVAL KAZIMIERZ DOLNY '2000
Organ music.
Organised by: the Cultural Centre in Kazimierz, the Town Office in Kazimierz Dolny, the St. Barthomolew Parish, the St. John the Baptist Parish
tel. 881 00 40
Month: June – August, every Saturday at 7pm. Place: the parish church

LUBARTÓW

THE INTERNATIONAL WIND ORCHESTRAS COMPETITION OF FIRE BRIGADES
Organised by: the Fire Brigade from Lubartów, the Town Office in Lubartów
tel. 855 30 81
Place: the park amphitheatre

NAŁĘCZÓW

DIVERTIMENTO
Organised by: the Municipal Cultural
Centre, tel. 50140 69
Month: May
Place: the Małachowski Palace

PUŁAWY

THE INTERNATIONAL JAZZ WORKSHOP
Organised by: the Cultural Centre
in Puławy known as "Dom Chemika"
ul. Wojska Polskiego 4
Information Bureau: tel. 886 20 24
Month: July
Place: the Cultural Centre in Puławy
– "Dom Chemika"

ŚWIDNIK

ŚWIDNIK JAZZ FESTIVAL
The International Festival under the
patronage of Elvin Jones.
Organised by:
the Municipal Cultural Centre
al. Lotników Polskich 24, tel. 468 67 80
Month: September
Place: the LOT Cinema (festival) Small
Stage Hall of the Municipal Cultural
Centre (workshop)

THE INTERNATIONAL WIND ORCHESTRAS
Festival Organised by: the Municipal
Cultural Centre
al. Lotników Polskich 24
tel. 468 67 80
Month: June
Place: the Avia Stadium

1 – *International Dance Theatre Meeting
(CK archives, Lublin). 2 – International Non-
-Stop Guitar Festival (archives, iM).
3 – Świdnik Jazz Festival (The Cultural Centre
archives, Świdnik). 4 – Masterpieces of small
Audience Music (The Province Gallery Foundation archives). 5 – 8 – International Theatre
Confrontations (archives, iM). 9 – The Song
and Dance Group of Wanda Kaniorowa (private archives). 10 – Biennal "Puppets in Lublin"
(archives, iM). 11 – International Folklore
Meeting of I. Wachowiak (A. Gauda).*

5

6

7

8

9

10

1

LUBLIN

THE BYSTRZYCA HOTEL
al. Zygmuntowskie 4a, tel. 532 30 03

THE TEACHER HOSTEL
ul. Akademicka 4, tel. 533 82 85

THE JEDLINA
Hotel the village of Motycz 331
tel. 503 19 19

THE LUBLINIANKA HOTEL
Krakowskie Przedmieście 56
tel. 532 42 61

THE PUMiS HOSTEL
ul. Pogodna 36, tel. 744 85 56

THE PZMOT
ul. Prusa 8, tel. 533 43 63

THE VICTORIA HOTEL
ul. Narutowicza 58/60, tel. 532 70 11

THE UNIA HOTEL
al. Racławickie 12, tel. 533 20 61

THE "POD KASZTANAMI" INN
ul. Krężnicka 94a, tel. 750 03 90

THE YOUTH HOSTEL
al. Długosza 6, tel. 533 06 28

THE ANNA MANOR HOUSE
Jakubowice Konińskie 28a, tel. 501 22 40

THE RELAX HOTEL
al. Mełgiewska 7-9, tel. 746 20 71

THE KASZTELAŃSKI INN
Płouszowice, tel. 502 09 66

KAZIMIERZ DOLNY

THE ARCADE HOTEL
ul. Czerniawy 1, tel. 810 00 75

THE HOUSE OF JOURNALIST
ul. Małachowskiego 17, tel. 881 01 62

THE HOUSE OF TOURIST
ul. Krakowska 59/60, tel. 881 00 36

THE HIGHLANDER LODGING HOUSE
ul. Krakowska 47, tel. 881 02 63

THE "POD WIANUSZKAMI" HOTEL
ul. Puławska 64, tel. 881 03 27

THE PIAST INN
ul. Słoneczna 3, tel. 881 03 51

KRAŚNIK

THE IWONA HOTEL
ul. Jagiellońska 14, tel. 825 21 65

LUBARTÓW

THE HOTEL TRADE
AND GASTRONOMY SERVICE
ul. Lubelska 104a, tel. 855 36 10

ŁĘCZNA

THE GOLDEN HORSESHOE HOTEL
Brzeziny, tel. 757 51 64

NAŁĘCZÓW

THE HOTEL "ENERGETYK"
ul. Paderewskiego 10, tel. 501 46 04

THE PRZEPIÓRECZKA HOTEL
ul. 1 Maja 8, tel. 501 41 29

PUŁAWY

THE IZABELLA HOTEL
ul. Lubelska 1, tel. 886 30 41

THE WISŁA HOTEL
ul. Wróblewskiego 1, tel. 886 27 37

LUBLIN

APOLLO
ul. Peowiaków 6, tel. 532 06 12

BORZYCE
ul. Krężnicka 163, tel. 750 09 22

BURGER KING
al. Racławickie 2A, tel. 532 97 22

CASA MIA PIZZERNIA
ul. Hryniewieckiego 70, tel. 524 37 14

DWOREK GRAFA
ul. Łęczyńska 150, tel. 746 35 542

EUROPA
Krakowskie Przedmieście 29, tel. 532 20 12

HELP
al. Spółdzielczości Pracy 36
tel. 0 601 35 35 63

JOLA
ul. Wieniawska 8, tel. 532 09 81

KALINA
ul. Lwowska 12, tel. 747 47 56

KARCZMA SŁUPSKA
al. Racławickie 33, tel. 533 88 13

LUBLINIANKA
Krakowskie Przedmieście 56, tel. 532 27 89

MCDONALD'S
Krakowskie Przedmieście 52
tel. 745 12 01

PAŁACOWA
Wierzchowiska II, nr 134, tel. 581 02 25

PIZZA HUT
ul. Nadbystrzycka 25, tel. 743 40 00

PZMOT
ul. Prusa 8, tel. 533 43 63

PRZYSTAŃ
ul. Kunickiego 143, tel. 744 10 97

RESURSA
Krakowskie Przedmieście 68, tel. 534 29 91

ZŁOTY SMOK
Krakowskie Przedmieście 30, tel. 534 44 88

GASTRONOMIC SERVICE
Małgorzata
Górniak-Mitrus
20-128 Lublin, ul. Lwowska 12

The Karczma Słupska
RESTAURACJA
Restaurant

al. Racławickie 22, tel. 533 88 13 Lublin

Opening hours: 10am – 10pm

KAZIMIERZ DOLNY

STAROPOLSKA
ul. Nadrzeczna 4, tel. 881 02 36

KRAŚNIK

JUBILATKA
ul. Lubelska 84, tel. 825 26 67

LUBARTÓW

„ROMANUM"
ul. Lubartowska 32, Firlej, tel. 857 54 26

NAŁĘCZÓW

PRZEPIÓRECZKA
ul. 1 Maja 8, tel. 501 41 29

PUŁAWY

POD DĘBAMI
ul. Norwida 2, tel. 886 37 92

Can there be a thing hotter
than a "French Lover" ?
Can there be a thing more amazing
than "a miraculous pork dish"?…

"Jola": a perfect combination of feminine
affection and masculine scent, taste
of home – made food. Convenient
central location.

"BORZYCE" – excellent place to choose
for an elegant official meal as well
as a long, lazy meeting with friends,
fireplace in the background

Preserve your memories – they keep
us all alive. Invite your friends
to be your guests and experience
the pleasure of being our guests.

We organise banquets, wedding parties,
birthday parties. Lots of fun guaranteed!
Our offer includes special discount prices
on Sunday family dinners.

Favourable discounts are also addressed
to organised groups of tourists,
bac-packers, members of conference
meetings etc. VAT invoices will be provided We accept credit cards
Visit us again!

Our address:
"JOLA"
20-071 Lublin
ul. Wieniawska 8
tel. 532 09 81

"BORZYCE"
20-515 Lublin
ul. Krężnicka 163
tel. 750 09 22

Follow your sense of taste!
Visit McDonald's

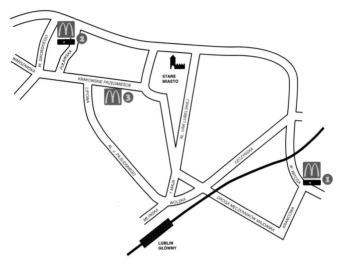

① McDonald's McDrive
the corner of ul. Chemiczna and ul. Witosa,
near Macro Cash&Carry open daily from 6am till 11pm

② McDonald's McDrive
the corner of al. Solidarnośći and ul. Puławska
open daily from 8am till midnight McDrive
open daily from 7am till 2am

③ McDonald's
Krakowskie Przedmieście 52 open daily
from 7am till 11pm Restaurant unlike any other!

**restaurant
near you**

CAFES

AMADEO
ul. Gliniana 60, tel. 525 66 40

BUON GIORNO
ul. Radziszewskiego 16, tel. 533 32 01

CUKIERNIA CHMIELEWSKI
Krakowskie Przedmieście 8
tel. 532 73 23

CZARCIA ŁAPA
ul. Rynek 19, tel. 532 03 44

HADES
ul. Peowiaków 12, tel. 532 87 61

HORTEX
ul. Lipowa 11, tel. 532 89 26

IMPULS
ul. Filaretów 44, tel. 528 01 35

LODZIARNIA-KAWIARNIA M. KULCZYCKI
Krakowskie Przedmieście 51
tel. 532 89 14

POD BASZTĄ
ul. Królewska 6, tel. 532 96 78

SZEROKA 28
ul. Grodzka 21, tel. 534 61 09

SOX
Rynek 7, tel. 0 601 35 00 50

U BIESÓW
Rynek 18, tel. 532 16 48

ZŁOTY OSIOŁ
ul. Grodzka 5a, tel. 532 90 42

ARIAŃSKA
Wojciechów, tel. 517 72 10

THE APOLLO
WINE BAR
20-007 Lublin
ul. Peowiaków 6   Phone
tel./fax 532 06 12   reservations

Winiarnia
APOLLO

Opening hours:
Sunday to Thursday 9am – midnight
Friday to Saturday 9am – 4am

DISCOS, SOCIAL CLUBS

ANDROMEDA
Płouszowice 137a, tel. 502 09 10

ART-BIS-CLUB
ul. Radziszewskiego 16, tel. 533 15 64

COLOSSEUM CLUB
ul. Radziszewskiego 8, tel. 534 43 00

MC
ul. M. Curie-Skłodowskiej 3, tel. 743 65 16

HELP DISCO
ul. Północna 22a, tel. 747 58 01

KLUB MEGIDO
ul. M. Curie-Skłodowskiej 13, tel. 533 75 91

KOTŁOWNIA
al. Racławickie 2a, tel. 532 28 46

POD CZWÓRKĄ
ul. Nadbystrzycka 42, tel. 535 32 01

STUDIO 32
Krakowskie Przedmieście 32, tel. 534 04 00

KRAŚNIK

ENIGMA
ul. Grunwaldzka 6, tel. 884 69 66

PUŁAWY

NOWA, ul. Powstania Styczniowego 13
Żyrzyn, tel. 881 43 49

ŚWIDNIK

MAX, ul. Racławicka 9, tel. 468 67 93

ANDROMEDA
Agnieszka Ceglarska

CAFE & DISCO
Płouszowice 137a, 21-008 Tomaszowice
tel./fax 502 09 10

TOURIST ATTRACTIONS, RECREATIONAL FACILITIES

THE FLYING CLUB OF LUBLIN
Radawiec Duży, tel. 503 10 44

THE WORKMAN'S FLYING CLUB
Świdnik, ul. Kolejowa 3, tel. 468 54 32

THE ACADEMIC SPORTS CENTRE
ul. Langiewicza 22, tel. 533 20 58

THE BYSTRZYCA SPORTS CLUB
al. Zygmuntowskie 4, tel. 532 30 03

THE GRAF-MARINA SPORTS CLUB
ul. Krężnicka 6, tel. 744 10 70

DOMED ICE RINK
ul. K. Wielkiego, tel. 528 01 13

RADOŚĆ
The Centre of Entertainment for Children
ul. Daszyńskiego 2, tel. 747 51 12

THE HORSE – RIDING CLUB OF LUBLIN
ul. Ciepła 7, tel. 532 60 11

THE MUNICIPAL CENTRE OF TOURIST
INFORMATION
ul. Leszczyńskiego 19, tel. 533 03 13

THE MUNICIPAL CENTRE OF TOURIST
INFORMATION
ul. Narutowicza 54, tel. 532 53 39

TOURIST SERVICE "SZOSTUR"
ul. 1 Maja 19, tel. 743 71 50

E & K TRAVEL AGENCY
ul. Radziwiłowska 5, tel. 534 56 54

TRAVEL & TOURIST AGENCY
"ALMATUR – LUBLIN"
ul. Langiewicza 10, tel. 533 54 55

ORBIS OFFICE LUBLIN
ul. Narutowicza 31-33, tel. 532 22 56

SCAN HOLIDAY
TRAVEL AGENCY
ul. Narutowicza 71/6a, tel. 532 55 01

THE MAIN RAILWAY STATION
pl. Dworcowy 1, tel. 531 56 42

THE MAIN BUS STATION
al. 1000-lecia, tel. 747 66 49

POLISH AIRLINES LOT
ul. Narutowicza 58, tel. 532 69 17

PUBLIC TRANSPORT SERVICE
tel. 525 97 42

THE COMPANY OF PUBLIC TRANSPORT
tel. 745 37 13

ALFA RADIO TAXI, tel. 747 44 07
DAMEL TAXI S.C., tel. 96 26
ECHO TAXI, tel. 96 62
HALO-TAXI, tel. 96 29
RADIO TAXI MERC SP. Z O.O., tel. 96 66
METRO-TAXI, tel. 96 23
RADIO TAXI CENTRUM, tel. 96 65
RADIO TAXI 919, tel. 919
RADIO TAXI EXPRES S.C., tel. 96 25
RADIO TAXI DWÓJKI S.C., tel. 96 21
RADIO TAXI LUBLIN, tel. 96 28
RADIO TAXI MAGNUM S.C., tel. 96 85
RADIO TAXI OK S.C., tel. 96 61
RADIO TAXI RYTM S.C., tel. 96 67

Transport Company

21-045 Świdnik, al. Lotników Polskich 1
tel./fax (+48 81) 751 25 95, tel. (+48 81) 468 05 05

- licence for international transport of goods – load weight 3 t and 24 t
- transport services (buses) – home and abroad
- home forwarding
- technical surveys
- car service
- bus connections from Lublin to Świdnik

 Przedsiębiorstwo ATON-re

20-122 Lublin, ul. Cyrulicza 3
tel./fax (+48 81) 53 253 59

ATON – re Service Company

TOURISM
INTERNATIONAL TRANSPORT SERVICES
RENT – A – BUS
PROFESSIONAL ADVICE
PROVIDED BY QUALIFIED INSURANCE
BROKERS

Anvi-Trans Ltd.
International Transport, tel. 532 35 89

Libra International Transport
tel. 743 33 65

AUTO-HELP

Help Car
ul. Spółdzielczości Pracy 48, tel. 090 276980

Renault Nazaruk
ul. Kunickiego 161, tel. 743 88 68

BORDERLINE CROSSINGS

Dorohusk
tel. (+48 82) 566 10 63
Customs Duty, tel. (+48 82) 566 10 07

Hrebenne
tel. (+48 832) 141 25

Kukuryki
tel. (+48 83) 376 10 26

Sławatycze
tel. (+48 83) 378 34 88

Terespol
tel. (+48 83) 375 24 41

Regionalny Inspektorat Celny
ul. Długa 5, tel. 743 83 94

BANKS

BRE BANK SA
Krakowskie Przedmieście 6, tel. 532 30 31

BANK GOSPODARKI ŻYWNOŚCIOWEJ SA
ul. 1 Maja 16A
tel. 531 91 00

BANK HANDLOWY W WARSZAWIE SA
ul. Kowalska 5
tel. 532 80 91

**BANK INICJATYW
SPOŁECZNO-EKONOMICZNYCH SA**
pl. Zamkowy 10, tel./fax 532 39 82

BANK OCHRONY ŚRODOWISKA SA
Krakowskie Przedmieście 56
tel. 532 83 59

BANK PEKAO SA
ul. Lubomelska 1/3, tel. 742 48 73

BIG BANK
ul. Kapucyńska 4, tel 532 44 13

BANK PRZEMYSŁOWO-HANDLOWY SA
Krakowskie Przedmieście 72
tel. 743 72 00

INVEST BANK SA
ul. Bernardyńska 3, tel. 532 56 39

KREDYT BANK SA
Krakowskie Przedmieście 37
tel. 743 70 02

LUBELSKI BANK REGIONALNY SA
ul. Sądowa 8, tel. 534 65 66

PKO BP
Krakowskie Przedmieście 14
tel. 537 32 00

PIERWSZY POLSKO-AMERYKAŃSKI BANK SA
ul. Probostwo 6a
tel. 534 68 11

**POWSZECHNY BANK KREDYTOWY SA
W WARSZAWIE**
Krakowskie Przedmieście 47, tel. 532 92 11

PROSPER-BANK SA
ul. Mełgiewska 2
tel. 746 15 89

WSCHODNI BANK CUKROWNICTWA SA
ul. Okopowa 1, tel. 532 22 20

BUSINESS

CENTRAL BROKERAGE HOUSE PKO SA
Krakowskie Przedmieście 62, tel. 534 43 36

BUSINESS CENTRE
al. Racławickie 12, tel. 533 20 61

CHAMBER OF COMMERCE
ul. Turystyczna 44, tel. 746 45 24

LUBLIN BUSINESS CLUB
Krakowskie Przedmieście 72, tel. 534 33 93

REGIONAL CHAMBER OF COMMERCE
Krakowskie Przedmieście 72, tel. 532 16 88

LOCAL MEDIA

PRESS

DZIENNIK WSCHODNI
ul. Zana 38c VIp., tel. 525 80 10

"GAZETA W LUBLINIE" Gazeta Wyborcza
Krakowskie Przedmieście 39
tel. 532 62 11

KURIER LUBELSKI
ul. 3 Maja 14, tel. 532 66 34

RADIO

AKADEMICKIE RADIO CENTRUM
ul. Radziszewskiego 16, tel. 533 08 33

RADIO ESKA S.A.
ul. Piłsudskiego 13, tel. 743 73 00

RADIO LUBLIN
ul. Obrońców Pokoju 2, tel. 532 80 61

RADIO MUZYKA FAKTY (RMF FM)
ul. Wieniawska 14, tel. 741 30 13

RADIO PLUS LUBLIN
ul. Jana Pawła II 11, tel. 527 55 90

RADIO PULS
ul. Skłodowskiej-Curie 5, tel. 532 72 23

TELEVISION

TELEWIZJA POLSKA SA o/Lublin
ul. Obrońców Pokoju 2, tel. 532 42 91

RADIO CAŁEJ
LUBELSZCZYZNY

Piaski - 102,2 FM
Łosice - 103,4 FM
Tarnawatka - 103,2 FM
Włodawa - 102,5 FM
Kazimierz Dln. - 99,60 FM

Polskie Radio - Rozgłośnia Regionalna w Lublinie
Radio Lublin SA

Lublin, ul. Obrońców Pokoju 2
tel. 0-81 532-80-61
faks 0-81 532-06-26
www.radio.lublin.pl
poczta@radio.lublin.pl

The Polish Radio – The Regional Broadcasting Station in Lublin
Radio Lublin S.A

Publisher: *idea*MEDIA. Agencja Wydawniczo-Reklamowa Ltd.
20-007 Lublin, ul. Peowiaków 12, tel./fax (+48 81) 442 55 77
Editor-in-Chief: Waldemar Żelazny
Type-setting: *idea*MEDIA
Printing and Binding: Zakłady Graficzne im. Komisji Edukacji Narodowej S.A.
Bydgoszcz, ul. Jagiellońska 1, tel./fax (+48 52) 321 26 71